Modern Love

Modern Love

*Romance, Intimacy,
and the Marriage Crisis*

David R. Shumway

NEW YORK UNIVERSITY PRESS
New York and London

NEW YORK UNIVERSITY PRESS
New York and London
www.nyupress.org

Library of Congress Cataloging-in-Publication Data
Shumway, David R.
Modern Love : romance, intimacy, and the marriage crisis / David
R. Shumway.
p. cm.
Includes bibliographical references and index.
ISBN 0-8147-9830-6 (cloth : alk. paper) —
ISBN 0-8147-9831-4(pbk. : alk. paper)
1. Marriage.   2. Marriage in popular culture.   3. Marriage in
literature.   4. Marriage in motion pictures.   I. Title.
HQ503.S54   2003
306.81—dc21   2003001968

New York University Press books are printed on acid-free paper,
and their binding materials are chosen for strength and durability.

Manufactured in the United States of America
10 9 8 7 6 5 4 3 2 1

For Heather

Contents

Preface

This book differs from much of my previous work not only in its subject matter but also and perhaps more surprisingly in its style and approach. Much of my writing has been explicitly theoretical. In *Modern Love*, I have attempted to translate the language of theory into an idiom shared by that most elusive of audiences, educated general readers. The theories that have influenced me continue to do so, but that influence exists here more often as a subtext. For example, my conception of discourse derives from Foucault, but I refer to him in that regard only once. My conception of how the discourses of romance and intimacy are related to larger social conditions is rooted in historical materialism, though some readers doubtless will not find it rooted deeply enough. One of the assumptions I hope this book will undermine is that the prominence of romantic love in our culture must be an ideological distraction, unworthy of any but the most obvious critical dismantling. Psychoanalysis also influenced me, but its influence is muted by the fact that it is part of the field I am investigating. While *Modern Love* is not written mainly from a psychoanalytic point of view, it is not written in opposition to psychoanalysis either. The most important theoretical influence on this text has been feminism, which is pervasive, though as with Foucault, I have not sought to contribute to that theory here.

Two theoreticians whom I do cite with some regularity—Anthony Giddens and Niklas Luhmann—are invoked here less for their theory than for specific historical and cultural analyses. Giddens's *The Transformation of Intimacy* was especially important in helping me to understand the historical shift on which this book is focused. My first sense of that shift came from discussions with students in my film and literature classes. I noticed that they often found romantic love in studio-era movies to be unconvincing. People don't fall in love so quickly, they said. Real love, many of them believed, came about only as the result of a process in which the couple came to know one another deeply. I would now say that, for these students, some elements of the discourse of intimacy defined the basic conditions of possibility for a relationship.

Giddens's book helped me to correlate my students' reactions to a larger pattern of changes in intimate relationships. My conception that the new discourse is best understood in terms of its privileging of intimacy came not from Giddens, however, but from reading the advice books. In them, *intimacy* has meanings that even Giddens's work doesn't comprehend. Moreover, these self-help books helped me to understand what was genuinely novel in the presentation of love in recent films and fiction.

Modern Love grew out of a conference paper on screwball comedies, and that work was a response to conversations with the late feminist philosopher Linda Singer that began after she had done a guest lecture on *It Happened One Night* and *Pat and Mike*. Linda would probably not find my book radical enough, but it is a great loss that she is not here to argue with. I am also indebted to Stanley Cavell's *Pursuits of Happiness,* a book that my essay "Screwball Comedies: Constructing Romance, Mystifying Marriage" (Chapter 3 is a revised version) criticized severely. I still disagree fundamentally with Cavell, but there are few books on film (or anything else) to which I have found myself profitably returning so often. Most film critics could learn something from the depth and detail of this philosopher's readings.

Since love, marriage, and relationships are subjects perhaps more likely to be discussed in personal than in academic contexts, many people have contributed to this book who had no idea they were doing so. I have probably discussed these issues with Anthony DeCurtis over a longer period of time than I have with anyone else. I have relied on his friendship for nearly thirty years in good times and bad. I have also been able to depend on the care and intelligence of another old friend, Patty Harkin, who perhaps first engaged me in critical analysis of love. Judith Schacter helped me get through the worst of times, and my thinking about some of the issues discussed in this book changed in response. The more than twenty years I spent with Linda Shumway had a significant impact on this book and, more important, made me a better person. Other friends and colleagues to whom I am indebted include Liahna Armstrong, Fran Bartkowski, Linda Charnes, Jim Creech, Kathe Davis, Jill Frederick, Henry Krips, Valerie Krips, Linda Levine, Ellen Messer-Davidow, Judith Modell, Kathy Newman, Nancy Spivey, Jim Sosnoski, Sarah Thornton, Joanne Pratt Todras, and Khachig Tololyan.

Those people who have read and commented on the manuscript in whole or in part have made invaluable contributions. Michael Ryan's reading of the whole manuscript was detailed and useful. The two anonymous readers for NYU Press suggested important revisions. Phil Mirrabelli's comments on an early draft of the introduction saved me from some embarrassing errors. Thanks also to Samantha Fenno, Lucy Fischer, Gerald Graff, Paul Gripp, Linda Kauffman, Jan Lewis, Brian McHale, Robert Myers, Richard Ohmann, Victoria Olwell, Peter Stearns, and Michael Witmore.

I am grateful to the many research assistants who have helped me with this project over the years, but especially to Denise Cummings. My students in several different seminars on romance in fiction and in film taught me a great deal. The librarians at the Kinsey Institute were most helpful. Gerald Graff, Phil Goldstein, Donald Pease, and John Schilb gave me the opportunity to present some of this material at their institutions. Some of it was also presented at the Center for the Humanities, Wesleyan University, where I was a fellow in 1992 and 1996. The center's staff and the other fellows helped to make for two very productive and enjoyable semesters of work on this book. Carnegie Mellon University helped to support the project with a Faculty Development Grant and several leaves.

It is hard to know how to express my thanks to Heather Scarlett Arnet for her brilliance, for her willingness to read and reread, for her faith, and for her love. This book is dedicated to her.

Part of chapter 1 was previously published as "Romance in the Romance: Love and Marriage in Turn-of-the-Century Best Sellers," *Journal of Narrative Theory* 29 (Winter 1999): 110–34.

An earlier version of chapter 2 was published as "Something Old, Something New: Romance and Marital Advice in the 1920s," in *An Emotional History of the United States,* ed. Peter Stearns and Jan Lewis (New York: NYU Press, 1998).

Chapter 3 is a revised version of "Screwball Comedies: Constructing Romance, Mystifying Marriage," *Cinema Journal* 30, no. 4 (Summer 1991): 7–23.

A few paragraphs of chapter 6 appeared in "Woody Allen, 'the Artist,' and 'the Little Girl,'" in *The End of Cinema as We Know It: American Film in the Nineties,* ed. Jon Lewis (New York: NYU Press, 2001).

Modern Love

Introduction

A Brief History of Love

Moonlight and love songs
Never out of date,
Hearts full of passion,
Jealousy and Hate.
Woman needs Man
And man must have his mate,
That no one can deny.
> —"As Time Goes By," Herman Hupfield (1931)

I can change, I swear, oh,
See what you can do.
> —"You're a Big Girl Now," Bob Dylan (1974)

The songs quoted above both deal with love and what we have come to call "relationships," a term that would not have had the same meaning for Herman Hupfield in 1931. We easily recognize "As Time Goes By" as a love song—it is one of the most well-known love songs because of its featured role in the film *Casablanca*. But we might not be so quick to call Bob Dylan's "You're a Big Girl Now" a love song even though it tells the story of a failed relationship. The lyrics quoted differ in one obvious way: one set is about things staying the same, while the other talks of change. The songs also differ in ways that these brief quotations don't clearly illustrate. "As Time Goes By" deals in generalities. It claims to be describing how love is, not just always, but for everyone. "You're a Big Girl Now" is from the album *Blood on the Tracks*, which according to most commentators was a response to the failure of Dylan's marriage. Most of the songs on the album are narratives about particular experiences of love. Moreover, the singer seems to be groping

1

for knowledge about love or about how to make a relationship better, reflecting on his own mistakes as much as complaining about hers. The two songs exemplify the discourses of romance and intimacy and in so doing call into question Hupfield's main idea. Love has changed.

Learning How to Love

How do we learn about courtship, love, and marriage? Many people can recall in detail the way they learned about the mechanics of sex and reproduction, but few of us can be so specific about how we came to expect that falling in love would be the desirable or even necessary prelude to a happy marriage. We may even assume that one doesn't have to learn such expectations, since they are part of "human nature." The lyrics of "As Time Goes By" illustrate with a variety of examples the assertion that romantic love is indeed timeless and natural. This is stated even more explicitly in the song's infrequently performed introduction (or verse), which refers to the rapid pace of progress and intellectual change—illustrated by a reference to Einstein's theory of relativity—and proposes "the simple facts of life" as a respite. Romance, this introduction implies, is natural in a way that even physics is not. Romantic love may be the chief example in our culture of what is natural, uncontested, obvious, as in the cliché "Love makes the world go 'round."

Love stories permeate our lives. Novels and films so predictably include a love story as at least a subplot that most people don't think to inquire into the significance of this repetition. If we give it any thought at all, we probably assume that all these representations of love are themselves a response to people's natural concerns and therefore a reflection of reality. In addition, novels and movies are typically understood as mere entertainment, worthy of concern only when a politician such as Dan Quayle notes some deviance from what he takes to be the norm. But it is in these mainly fictional genres that love and marriage have been most frequently depicted. Historically, explicit instruction about love, courtship, and marriage has been much less common. Many people doubtless learned things about love from religious teaching and from the advice and example of elders and peers, yet such advice or influence was for many probably not as frequent or as powerful as the experiences of love that fiction provided.

My assumption is that these fictional narratives do in fact teach readers and viewers even if they are often unaware of the lesson. *Modern Love* explores what it is that stories about love and relationships have been teaching. My argument is that the kinds of stories that our culture has told itself have changed. For most of the twentieth century, such stories were written in the discourse of romance. "As Time Goes By," with its references to "passion, jealousy, and hate," but also to a world in which "lovers" will always be welcomed, is typical. Romantic stories deal with love that leads to marriage or love outside marriage, but not love in marriage. The expectation that marriage will be a continuation of the romantic state has been attributed to the influence of these romantic stories.

While most Americans still assume romance to be natural, the idea that romance is specific to the cultures of Europe and the West is not new. The existence of a competing discourse, however, has not generally been recognized. This new discourse, which I call "intimacy," emerged in the last third of the twentieth century, partly in response to the marriage crisis. The most typical instance of intimacy discourse is the instructional manual, and the very popularity of self-help books about relationships, the most popular of which now typically outsell the leading novels, is evidence of a cultural shift.[1] This discourse claims to be able to explain how marriage and other relationships work. "You're a Big Girl Now" is representative in that it states a plea to "work on the relationship" and expresses faith in the possibility of change. The discourse of intimacy makes emotional closeness, rather than passion, its Holy Grail. Intimacy, however, does not replace romance but coexists with it. Many stories of the later part of century are told as mixtures of intimacy and romance, which often function in tension with each other.

I call romance and intimacy "discourses" not to restrict my discussion to mere thoughts or words but to emphasize the role that stories and other representations play in shaping experience. Discourses are not doctrines or systems of ideas but rather groups of related narratives in terms of which men and women have projected the "natural" course of their lives. Discourses are not simple sets of prescriptions; rather than dictating particular beliefs or behaviors, they provide sets of terms in which differing thoughts might be formulated. Discourses produce many variations but at the same time exclude others entirely. For example, the discourse of romance includes both the position that love outside marriage is sinful and best avoided and the position that it is ennobling and highly desirable. It excludes the view that love is a form of affection or care that differs little whether it occurs within a family, between friends, or between lovers.

A *discourse* differs from an *ideology* in a number of ways depending in part on which definition of the latter one has in mind. In the Marxist definition of *ideology,* widely used in other theoretical contexts, the term implies a motivated misunderstanding of the world. Thus, "bourgeois ideology" is a set of assumptions or ideas that not only are the way the bourgeoisie conceive reality but also are a reflection of their interests as a class. Romance has often functioned ideologically in this sense. As any number of feminists have argued, romance has served the interests of men while seeming to represent the natural needs and desires of women.[2] While *Modern Love* will regularly observe romance in this role, the book will also show why romance is not restricted to it. It is not my intention to debunk romance as merely a pernicious illusion.[3] As for *ideology* in the second common usage, a systematic and typically rigidly held body of ideas, romance does not fit the definition. Romance has not usually been advocated as a doctrine, and its conceptions are too dispersed and even contradictory to qualify as a system of this kind.

Poststructuralism has caused us to question the assumption that we speak discourse, insisting that it speaks us. As Michel Foucault puts it, "Discourse is not the majestically unfolding manifestation of a thinking, knowing, speaking subject, but, on the contrary, a totality, in which the dispersion of the subject and his discontinuity with himself may be determined."[4] By placing the knowing subject in discourse, this body of theory has helped to make us aware that we are not capable of bringing to consciousness all of the background assumptions we must hold in order to function in a society. While not strictly poststructuralist, a remark on marriage by the French sociologist Pierre Bourdieu illustrates the point: "The constraints surrounding every matrimonial choice are so numerous and appear in such complex combinations that the individuals involved cannot possibly deal with all of them consciously."[5]

The danger of the poststructuralist position is that it seems to deny people the ability to make *any* rational evaluation of discourse and sometimes seems to ignore the diversity of discourses in which we typically find ourselves. Foucault claims that discourse is a "totality," but no one lives under a unified, coherent one. Rather, there are competing, contradictory discourses that sometimes allow us to use one to get a purchase on another. The theory of discourse I am assuming rejects the traditional alternative that texts either *influence* people—and thus cause behavior—or *re-*

flect preexisting realities. To say that novels and films teach us about love is not to say that we consciously learn their lessons or that it is impossible to reject or ignore them. Film scholar Virginia Wright Wexman describes Hollywood film as "modeling appropriate courtship behavior."[6] This is exactly right, if one understands "behavior" to include not just activity but also ideas and emotions. Such models typically are followed without an awareness of them as models. The fact that romance narratives are usually consumed as entertainment and often explicitly regarded as fantasy does limit the degree to which readers are likely to accept them as true, but this skepticism may not prevent a repeated pattern found in these texts from functioning as a model. Conversely, as sociologist Anthony Giddens has suggested, the fictional status of a narrative may enable it to be used by the reader consciously as a hypothetical model.[7] In other words, because the narrative does not claim literal truth, it is more available for testing against the reader's experience. In the theory I am arguing here, discourses define who we are and limit what we can say, while at same time allowing us to become someone different by enabling new things to be said.

Discourse understood in this way must exist at some remove from the social practices or behavior contemporary with it. Bourdieu and the German sociologist Niklas Luhmann treat discourses, or "codes," as Luhmann calls them, as constitutive of differing social practices. In this conception, changing patterns in fiction are taken as evidence for changing patterns of behavior. I'm not insisting on such significance for the books and films discussed below. Rather, these works are taken to be evidence of the existence and reach of the discourses of romance and intimacy. The discourses provide models for behavior that have been more or less accepted in different eras and that always exist in tension with models deriving from other discourses. What individuals actually do with these various models differs. Thus, neither discourse can be considered identical with the practice of courtship and marriage, which can differ significantly from the model.

That both discourses do function as models—and that they differ from each other—has been powerfully demonstrated by the feminist Sharon Thompson in *Going All the Way*. Thompson interviewed four hundred teenage girls, asking them to talk about their experiences of sex and romantic love. Not all the girls Thompson talked to were caught under the spell of love, and some were quite adept at using it for their own purposes. One group, however, Thompson calls "victims of love." Some of these girls held explicitly romantic visions of the lives they hoped to live. One interviewee, Tracy, regards sex as something to be bartered for love:

> She considered first sex an extremely serious experience in itself as well as an augury. If she had the ability to transform desire into love through the alchemy of sex, she could look forward to a marvelously romantic future and ultimately to marriage. If she didn't, if she couldn't even exchange virginity for love, what was she going to make a life worth living out of?[8]

This romantic conception of the future coexisted, however, with the influence of the discourse of intimacy. When Tracy finally did decide to have intercourse for the first time, it was in the context of what she described as a "meaningful relationship." "The meaningful relationship was almost as prevalent in the 1970s and '80s as going steady was in the 1950s."[9] According to Thompson, Tracy's "version of the meaningful relationship was really just a slight modification of the old idea of one true love that lasts forever."[10] Other girls, however, seem to have taken over more of the discourse of intimacy:

> They were . . . highly conversant with the language of therapy, and the therapeutic model was much in evidence when they talked about their expectations for a meaningful relationship. . . . Their accounts gave dominance to problems like feeling marginal or being wounded or disoriented by parental divorce. A combination of meaningful talk and sex could unravel and heal such problems, these narrators believed, and this was the role of the meaningful relationship. Practitioners expected their partners to "work on issues," "deal with problems," "talk things out," discuss pain, alienation, being different or alone or anxious and to be sensitive, responsive lovers. The relationship would last as long as the partners were able to shed a healing or clarifying light on each other's problems or perhaps even generate new problems to work on. Other relationships might also involve meaningful talk; the meaningful relationship simply produced the most meaning. This was the sense in which it was true love.[11]

While practitioners of this discourse conceived of love differently than the more traditionally romantic girls did, they continued to put enormous store in love. They were just as likely to regard "romantic failure as . . . one of the worst 'horrors of a teenage life.'"[12]

Thompson's book strongly suggests, although it does not explicitly argue, that the discourse of romance influences teenage girls across boundaries of class, race, and sexual orientation. Romance seems to be most important and most destructive to working-class girls like Tracy. Thompson attributes this to their seeing no choices for themselves besides marriage, but it may also be that romance continues to be at odds with other patterns of working-class life. Historians have long connected the rise of companionate marriage and the later association of romantic love and marriage to the rise of the bourgeoisie. The aristocrats needed marriages of alliance to preserve their power and wealth, and the working class typically married for the economic advantages that extra hands brought to a household. In the period with which I am concerned, however, the true bourgeoisie are no longer the innovators in matters of love and intimacy. It is rather the new middle classes—the petite bourgeoisie and the professional managerial class—who are positioned economically and educationally to develop new patterns of love and intimacy. The expansion of the professional managerial class throughout most of the twentieth century is one of the conditions that enabled the discourse of intimacy to develop. This fact is ratified by the upper-middle-class setting of the relationship stories and marriage fiction that I discuss in Part II.

The true bourgeoisie tend to revert to aristocratic patterns of marriage—as Edith Wharton's novels illustrate—while in the working class the separate spheres of the Victorian age continue to define heterosexual relationships. Among the working class, the divide that Giddens notes between men's and women's responses to romantic love would seem to be especially acute.[13] For both the bourgeoisie and the working class, economic considerations play a larger role than they do for the middle classes, who are freer to experiment. *Modern Love* does deal with some works that depict a bourgeois milieu—most screwball comedies, for example—but this setting is almost never meant to distinguish the characters' habits of love or marriage, which are middle class. I assume that the most ready audience for the lessons these texts teach is also middle class.

The films, novels, and advice manuals I'm concerned with depict heterosexual relationships and most directly hail heterosexual men and women; my focus is on what these people are likely to learn from them.

Gay men and lesbians do, I think, also learn from stories devoted to heterosexual relations, but what they learn is also transformed in complicated ways. Romance is not, as is often alleged, an exclusively heterosexual discourse in our society, but its narrative patterns that take marriage as a defining category cannot have the same meaning for those whom that category excludes. It is also true, of course, that gay and lesbian experience and representations of it have had an impact on heterosexuality. Moreover, gay artists have given us some of the most popular representations of heterosexual love, such as the songs of Cole Porter and the films of George Cukor—though just how these men's private sexual orientation made an impact on their work remains to be determined. The increasing visibility of and tolerance for homosexual practices has doubtless had an impact on the meaning of various kinds of heterosexual relations. According to Giddens, because gays could not marry they "have therefore been forced to pioneer the more open and negotiated relationships which subsequently have permeated the heterosexual population."[14] Explicitly gay or lesbian fiction and films have remained limited enough in their reach, however, that they cannot be regarded as a significant source for heterosexuals' conceptions of love and relationships.

In another road not taken, this book could have surveyed the literature and film of various ethnic minorities for their representations of love, courtship, and marriage. Immigrants often bring with them practices that differ markedly from those dominant in the United States, including, for example, arranged marriage. Other ethnic groups' patterns of courtship and marriage differ from those of the white, Anglo middle class. Sometimes, as in *Crossing Delancey* (Joan Micklin Silver, 1988) or *Mississippi Masala* (Mira Nair, 1991), this conflict becomes the subject of an independent film or a novel, but it is seldom the focus of mainstream treatments of love and marriage.

African Americans' experiences of slavery and racial oppression have had an impact on how love and marriage have been depicted in the novels and films they have produced. As literary scholar Ann duCille notes, "Marriage is necessarily a historically complex and contradictory concept in African American history and literature. . . . [F]or nineteenth-century African Americans, recently released from slavery and its dramatic disruption of marital and family life, marriage rites were a long-denied basic human right—signs of liberation and entitlement to both democracy and desire."[15] As a result, African American fiction, while continuing to make use of marriage plots, is much less prone to specifically romantic treatments of love and marriage. As duCille concludes, "The particular history of African Americans has complicated the marriage stories black authors have told and continue to tell. Alice Walker's first novel, *The Third Life of Grange Copeland* (1970), for example, highlights the disparity between the implicit promises of the marriage ideal . . . and the explicit impossibilities of the actual social and material conditions of . . . most black Americans."[16] Films focusing on African American culture tend to reflect the working-class gap between men's and women's attitudes toward love and marriage, and, as a result, they tend to fall outside the patterns of the screwball comedy or the relationship story.[17] Films that deal with interracial marriage typically fail to do anything else very interesting with love because they focus on the conflicts that the relationship generates in or between the couple's families.[18]

If racism and racial conflict are not my subjects, and conflicts of sexual orientation and class are more background than foreground for this study, gender conflict is of central concern in *Modern Love*. The book is partly motivated by the belief that gender inequality is one of the chief barriers to successful heterosexual relationships. Each chapter explores the nature of that inequality and its effects on love, courtship, and marriage. The book does not assume, however, that it is the main function of the representations of these in film or fiction to perpetuate that inequality. While that is doubtless part of the cultural work of many of the texts I discuss here, many of them also contribute to or at least reflect changes in the culture that have made gender relations more equal and gender roles more flexible. Part of the story this book tells is of the decline of patriarchal power and of the success of women's struggles.

Academic fields such as women's studies, African American studies, and gay and lesbian studies have made us aware that the white, the male, and the heterosexual cannot be treated as normative. While these studies have assumed and critiqued the illegitimate domination of whites, men, and heterosexuals, they have also tended to take the character of the dominant for granted and to focus their interpretive energy on the works of the marginal and oppressed. Lately, however, cultural studies has begun to return to the dominant, now relativized by the existence of historical and cultural difference. I have chosen texts—a few canonical, most not—that best illustrate romance and intimacy and that by their popularity demonstrate the cultural reach of these discourses. It is not my goal to canonize these texts but to treat them as artifacts of the culture that produces and consumes them.

If I have chosen mainly popular books and films, I have not devoted chapters to other media that reach larger audiences because I believe they have been less important to the development and spread of romance and intimacy. Television, with the exception of the soap opera, has from its inception been much less focused on romantic love than film. In recent years, since it became possible to deal with sex openly on television, romance has been more in evidence, but it still does not play the dominant role here that it does in other popular media. The more routine way in which television is used by consumers may make it less a source of deeply internalized narratives than novels or movies. The talk show boom of the 1980s and 1990s has doubtless contributed to the spread of the discourse of intimacy, but the talk show is not a site in which the complexities of this discourse can easily be observed or analyzed. Similarly, while it is true that popular songs have long been predominantly concerned with love, their form makes them less useful texts for the interpretive work I am engaged in here. The limited number of words a song contains restricts what it can communicate, and throughout most of twentieth century, popular songs were not typically narrative. Popular songs have reinforced the cultural power of romance and intimacy, but the way in which popular music is used may make it less significant in spreading these discourses. Popular songs are most often experienced as ephemeral and transient, the background rather than the focus of the listener's attention.

Fiction and film are experienced quite differently from television and popular music. Novels especially demand a commitment of considerable time and attention. Moreover, they encourage emotional involvement. Readers often report that they find themselves transported out of their mundane reality and into the fictional world that the novel evokes. Movies also command identification from the viewer, and the star system, Hollywood's practice of building films around two or more carefully nurtured and promoted personalities, has helped to transfer such identification from fictional character to actor, thus maintaining it from film to film. The physical beauty and glamour of the stars reinforce the allure of the romance that their films typically portray. And, like novels, theatrical films are experienced apart from mundane reality, in this case literally apart in a special darkened space where both sight and sound are larger than life.

Love's Prehistory

Most of us probably don't normally think of love as having a history, much less a prehistory. We assume, with "As Time Goes By," that love, desire, sex, and marriage are eternal and that they don't vary significantly from culture to culture. There are senses, I believe, in which it is proper to speak of love as an experience that most humans share. Like other mammals, humans typically begin life in an emotional attachment with one or both parents. The capacity for such attachment presumably is at the root of all of the psychological bonds that humans form later in life, including those with siblings, relatives, friends, lovers, spouses, and even pets. But while such bonds can have very different degrees and qualities, the capacity to bond does not by itself account for the experience of love usually associated with romance. Yet anthropologists have discovered that experiences like those we name "romantic love" or "romantic passion" are recorded across a wide range of cultures.[19] The anthropologist Helen Fisher describes the elements of this experience, including patterns of courtship behavior and feelings she labels "infatuation," which seem to represent another capacity available to most human beings.[20]

Let us grant that there exists a more or less universally human capability, "infatuation," and distinguish it from "romantic love," a way of writing, thinking about, and experiencing love that is distinctive to the cultures of Western Europe.[21] "Romantic love" in this sense is best understood as a culturally specific discourse. The point is not that humans elsewhere lack the capacity to experience what we typically call romance or that they never do so. Rather, it is that the place that passionate love is given in Western culture and the specific form it has taken there are not universal.

The idea that love has a history is not new even if it is fairly recent. Denis de Rougemont's *Love in the Western World* might be taken to mark the emergence of a specifically historical treatment of love,[22] though Sigmund Freud and sexologists such as Richard von Krafft-Ebing had early in the century already at least implicitly relativized love by naturalizing sex. Since Rougemont, we have seen studies such as *Love as Passion,* by the German sociologist Niklas Luhmann, and *The Transformation of Intimacy,* by the British sociologist Anthony Giddens, argue for fundamental historical shifts in the experience of love. The literary scholar Joseph Boone and the film scholar Virginia Wright Wexman have treated the history of love as expressed in the particular cultural forms they study.[23] In spite of these books, most people in the United States now so routinely associate love and marriage that it is easy to forget that they have not always been so connected.

Marriage in most cultures has been understood mainly as a social institution and a property relation rather than a personal commitment and an emotional relation. The traditional meaning of *love* is not romance but social solidarity; it corresponds to the capacity for bonding rather than the capacity for infatuation. For most of Western history, as Luhmann argues, "What was considered important is not living out one's own passions, but rather a voluntarily (and not compulsorily or slavishly) developed solidarity within a given order. And the master was thought of as someone who loved his property, i.e., his house and home, wife and children."[24]

Representations of love from such cultures are often read today as dealing with romance, but to do so is to misunderstand what these texts meant to their original audiences. The literature of ancient Greece, for example, is full of sexual intrigue and passion, yet it does not typically follow the pattern of romantic narratives, the overcoming of the obstacles that stand in the way of true love. In Euripedes' *Medea,* for example, the protagonist kills her children because her husband has left her for another woman. The act demonstrates her passion, yet it is not primarily the loss of Jason's love that she avenges but the loss of power and privilege that the marriage provided. By killing his children, Medea deprives Jason of the one thing he valued from the marriage. The most famous triangle in ancient Greek literature, that of Oedipus and his parents, is again not romantic. The issues here are fate and incest, and Sophocles' *Oedipus Tyrannus* tells us nothing of the characters' desire, passion, courtship, or marriage. Even the so-called "Greek romances" are not about love triangles typical of the Middle Ages and later. Rather, they seem to be about the exchange of women between fathers and husbands. Greek New Comedy is also about such exchange, as revealed by its typical focus on the objections of the woman's father. Yet Greek comedy probably provides the ur-story of the romance discourse, since it is about courtship and ends in marriage. It remains unromantic, however, because its chief concern is the renewal of society and not the passion of the lovers.

Not only literature but also the actual practice of love and marriage has differed significantly over the course of history. In ancient Rome, "Love in marriage was a stroke of good fortune; it was not the basis of the institution."[25] In the early Middle Ages, though the Church insisted on monogamy and indissoluble marriage, these did not become common practice until the tenth century. And marriage was still not founded on love, which was regarded as a destructive passion. The term *love* was not used in connection with official marriages. The proper attitudes between a married couple were said to be tenderness, friendship, and respect, but misogynist attitudes doubtless made such feelings difficult and perhaps rare.

The direct precursors of the literature of romance in Europe were probably written in Arabic and Persian. *Layla and Majnun,* a Persian poem of the twelfth century by Nizami, describes the obsessive love of the poet Majnun for his cousin Layla. The very extremity of Majnun's love leads Layla's father to prohibit their marriage even though Layla also loves Majnun. Like medieval European romances, this narrative tells of an impossible love. But unlike them, it clearly depicts passion as a misfortune. Majnun's love is so extreme that it drives him mad, making him unfit to be a husband.[26] Passion here is treated in a way that is consistent with its treatment in the ancient world. If there is a change, it is in the focus on the experience of passion; the judgment of it remains the same. Moreover, in *Layla and Majnun* the obstacle to the lovers' union is the father's prohibition, as it typically was in ancient comedy. Marriage here continues to be depicted as exchange between men in which the woman's wishes are ultimately irrelevant.

Courtly Love and Medieval Romance

Romance emerged as a counterdiscourse representing at least a theoretical alternative to the repressive character of officially sanctioned marriages among the aristocracy. The rise of the literature of romance, which includes both lyric poetry and narrative romances, corresponds to shifts in manners and morals in the courts of feudal Europe. One of these changes was that women, who had been assumed to be corrupt and corrupting, came to be idealized, and love was idealized in the process.[27] Historians today suggest that this idealization probably caused little immediate change in marriage or in women's lot, though its impact was felt in the long run. The idealization of love was one of the conditions for the emergence of the discourse of romance, but this elevated sense of love was not then connected to marriage. "Whether love and marriage were compatible was the great question that agitated the courts of Champagne and

Ile-de-France."[28] The creed of courtly love argued that they were not; as Andreas Capellanus's twelfth-century treatise, *The Art of Courtly Love,* insists, "Everybody knows that love can have no place between husband and wife."[29] As this text describes it, love at its most pure will exist between a knight and a lady of higher rank. While this love is passionate, it is to be unconsummated. But as Boone notes, "The extent to which *amour courtois* [courtly love] existed as a real phenomenon beyond literary convention remains open to speculation."[30] French historian Georges Duby describes it as a "great game" in which "the Lord's wife was coveted, and the desire she inspired, sublimated into a sophisticated form of love, was used as a means of disciplining young knights."[31] Duby believes that this game only infrequently resulted in actual adultery, but the lyric poems and romances of the period often describe explicitly or implicitly consummated adultery between such partners.[32]

The first two books of *The Art of Courtly Love* may have been a hoax; the text does a complete reversal in Book 3 and ends by criticizing the extramarital love it originally had endorsed, but this failure to endorse the love it first claimed to instruct is typical of the discourse that will develop after it. Romance has seldom been expressed as a doctrine or explicitly used as the basis for moral instruction.[33] But romance did produce a raft of new literary forms. It is no coincidence that the name *romance* means, in addition to a kind of love, a kind of story. These two definitions stem from the fact that romantic love was originally disseminated most widely in the extended narratives we call medieval romances.

The structure of these medieval romances is distinct from the structure typical of the narratives that precede them. Their specific narratological structure was discovered by literary scholar Donald Maddox in the *Lais* of Marie de France. Maddox argues that short narratives in the Middle Ages had been dyadic, involving an exchange between two subjects. Marie's *Lais,* on the contrary, feature a triadic structure, including a pair of subjects and an excluded third subject. Maddox illustrates the structure as a triangle with each member of the pair at an angle on top and the third term at the bottom (see figure 1). Narrative succession occurs because the excluded subject always seeks to be included in the pair. When he or she is included, this will necessarily displace someone else.[34] In most romances, the narrative structure is actually represented by a triangular set of relationships among lovers, but the narrative structure is not identical with the love triangle, since other relationships—for example, fa-

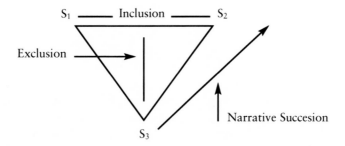

Intersubjective relations and narrative succession in the discourse of romance. Adapted from Donald Maddox, "Triadic Structure in the *Lais* of Marie de France," *Assays* 3 (1985): 22.

ther/daughter or king/court—may be represented. Maddox describes this narrative structure as *intersubjective* because all three subjects of the narrative are represented as both desiring and desirable. The intersubjective character of romance helps to explain its extraordinary power to generate emotional investment. The reader of a romance is positioned to identify with the excluded subject and experiences his or her desire, motivating and structuring the reader's attention.

The triadic structure of romance enshrines the obstacle as the indispensable element of such a narrative. Love stories are seldom simple celebrations of ecstasy. While they may have ecstatic moments, these at best punctuate a series of events that keep the lovers apart. Historically, the discourse of romance transformed passion from a pain that it was best to avoid into an experience to be sought. The view of passion as a misfortune continues to be present in some of the early European romances, such as *Tristan,* but in them, this view is undermined by the events of the stories they tell. *Tristan* is ultimately a tragedy, but it is a marvelous adventure first. It celebrates the lovers' passion before it shows the consequences of that passion, the lovers' deaths. Moreover, it is a tale of mutual love, in which the woman's desire is every bit as important as the man's desire. As in most other European romances, the obstacles standing between Tristan and Isolde result from the fact that she is married to someone else. *Tristan,* unlike *Layla and Majnun,* is not a story of love that can never be consummated; it is a tale of an adulterous affair. What is impossible for Tristan and Isolde is not love but marriage.

Early Modern Love

Rougemont famously claims that "happy love has no history."[35] While this is an accurate account of the medieval discourse of romance, it is a vast overstatement when it is applied to the entire history of Western culture. Rougemont ignores several important genres that contradict his point. The earliest of these is Shakespearean romantic comedy, which, it has been suggested, expresses a new, middle-class myth that links romantic love and marriage.[36] Unlike ancient comedy, Shakespeare's is concerned with marriage as a matter of individual happiness as much as a rite of social renewal. Perhaps even more germane to the history of love, his comedies not only embody a new pattern that unites romance and marriage but also reflect the old practice of marriage as alliance.

The two couples in *Much Ado about Nothing,* for example, seem to embody two conflicting conceptions of marriage that correspond to their different creative origins. Shakespeare is believed to have borrowed the basic outline of *Much Ado* from an earlier play that itself made use of a story found in various sixteenth-century sources, including *The Faerie Queene* and an Italian novel by Matteo Bandello. These sources contain the story of Hero and Claudio, the first marriage to be planned in the play, which is quite explicitly arranged. Don Pedro courts Hero and wins her for Claudio. It is significant that Hero is Claudio's choice, but we the audience see nothing that would help us to understand this choice. The lack of knowledge that each has of the other is the condition of Don John's temporarily successful slander of Hero. This story gives a picture of the traditional marriage of alliance, albeit with a comic aura that largely disguises its political foundation.

The story of the play's other couple, Beatrice and Benedict, is Shakespeare's own invention, and it reflects the emerging ideal of marriage based on the needs and desires of increasingly individualized persons. It is true that Beatrice and Benedict are tricked into believing that each loves the other, yet this "arrangement" only works because the two already know each other deeply. That knowledge is expressed in the couple's verbal sparring, and this competition grants a degree of equality between these two lovers that is not depicted between Hero and Claudio. Beatrice and Benedict's sparring serves as both obstacle and enticement to their love, a combination perfectly consistent with the discourse of romance. We will see this device again in Hollywood's screwball comedies. The difference between this early modern version of that discourse and the one we observed in the Middle Ages is that Beatrice and Benedict do get married, and we are meant to believe in their living happily ever after.

Much Ado about Nothing is probably more a utopian vision of marriage and courtship than a reflection of widespread change in practice, and it certainly does not give us grounds for assuming that a courtship like Beatrice and Benedict's was typical. Still, historians are divided about courtship practices in the sixteenth and seventeenth centuries. Lawrence Stone argues that "for all classes who possessed property, that is the top two-thirds economically, marriage before the seventeenth century was arranged by the parents, and the motives were the economic and political benefit of the kin group, not the emotional satisfaction of the individuals."[37] But Richard Adair asserts that "even among the aristocracy . . . a certain degree of choice was always extended to children, particularly sons, and it was rare for them to be forced into marriage with an unwanted partner."[38]

Historians are also divided about the character of early modern marriages. Stone believes that before about 1660, they typically lacked even affection, but it has been claimed that "diaries, letters, ballads, and church court cases" prove otherwise.[39] Romantic love was a frequent literary concern but was uncommon in life except for one social group, "the one in which it had always existed since the twelfth century, that is the households of the prince and the great nobles."[40] And in these households romantic love existed outside marriage and was often adulterous; only by chance might it lead to marriage. Other historians believe that romantic love was much more commonly associated with marriage in Shakespeare's time, and they cite literature as evidence.[41]

There is more agreement that in the seventeenth century, a new form of marriage emerged in England that Stone names "the companionate marriage."[42] Unlike the sort of marriage proposed under this name in the twentieth century, this form was not based on romance. In companionate marriage, "the choice of spouse was increasingly left in the hands of children themselves and was based mainly on temperamental compatibility with the aim of lasting companionship."[43] Marriage now assumed friendship or affection rather than passion as its basis, and it entailed more legal equality between the partners. As feminist literary historian Nancy Armstrong describes it, this modification of patriarchy took the form of an exchange in which the woman ceded her political power to the man in return for control of the domestic sphere and emotions.[44] This bargain continued in force well into the twentieth century, and the Victorian doctrine of "separate spheres" can be understood as an outgrowth.

During the time the British were practicing "companionate" marriage, there developed among the French aristocracy an elaborate social code for adulterous love that Luhmann labels *amour passion*. Manuals printed during this period taught readers how to seduce and be seduced: Seduction becomes a game with two players, at which point it can only be a game that both parties see through—that is, a game in which they take part only because they wish to take part. Players agree to subject themselves to the code and its rules and allow themselves to be seduced or at least play for a while with fire. The game's fascination lies in this quality of its conceivably getting out of control—from the points of view of both players.[45]

Where medieval discourse had idealized love, the Classical Age "paradoxicalized" it. "The special sphere accorded to love relations makes it clear that here *the code is 'only a code' and that love is an emotion preformed, and indeed prescribed, in literature,* and no longer directed by social institutions such as family or religion."[46] In this system, love is not merely opposed to marriage; society has created a separate social arrangement in which love can flourish. We don't remember the literature of *amour passion* very often these days, but the literature of reaction against it from the late eighteenth century is quite familiar. Mozart's opera *Don Giovanni* and Laclos's novel *Les Liaisons Dangereuses* are representations of *amour passion* from the point of view of romantic love, its successor in cultural dominance. The seducer now is either an evil exploiter of innocence and/or a romantic who is unaware of him- or herself.

The Triumph of Romance

The emergence of the discourse of romance as the dominant way of conceiving love and marriage depends upon the historical evolution of the individual. As capitalism dissolved more and more of the social bonds that had structured traditional societies, persons became increasingly individualized. Individuals are persons who are understood to be differentiated from all others and not to be defined by membership in a class or caste. To be an individual is to have a distinctive inner life or psychology. To be sure, the traditional view of personhood assumed a substantial soul, but the soul's distinctiveness was known only to God. In the feudal era, nobles were more individualized than members of other classes were. The rise of capitalism not only extended individualization, first to the bourgeoisie and then to other classes, but made persons of these classes more individualized than medieval lords and ladies. Romantic love accompanied the dawning of individualization among the bourgeoisie, and it became a dominant discourse only when individualization was widespread.

It was only in the nineteenth century that romantic expectations began to be commonly attached to marriage. As Stone puts it,

> It was not . . . until the romantic movement and the rise of the novel, especially the pulp novel, in the nineteenth century, that society at large accepted a new idea—that it was normal and indeed praiseworthy for young men and women to fall passionately in love, and that there must be something wrong with those who have failed to have such an overwhelming experience some time in late adolescence or early manhood [*sic*].[47]

Yet this shift in cultural values does not mean either that marriages suddenly became more passionate or loving or that romance now ruled the emotional world without opposition. While the separate spheres that men and women were encouraged to inhabit probably helped to foster a romantic conception of marriage by making the other gender more mysterious, this separation also must have inhibited marital love. Victorian sexual repression meant that men continued to look for sexual satisfaction outside marriage. We have evidence from such sources as letters and diaries that romantic love was indeed increasingly the dominant conception of the grounds for marriage during the nineteenth century.[48] In these letters and diaries people use the romantic language of novels to describe their own experience of love. At the same time, marriage manuals consistently warn their readers against the illusions of romantic love. Both religious and "scientific" advice books of the period depict the ideal marriage as something like a successful business arrangement. Love is often identified with devotion and friendship rather than romance or pleasure. Conceptions of love and marriage in the nineteenth century were divided among those deriving from romance, from companionate marriage, from more traditional economic and social considerations, and from other sources.

As long as the opposition between love and marriage remained dominant in society, fiction continued to follow the pattern Rougemont describes. When, as Luhmann puts it, "passionate love [was proclaimed] to be the very principle upon which the *choice* of a spouse should be based," the typical narrative of romance also changed: "the old thesis of the incompatibility of love and marriage had to be covered up; the end of the novel was not the end of life."[49] While the medieval and early modern models assumed a fundamental incompatibility between romance and marriage, the romantic ideology of the nineteenth century assumed their inseparability. It is this later version of romance that was dominant in America in the late nineteenth and twentieth centuries. The most popular narratives of this era, both in print and on screen, unite romantic love and marriage more explicitly than was typical even in the early nineteenth century. This version of the discourse of romance holds that there is a right man or woman for each person. It projects a life story that involves meeting that individual and living with him or her in marriage.

There is general agreement among historians of love and marriage that novels were the primary means by which a romantic conception of marriage came to be widely held.[50] Since the fictional status of novels and movies is often taken to compromise any claim to truth that they may seem to make, we may wonder why fiction could have served this function. We call the cognitive attitude that a typical consumer of fiction takes toward a story "suspension of disbelief." The reader or viewer knows that what he or she is experiencing is "only a story," but the full experience of the narrative depends on a temporary forgetting of this knowledge. If the story is successful, most readers or viewers will not merely comprehend the words or images but also live with and through the characters for the duration of the narrative. In surrendering to the story, the reader or viewer typically accepts the point or points of identification that the text offers. So readers, male or female, of *Jane Eyre* usually identify much more with Jane, the narrator and protagonist, than with any of the other characters. Literary and film theorists describe this effect as the "positioning" of the reader or spectator. Such positioning involves more than emotional identification with a character; it can entail the acceptance of a whole range of assumptions associated with the character. The reader of *Jane Eyre* is positioned not merely to want for Jane what Jane herself most wants—to marry Rochester—but also to accept, at least while in the world of the novel, that the desire to marry for love is natural. Such positioning is all the more effective and consequential when, as is the case here, it reinforces the positioning of discourse in general social circulation.

After the story is finished, "disbelief" is resumed. The reader, having finished the novel, doesn't believe that Jane Eyre is a real person. The reader's emotional experience produced by the novel is real, however. If, in seeking similar experiences, a reader repeatedly experiences the same kind of narrative pattern, might that not also come to seem real or true even if the characters and events are never held to be factual? And if the narrative pattern confirms or illustrates more broadly held beliefs or expectations, then it would in a sense be "true" in advance of the reading. We can assume that, so long as fictional romance was at odds with social practice, it would typically have been regarded as fantasy and would not usually have led people to expect to experience the pattern in their own lives. But as the traditional practice broke down and individuals increasingly chose their own partners, the fictional discourse no longer seemed so fantastic. Moreover, the breakdown of the traditional practice increased interest in fictional romance, and technological innovation in the nineteenth century meant that that interest could be indulged as never before. We can't say that fiction by itself changed the practice of courtship and marriage, but we can say that it was part of the context that helped form new practices.

In the nineteenth century, romance became grafted onto marriage, but it has never become entirely at ease with the union. This combination produced a tension within the discourse because its essential characteristics derive from adulterous love. As the chapters in the first section of this book will show, narratives written in the discourse of romance contain in some form, however repressed or vestigial, what Luhmann called "the old thesis" of love's incompatibility with marriage. Because the fundamental structure of romance narratives is triadic, the form does not lend itself to accounts of the couple. The stories that romance narratives tell now more often than not endorse marriage, but the endorsement typically relies on the excitement and adventure of illicit love. Often the entire story is taken up with overcoming obstacles, so that only in the end, offscreen, as it were, do the lovers fulfill their desire for each other.

Thus, the last and perhaps most important characteristic of the discourse of romance: whatever its attitude toward marriage, it does not depict it. Romance may describe chaste courtly love, it may revel in adulterous passion, or it may give an account of an extended courtship ending in a marriage made in heaven, but it cannot tell the story of a marriage. It is in part because of this inability that the discourse of intimacy arose.

The Marriage Crisis

The growth of capitalism not only made people into individuals; it also caused older social relations to dissolve. Where marriage had previously been a central structure in which property could be preserved or augmented, under capitalism it tended to lose this role. As institutions such as the corporation replaced the family as the major repositories of wealth, marriage was increasingly freed from the necessity of being a financial alliance. Historian John Gillis has argued that even the rituals associated with marriage became increasingly private, as weddings, kissing, and other behaviors retreated from public spaces.[51] Marriage became more private as its social function became less significant.

The social expectation of marriage had always been binding on women in a way that it had not been on men. Marriage was expected because women had few if any socially acceptable alternatives. But as women began to envision life projects beyond those of wife and mother, marriage became not only an option rather than a rule but also an option that might get in the way of a career or of a quest for personal fulfillment. While the vast majority of women still married, they were increasingly unwilling to accept unhappiness as the price for keeping a marriage together. Until the twentieth century, divorce, which Milton had argued in the seventeenth century was a necessary condition for loving marriages, remained socially taboo even when and where it became legal.

Paradoxically, it was only when marriage became a choice that expectations of it radically increased. Marriage became both a bigger—or at least different—site for emotional investment and a more fragile bond. As long as marriage functioned as the cornerstone of the social edifice, divorce had to be prohibited or strongly discouraged. Traditionally, this state of affairs was accepted because marriages were not assumed to provide the benefits of romantic love or indeed to exist for the purpose of making individuals happy. But with marriage now being less a social necessity and with more individualized persons demanding happiness, divorce became more acceptable and more common. The new vision of romantic marriage engendered expectations that many marriages did not fulfill, in part because romance offered no vision of how marriage might fulfill them.

According to May, the result was a massive shift in patterns of marriage and divorce. "During the late nineteenth and early twentieth centuries, American marriages began to collapse at an unprecedented rate. Between

1867 and 1929, the population of the United States increased 300 percent, the number of marriages 400 percent, and the divorce rate 2,000 percent. By the end of the 1920s, more than one marriage in six ended in divorce every year."[52] If divorce had been increasing since the nineteenth century, it continued to do so in the twentieth. Between 1910 and 1940, the divorce rate nearly doubled, in spite of a slight decline in the 1930s.[53] Debate over the causes of the crisis raged in newspapers, magazines, and scholarly journals. Many explanations were offered, ranging from women's emancipation and liberal divorce laws to the general conditions of urban life. May's explanation is that rising expectations of personal satisfaction and happiness put an increased burden on marriage that it was unable to bear. May seems unaware, however, that a version of this explanation was also articulated at the time. Several studies related the failure of marriages to expectations engendered by romance.[54] If, as Luhmann notes, this explanation remains speculative, May's analysis of divorce cases goes some way toward supporting it.[55] May adds to the traditional sources of romance the example set by movie stars, such as Douglas Fairbanks and Mary Pickford, who became identified "with an entirely new type of home."[56] While the home had traditionally been identified as an institution that demanded sacrifice and communal values, the new home was "self-contained" and "geared to personal happiness."[57]

That the rise in the divorce rate should be considered a crisis shows that older views of marriage, both religious and secular, persisted. Even though sociologists recognized that marriage no longer played the same role that it used to, they continued to see it as a fundamental social building block. While there were critics of marriage who thought that the institution should be abolished, most of the discussion of the crisis involved proposals for trying to save it. As we will see in chapter 2, feminists like Elinor Glyn and Marie Carmichael Stopes continued to treat marriage as the only legitimate form of relationship. More than this, they treated marriage as having the potential to yield a transcendent happiness available from no other source. Thus marriage, increasingly freed from its social obligations, also came increasingly under the pressure of ever-greater personal expectations. The discourse of romance narrated these expectations, but it was not by itself responsible for their rise. Rather, increasing social fragmentation meant that marriage had to fill in the emotional gap left by the demise of other relations. As individuals found themselves ever more alienated from each other and from their work, they made marriage the refuge of human connection.

Intimacy

Sociologist Francesca Cancian remarks of early nineteenth-century America that "marital intimacy, in the modern sense of emotional expression and verbal disclosure of personal experience, was probably rare. Instead, husband and wife were likely to share a more formal and wordless kind of love, based on duty, working together, mutual help, and sex."[58] My investigation into the discourses of love supports Cancian's contention, for emotional expression and verbal disclosure of personal experience were not typically understood to define a good marriage in the nineteenth century. In her study of nineteenth-century American love letters, the American studies scholar Karen Lystra finds that "self-disclosure" was understood to be an important aspect of courtship but finds much less of it in letters written by couples after they married.[59] While romantic love urged emotional expression outside marriage in courtship or adultery, it didn't provide a model for the continuing expression of emotion. As historian Peter Stearns has shown, Victorian culture did value intense emotional experience and its expression in poetry and other arts, but within a marriage, the need for "serenity" demanded "emotional repression."[60] Cancian names qualities that we have come to expect in marriage only since the twentieth century.

The discourse of intimacy is both an expression of these new expectations of marriage and a response to the crisis that they in part provoked. The new desire for intimacy, a special closeness founded on verbal openness, has its roots in alienation caused by social fragmentation under capitalism. But this desire was in the beginning formulated in terms of the discourse of romance. It was psychotherapy, especially psychoanalysis, that enabled a new discourse to emerge. Since therapy is by definition a response to an illness, a crisis, the application of it to marriage could come only after a crisis or problem in marriage was widely perceived. At one level, the discourse of intimacy arose because many people—including social scientists, public moralists, politicians, and psychoanalysts, but also private individuals—were troubled by the failure of marriages to last and to satisfy. But the discourse of intimacy is also a more direct response to the reduced social role of marriage. Since marriage was increasingly seen as a private matter, it could no longer be justified as the exclusive legitimate context for sexual relations. People began experimenting more openly and in larger numbers with various alternatives to marriage, including heterosexual and homosexual practices. From the late nineteenth through the mid-twentieth centuries, courtship and marriage continued to be the very powerful norm, but by the 1960s, a new term, *relationship*, had emerged to cover the new variety of commonly practiced erotically invested bonds between individuals. Marriage was now only one alternative, albeit still the dominant one, in which intimacy might occur.

In that last sentence, *intimacy* is used ambiguously. It could mean in the context either "sexual relations" or "emotional closeness." While both of these meanings persist today, the connotations of the word *intimacy* have subtly changed during the twentieth century. From the seventeenth century through the nineteenth century, it was, as it still is, a euphemism for sexual relations. But its primary meanings were, according to the *Oxford English Dictionary,* "the state of being personally intimate; intimate friendship or acquaintance; familiar intercourse; close familiarity; an instance of this." Thus, in Jane Austen's novels, intimacy was what a family shared and what it might extend to specially favored others. Intimacy was not what Elisabeth Bennet, say, expected to achieve in her marriage to Darcy; it was rather a simple condition of the married state. By the late twentieth century, however, intimacy had become a quality by which a marriage could be measured. Thus, a typical formulation from an advice book states that "of all the components of marriage, intimacy is probably the quality most longed for, and often the most elusive."[61] Intimacy was once what distinguished marriage and family from most other social relations; it is now a quality that marriages may or may not have and that couples are told they must work to attain.

If love is a duty, as it was conceived in the traditional view of marriage, then in principle anyone is capable of performing it. If love is something that befalls one, as the discourse of romance would have it, then whether a couple loves is beyond their control. It is the premise of the discourse of intimacy that love is something that happens between lovers. While it is partly a function of who they are as individuals, it is also a function of how they behave in the relationship. In the early part of the twentieth century, popular advisers such as Dorothy Dix began to pave the way for the new discourse. These advisers reflected an increasingly widespread belief that some individuals are suited psychologically for each other, while others are unsuited and should not marry. Moreover, advice columnists probably helped to condition the population to accept the idea that a marriage could be "worked on," even though their recommendations tended to be fairly limited in scope. We get the first hints of a deeper analysis of marriage and its problems in the 1920s, but these advice books remain mainly within the discourse of romance; their novelty lies in applying that discourse explicitly to marital relationships. It is only after World War II, and mainly after the 1960s, that intimacy as a distinct discourse develops, producing new descriptions of and prescriptions for the "relationship." It also has produced a distinctive narrative form. Besides exposition and instruction, intimacy manuals typically rely on the case history as a major element. The case history has been picked up by novelists, filmmakers, and even songwriters and has been transformed into new genres telling new kinds of stories that are increasingly influential.

Readers will, I am sure, be aware that the discourse of intimacy has not "solved" the crisis of marriage. Divorce rates have leveled off, but they have not receded. What's more, there is now evidence that fewer people are getting married. Some feminists and others on the left have long considered marriage an inherently oppressive institution. More recently, advocates of same-sex marriage are challenging some of the basic terms in which marriage has been understood. Our society is increasingly accepting of a diversity of intimate relationships, yet the widespread influence of the discourse of intimacy suggests that most Americans still value marriage very highly. It is certainly true that none of the alternatives to marriage seem satisfactory replacements for it. Intimacy discourse thus finds itself caught between its bias toward marriage and its assumption that marriage is just one kind of relationship. In the examples discussed below, we will see both sides of this tension explored. The new film genre, "the relationship story," takes the nonmarital relationship as its focus. Fiction by the writers John Updike and Alison Lurie, on the contrary, looks at marriage with a brutal honesty that was not possible when marriage seemed to hold society together. In both genres, marriage is presented as difficult and likely to fail, yet happy marriage remains at least the implicit goal of the characters depicted.

Even in its most distinct expressions, the discourse of intimacy has not banished romance, which remains an element of the other discourse. Romance is in intimacy a stage in the relationship, or a reproducible experience that a couple can make or purchase.[62] Moreover, the discourse of romance continues to exist on its own. There is much evidence in contemporary novels and movies to show that romance is more influential than ever. The success of romantic films such as *Pretty Woman* (Garry Marshall, 1990), a modern Cinderella story, and the massive industry that the formula romance has become demonstrate this beyond reasonable doubt.

While the two discourses are in part contradictory, the differences between them often go unrecognized because they coexist with each other and most of us are influenced by both of them. Both discourses promise a great deal in the name of love. Romance offers adventure, intense emotion, and the possibility of finding the perfect mate. Intimacy promises deep communication, friendship, and sharing that will last beyond the passion of new love. As we will see, both discourses cover over internal contradictions that they cannot resolve, making their visions of love seem more complete and adequate than they are. By recognizing the gaps in these conceptions, it is more likely that one can approach relationships with appropriate expectations.

The connection between romance and marriage forged in the nineteenth century was an expression of individualism, of the growing freedom of the individual from traditional social structures. The development of the discourse of intimacy represents both the intensification of that process and a reaction against it. Where romance championed the autonomous individual, intimacy insists on a balance between autonomy and attachment. Thus, intimacy at the start of the millennium has become perhaps the most significant refuge from the social fragmentation of late capitalism. Unfortunately, it is a purely private refuge, and thus no solution to the degradation of society.

PART I

Romance

1

Romance in the Romance
and the Novel

American culture has in an exceptionally intense way emphasized . . .
romantic love as the basis for marriage.
—Werner Sollors, *Beyond Ethnicity: Consent and
Decline in American Culture*

    The discourse of romance has always been primarily ex-
pressed in fiction, and, until the twentieth century, the vast majority of fiction was experienced in books and magazines. In the nineteenth century,
new habits of reading, which had only recently emerged, became commonplace as women in particular increasingly read in private for pleasure. The spread of this pastime was enabled by technological innovations that consistently lowered the cost of books as the century pro-
gressed, so that the novel became a medium of mass entertainment. The
novel was well suited to performing the role historians have granted it—
the dissemination of the nineteenth-century version of the discourse of romance that linked romantic love and marriage—because, as literary historian Ian Watt argues, of its "access to the inner life."[1] Without ques-
tioning the ability of readers to distinguish novels as fiction, one can
argue that it was the capacity of the novel to engender emotional involvement in the reader, especially in the form of identification, that made
the novel so successful and so powerful. By living fictional love stories vic-
ariously, readers came to desire romantic love in their own lives.
    However, it is important to understand that fiction cannot be regarded
as the ultimate source of the change in patterns of practice in love and
marriage. In the first place, we need to ask why fiction itself changed in
the eighteenth and nineteenth centuries from a form that opposed love
and marriage to one that linked them. Second, we should wonder why

audiences were now receptive, since the discourse of romance had been around for six or seven hundred years without causing large numbers of people to change their values or behavior. The most important cause for these changes is the spread and development of capitalism and the rise of the individual, but we could also add the slow decline of domestic production, the rise of social institutions such as public schools, and the shift in control of wealth from the family to the corporation. The discourse of romance became dominant because it suited the social system in which it flourished.

As was noted in the introduction, the word *romance* names, on the one hand, a certain kind or experience of love, and, on the other, several genres of fiction. Since the word means so many different things, most of which are relevant to this chapter, it is important to distinguish carefully the several different definitions of *romance* that will be used here. *Romantic love,* as I have stipulated, designates here, not a general human capacity to experience passionate love, but rather a way of writing, thinking about, and experiencing love that is distinctive to the cultures of Western Europe. Romantic love is related historically to literary romances, but to call a literary work a romance is not necessarily to say anything about how it depicts love. Having defined at some length the discourse of romantic love in the introduction, I will here focus on distinguishing among three different genres that go by the name of *romance*. First, the *medieval romance* is a narrative—in prose or poetry—that tells of fantastic events and adventures. The form is the ancestor of the novel, and it continued with certain modifications to be a significant popular genre into the eighteenth century. Romantic or courtly love is a typical feature of the medieval romance. The novel was invented in opposition to this sort of romance. *Don Quixote* (1605–1615), often regarded as the first novel, sets itself explicitly against the tales of knight-errantry typical of the medieval romance. The novel in English is often traced to Samuel Richardson, who believed himself to have invented a new prose form in *Pamela* (1740), which he regarded as a more truthful alternative to the fantasies of romances.

Second, in the nineteenth century, a new subgenre, the *romance novel*, emerged under the name *romance,* typified by the work of Scott and the Brontës. While such works are often today accused of a lack of realism, they claimed the same truth status as other novels. Scholars have since tended to reject that claim. They have defined the novel proper, or, as it is sometimes specified, the "novel of manners," as dealing with the social reality of the historical present in which it is produced. That reality may be described in broadly political or economic terms or in psychological and interpersonal ones, but in any case it is a particular social setting that is represented in the fiction. Those novels called romances are distinguished mainly by their being about something other than a specific contemporary social reality. Thus, romance novels are set either in the past, or, beginning in the late nineteenth century, in the future. Or they may be set far away from society in the wilderness, on the high seas, or in another remote location. It is often said of the romance novel that it is about mythic or metaphysical "reality," but novels may also be classified as romances simply on the grounds of a lack of realism. Romance novels need not be about passionate love, and some of the most familiar examples of the genre, such as Cooper's Leatherstocking series or *Moby Dick,* are not. The historical romance I discuss below is one version of this genre. A third genre of romance is defined by its use of romantic love. This genre, which is a subgenre of the romance novel, includes the formula romances marketed under trade names such as Harlequin but also older works such as *Gone with the Wind* or *Rebecca.* In this genre, the love story is always foregrounded, and the presumed audience for these romances is almost exclusively female. I will call this genre the *women's romance.*

What I have been calling the discourse of romance is important to all the genres I have just discussed, including the novel proper. It is not just the romance novel that has dealt with love and courtship. Historians of the novel have long recognized that it also has been overwhelmingly devoted to those subjects.[2] From Richardson in the eighteenth century on, the novel is strongly identified with the "marriage plot," in which the action of the story moves toward the wedding of the hero and heroine. The romance novel and the novel proper typically deal with courtship differently, the latter often being more ironic or distanced in its treatment, but both genres helped to build the association between romantic love and marriage. By the late nineteenth century, a new sort of novel emerges that can be called an antiromance in a new sense. *Madame Bovary* might be the founding text of this movement, and it is perhaps the most explicitly antiromantic. Many of Emma Bovary's problems are attributed to her having read and internalized the stories and values of romances. Moreover, these antiromances are more likely actually to deal with a marriage, as does Flaubert's novel. Even when such fiction does focus on courtship, as in Henry James's *Washington Square* and many other works, it does not treat the phenomenon romantically. Courtship here neither leads to a "happily ever after" nor is it tragically interrupted. Critics often identify the novel of manners with a Jamesian, antiromantic perspective, but one should remember that Jane Austen also wrote novels of manners, and there courtship always produces a "happily ever after."[3]

Novels such as those of Flaubert and James lie outside the discourse of romance, though their existence testifies to the influence of that discourse. In this chapter, I'm concerned with fiction that remains within it. The first section deals with best-sellers of the turn of the twentieth century. These historical romances are works that both spread and reinforced the connection between romantic love and marriage.[4] They reflect, I argue, the most commonly held conception of romance among middle-class Americans, not just of that period, but at least until the 1950s or 1960s. It is a conception that remains powerful today. While print fiction will in the 1920s lose its role to movies as the most powerful medium of this version of romance, the basic narrative pattern will continue to be reproduced and absorbed. The second section will concern novels that present a different version of the discourse of romance. These critically acclaimed works depict romance in opposition to marriage. They present the dark side of the discourse of romance, yet they are not fully tragic works of the sort Rougemont has found in European fiction. They are, rather, "American" tragedies, tragedies that are less than tragic, testifying to the power of the connection between romance and marriage in American culture.

In each section, my goal is to explore what these different kinds of novels teach us about love and marriage. Some of what they teach is apparent to any reader, but much of it is covert and needs to be brought to the surface. Both sets of texts function ideologically, but the ideological work they perform is contradictory. These works doubtless reinforced most of their audiences' assumptions about gender roles, but they also open up spaces in which the expectations such roles entailed might be questioned. While we might expect that the best-selling romances would be more restrictive in their vision than the canonical novels, I will suggest that the opposite may be true.

Romance in the Romance

During the 1890s, the most popular genre of prose fiction was the historical romance. According to Frank Luther Mott, a standard authority on the history of American best-sellers, 50 percent of the best-sellers of that decade fit this category, and historical romances continued to be the leading category of popular fiction until about 1914.[5] When such fiction is remembered in literary history, however, it is mainly as the butt of attacks by William Dean Howells and other realists. And even in being remembered in this way, the cultural significance of turn-of-the-century romances is misunderstood. For one thing, Howellsian realism most often is understood in opposition to the genteel critics' championing of romance. As literary scholar Amy Kaplan observes, however, Howells conflated under the term *romance* "elite culture, as a form of upper-class leisure, with popular culture, as a form of mass consumption."[6] Howells saw himself as attacking an outmoded literary form even as this form was most likely to appear as a new kind of product in a rapidly changing literary market. It was the broad reach of this mass market fiction that Howells's feared, claiming that novels "form the whole intellectual life of such immense numbers of people" and shape "the modern human being."[7]

Howells was not the only one to take notice of the exploding popularity of fiction. Turn-of-the-century novels were being marketed on a scale that could not have been imagined just a few years before. According to one historian of the publishing industry, "Between 1890 and the First World War, the reading of fiction in America became something of a mania. Novels were devoured as much as read, and the public appetite appeared to be insatiable." The fiction market had begun expanding in the 1850s and expanded again in the 1870s. By 1880, "the flood of fiction was so strong that the backlash of reaction had set in from those who were convinced . . . that novels were the opiate of the masses and productive of social degeneracy. . . . A magazine called *The Hour* warned . . . , 'Millions of young girls and hundreds of thousands of young men are *novelized* into absolute idiocy.'"[8] Writers of popular fiction often seem to respond to this kind of attack by making their characters into readers or even oppressed readers. For example, Paul Leichester Ford's best-selling historical romance of the American revolution, *Janice Meredith* (1900), opens with its young heroine being punished by her highly religious mother for reading a novel on the Sabbath. Fiction was perceived to be the same kind of powerful influence that movies and television have more recently been taken to be.

The novel was never a more powerful influence than during the period under discussion here, and not only because of its popularity. It is important to understand that, although the popularity of novels did arouse fear in some quarters, novels had a cultural advantage later popular forms would lack: their association with literature. If Howells could mistake popular romances for elite culture, surely much of the reading public did as well. What needs to be kept in mind is the enormous influence of all kinds of writing during this period. By this time, the literary had already acquired a new class valuation in what Raymond Williams describes as a vast transformation in the cultural significance of writing. To put it succinctly, literature had once been associated with learning but was now the bearer of class-identified taste, national tradition, and "aesthetic" relief from increasingly rationalized labor. Literature had been systematically reduced in scope to include only imaginative works of aesthetic value or cultural significance. In the United States, this transformation was not quite complete, and the new conception of literature was rivaled by a broader one that could encompass most writing, even journalism. Yet this larger conception traded on the prestige of the first. Together, they constituted a cultural force of enormous power. The power of the literary may seem less surprising if we remember that the other media that now dominate mass culture were then barely in existence. Though such comparisons are hard to substantiate, it is at least arguable that the literary was the dominant cultural sector, having more power than the church, political parties, or education while at the same time serving all of these.[9] The best-sellers I am discussing here were all the more influential given the power of literary culture. Historical romances were able to trade on this power because most critics did not regard them as pernicious or even as aesthetically inferior. Howells's opposition to the romance was far from universal among the literary elite, and, while this group generally condemned what they saw as declining literary values, they differed about what kinds of works illustrated this decline. Leading elite magazines such as the *Atlantic* and *Harper's* could publish Howells's attacks on romance in one section and serialize the latest historical romance in another. Authors of novels—whether romances or not—were in general accorded great respect and held cultural authority. Because of this, we cannot dismiss these works as mere entertainment.

Scholars typically focus on the late eighteenth and early nineteenth centuries as the moment when the novel and love were both transformed. Works from this period did have important influence, making the formal innovations that will have become standard practice in the books I'm discussing here. The popular fiction of the turn of the twentieth century, however, is important in its own right. Though it was not in the least innovative, it was much more widely read and disseminated. The very repetitiveness of the books themselves and of the experience of them suggests that the romantic discourse they convey would have been more likely to be internalized. Moreover, if you compare the turn-of-the-century historical romances to earlier examples by Walter Scott, James Fenimore Cooper, or the Brontë sisters, the more recent works are in many respects closer to realism. While they make use of historical settings, those settings are much less likely to be wild or dangerous. The discourse of romance was thus presented in a more mundane or "normal" context, making it seem less a fantasy and more a "natural" part of life.

Historical romances of the turn of the twentieth century predictably include a plot line involving romantic love. This is true not only of romances that we would recognize as "love stories" but of many that we would not. Consider one of the most popular late nineteenth-century historical romances, *Ben Hur,* published in 1880. As an explicitly Christian work, the novel's focus could hardly be on passionate love. Yet the protagonist is involved in a love triangle, finding himself attracted to two women, Esther and Iras. Now, neither of these relationships is very important to the novel as a whole, but that is precisely my point. The love story in *Ben Hur* is evidence that romantic love and its typical triangular pattern is a fundamental convention of prose fiction rather than a mere topic or generic variation.

Nor were historical romances the only popular fiction to depend on the discourse of romance. As Richard Ohmann has shown, the new mass market magazines of the turn of the twentieth century featured, in addition to serialized historical romances, a particular genre or formula of short story. The "courtship story" was the most common type published in *McClure's, Munsey's,* and *Cosmopolitan.*[10] As Ohmann describes these stories' motive, it is "to give words to the heart's desire and fulfill it in marriage," and he links these stories to what Northrop Frye calls the "mythos of comedy," which also informs the typical historical romance.[11] According to Frye, the mythos, or plot, of comedy derives from

> the plot structure of Greek New Comedy . . . [that] has become the basis for most comedy, especially in its more highly conventionalized dramatic form, down to our day. . . . What normally happens is that a young man wants a young woman, that his desire is resisted by some opposition, usually paternal, and that near the end of the play some twist in the plot enables the hero to have his will.[12]

Courtship stories, as the name implies, involve the meeting and uniting of a young man and woman, almost always of the middle or professional managerial classes. Unlike romance novels, these stories are almost always set in the present, though often in a place remote from the world of work or business. Because these stories are quite short, a love triangle is often merely suggested, with one of the characters believing the other to be already attached, but it is usually present in some form. The courtship story might be described as the simplest expression of the dominant version of romance discourse.

These genres of fiction demonstrate by their popularity and their very predictability the reach and penetration of the discourse of romance. Courtship stories and the historical romances, because of their repetitiveness, would have been likely to provide models of love and courtship for their readers. Such models were not the only ones available, but they were the most powerful. Unlike hygienic or moral instruction, fictional works position their readers to identify with the romantic subjects they present.[13] Romances imagine the lives of individuals in terms of the natural pairing of love and marriage or the tragic failure of this pairing. The reader is not just an observer of a love affair but an emotional participant in it who becomes through reading a subject of romance just like the hero and heroine.

These best-sellers featured a particular variation of the romantic discourse that was dominant in America, especially among the middle class at the turn of the century, which I will call the "fairy-tale" version. It assumes that there is a right man or woman out there for each person. It projects a life story that involves meeting that individual and living with him or her in marriage. The assumption of the naturalness of the connection between passionate love and marriage, and of the possibility of achieving through them a happiness available by no other means, meant that romantic love would have a powerful but different hold on both men and women. Yet the traditional form of the discourse, which saw romance in terms of suffering and death, was still very much available. This darker variant of the discourse was more typical of works like *The Great Gatsby* that end up getting classified as great literature. While novels featuring this darker conception of romance didn't often reach the best-seller lists, they sometimes did. One of them, Elinor Glyn's *Three Weeks,* I will discuss at some length in the next chapter. The opposition of love and marriage was never entirely absent, however, even from the novels that assumed a natural link between romantic love and marriage, for love triangle plots continued to structure these works.

To illustrate the way that the discourse of romance functioned in the historical romance, I will present a detailed analysis of a single best-seller, Winston Churchill's *The Crisis*. To understand how historical romances function, it is necessary to see that their cultural significance cannot be read in terms of the discourse of romance alone. *The Crisis* was published in 1901 and was one of the leading sellers of its year and its decade. It is the second of Churchill's historical romances, a sequel to *Richard Carvel,* which established the author's reputation. Both books deal with American history, *Richard Carvel* with the American Revolution and *The Crisis* with the Civil War. Novels about American history seem to have been especially popular around this period, although earlier settings were common as well. According to Mott, Churchill's books were "mid-Victorian" in their restraint and leisureliness, and Churchill was "the great popular novelist of middle-class American readers."[14]

Not all best-sellers shared such restraint. Some clearly aimed to titillate, however slight such titillation might seem to us today. Charles Major's *When Knighthood Was in Flower* (1898) uses the story of King Henry VIII's sister Mary and her love for a commoner for such purposes. As a result, this romance reveals the power passionate love was presumed to have:

> It would be bad enough should Brandon fall in love with the princess, which was almost sure to happen, but for them to fall in love with each other meant Brandon's head upon the block, and Mary's heart bruised, broken and empty for life. Her strong nature, filled to the brim with latent passion, was the stuff of which love makes a conflagration that burns to destruction; and could she learn to love Brandon, she would move heaven and earth to possess him.[15]

While this novel contains no literal sex, it does feature kissing, passionate embracing, and a few risqué situations.

None of these are to be found in *The Crisis,* the story of Stephen Brice, the impoverished son of a Boston aristocrat who has come to St. Louis in the late 1850s to study law with a family friend, Judge Whipple, an abolitionist. Even before we are introduced to the hero, however, we have met Colonel Carvel, a St. Louis merchant and southern gentleman; his daughter, Virginia; her cousin and beau, Clarence Colfax; and the Colonel's employee, Eliphalet Hopper, a Yankee and would-be capitalist. These are the central *fictional* characters in the novel, but during its course our hero comes into contact with Abraham Lincoln, Ulysses Grant, and William Sherman. He manages to witness one of the Lincoln-Douglas debates, the end of the siege of Vicksburg, and Sherman's march through Georgia. Stephen is also present at important but less nationally familiar events in Missouri in which that state is prevented from secession by federal troops. There are some scenes of high adventure, but this is not mainly a novel of individual valor and it is only peripherally a novel of military engagement. Stephen is most often little more than a witness, and his moments of action often involve interceding on behalf of Southerners.

It has been argued that Civil War novels of the period often featured the theme of "healing wounds between the sections . . . through the device of 'reunion by marriage' of a Southerner and a Northerner."[16] *The Crisis* certainly lends itself to such an allegorical reading. The story ends in the marriage of a Northerner and a Southerner, and the other characters can be assigned equally clear allegorical functions. The two father figures, Judge Whipple and Colonel Carvel, illustrate what is best about the sections of the country they represent, each having a different high moral standard. Furthermore, their friendship represents the old union and foretells the possibility of reunion. Clarence and Eliphalet represent potential evils that each section is prone to produce. One of the first things we learn about Clarence is that he is too prone to fight; in the war he serves with valor but without success. He represents the heroic but outmoded ways of the old South. Eliphalet is Clarence's opposite number; he represents the danger of unrestrained capitalism. His exclusive concern is with making money, which he does successfully but at the cost of abandoning all other values. Clarence and Eliphalet are rivals, as the latter explains when he asserts that Clarence plans to own the town some day, a plan Eliphalet doubtless also harbors. Neither one achieves his goal, for the war bankrupts Clarence, and Eliphalet is charged with profiteering and with selling contraband to the rebels. Each of these men is a potential mate for Virginia, and each is ultimately unsuitable. The marriage of Stephen and Virginia represents moderation rather than the excesses exhibited by Clarence and Eliphalet, and it is a perfect ideological resolution of the conflict between the two social systems that the latter represent.

When *The Crisis* was written, however, that conflict had already been won by the Eliphalets of the world. The decade of the 1890s had been one of almost perpetual economic crisis. The competitive capitalism of the Civil War era had given way to the monopoly form, as business leaders invited government to help to protect them from destroying each other. Investment in railroads and other capital-intensive enterprises had slowed, and business increasingly looked to the production of consumer goods to absorb surplus value. The economic strife and the increasingly rationalized world of work of the turn of the century must have made the simpler lives and genteel values of Stephen and Virginia seem quite appealing. Though Churchill's novel deals with the nation's worst political crisis and most destructive war, the period is depicted nostalgically. *The Crisis* could even be read as offering Stephen and Virginia's moderation as a solution to the contemporary economic crisis. This would connect the book to Churchill's later, explicitly Progressive novels, which directly attack the excesses of business and urge government control and reform.

As this account shows, *The Crisis* does not present itself primarily as a love story. While it is the epitome of the historical romance, it differs from novels popularly called simply "romances" (the genre I have designated the women's romance)—from *Gone with the Wind* through the most recent Harlequins—in that it seems to be about political history more than about private emotion. But I have not yet described the most important line of action in the narrative. That is the question of whom Virginia Carvel will marry. This question is not merely of allegorical interest; it goes to the novel's fundamental structure. We discover early on that Clarence, Eliphalet, and Stephen all desire Virginia. In most chapters, one of these three characters interacts in some way with her. We are frequently made privy to Virginia's thoughts about her suitors and her friends' thoughts about her feelings about them. Throughout most of the novel, Virginia is leaning to Clarence, though the novel lets us know that she is attracted to Stephen even if she won't admit it to herself. The effect of this is to create a tension, a desire in the reader, a desire that is fulfilled when, in the last pages of the novel, just before they hear that Lincoln has been assassinated, they get married. Like most historical romances of this period and perhaps most novels, *The Crisis* is above all else a love story, even if it doesn't appear on the surface to be one. If that love story may be read allegorically to refer to problems of sectional politics and changing modes of production, it can and should be read as representing the realities of sex and gender, a pair that are not here meant as synonyms.

In this regard, I want to quote at some length from the conclusion to *The Crisis*, for here, in unusually explicit form, the fairy-tale version of the discourse of romance is articulated. This scene takes place in President Lincoln's office. Virginia has come to plead for Clarence's life and finds that Stephen has already arranged for clemency. Lincoln leaves the two of them alone:

> Then overcome by the incense of her presence, [Stephen] drew her to him until her heart beat against his own. She did not resist, but lifted her face to him, and he kissed her.
>
> "You love me, Virginia!" he cried.
>
> "Yes, Stephen," she answered, low, more wonderful in her surrender than ever before. "Yes—dear." Then she hid her face against his blue coat. "I—I cannot help it. Oh, Stephen, how I have struggled against it! How I have tried to hate you, and couldn't. No, I couldn't. I tried to insult you, I did insult you. And when I saw how splendidly you bore it, I used to cry."
>
> He kissed her brown hair.
>
> "I loved you through it all," he said. "Virginia!"
>
> "Yes, dearest."
>
> "Virginia, did you dream of me?"
>
> She raised her head quickly, and awe was in her eyes.
>
> "How did you know?"
>
> "Because I dreamed of you," he answered. "And those dreams used to linger with me half the day as I went about my work. I used to think of them as I sat in the saddle on the march."
>
> "I, too, treasured them," she said. "And I hated myself for doing it."
>
> "Virginia, will you marry me?"
>
> "Yes."
>
> "To-morrow?"
>
> "Yes, dear, to-morrow." Faintly, "I have no one but you—now."[17]

Several pages later, after the couple are married, and just a day before they receive news of Lincoln's assassination:

> "Virginia," he said, "some force that we cannot understand has brought us together, some force that we could not hinder. It is foolish for me to say so, but on that day of the slave auction, when I first saw you, I had a premonition about you that I have never admitted until now, even to myself."

She started.

"Why, Stephen," she cried, "I felt the same way!"[18]

We find in these passages virtually the whole fairy-tale version of romance in a nutshell. Love is tested against a series of obstacles. It leads inevitably to marriage, and both love and marriage are somehow foreordained. The marriage is not merely good or loving but cosmically meant to be. The couple is defined against the rest of the world, including their own parents. They have only each other, but that is exactly what they should have. Other ties would merely interfere with their love. Though this novel has been set against a great social struggle, it ends with an absolutely private resolution, a retreat from social life to the promise of conjugal bliss and, implicitly, the creation of a nuclear family.

The conventionality of these passages—in both style and content—raises again the issue of the epistemological status of romance. If the book were understood by its readers merely as a romance—in other words, as not telling the truth about the world but just being a pretty story, or telling only a symbolic truth—then it would be hard to maintain that readers would accept its depiction of sex, gender, or love as the truth. But there is little in *The Crisis* that would lead a reader to regard it as being, like a myth or a fairy tale, capable only of symbolic truth. In fact, one would be hard put to classify the work as fitting what Frye calls the romantic mode, in which the hero is "superior in *degree* to other men and to his environment. . . . The hero of romance moves in a world in which the ordinary laws of nature are slightly suspended."[19] In these terms, the typical historical romance is much closer to the high mimetic mode, in which the hero is not superior to his environment but precisely to other men, or the low mimetic mode, in which the protagonist is defined by his common humanity.[20] This is not to say that the novel seems realistic in Howells's terms. In fact, one could argue that it fits very well the aesthetic Howells caricatured when he complained of literary idealists having a preference for a "wire and cardboard" grasshopper over a grasshopper found "out there in the grass." The former is "very prettily painted in a conventional tint, and . . . perfectly indestructible. It isn't very much like a real grasshopper, but it's a great deal nicer, and it's served to represent the notion of a grasshopper ever since man emerged from barbarism."[21] *The Crisis* is full of wire and cardboard grasshoppers. Its characters are almost perfectly consistent. Southern gentlemen are always honorable, presidents are wise and fatherly, generals are devoted to their troops, and so on.[22] But if the ideal seemed unreal to Howells, it did not to many others, and not merely to naive readers but to the critics with whom Howells was arguing. While all fiction is understood as conveying something other than literal truth, novels such as *The Crisis* present themselves, not as mere fantasy, but precisely as a version of historical reality. In other words, Churchill's "romance," just like the "romances" of Scott and the Brontës, claims to be a "novel"—that is, to be true.

And what these romances present as their truth is the natural connection between romantic love and marriage. The end of most of the best-sellers of this era is not the end of life but the beginning of marriage. And since marriage is often the goal toward which everything else in the novel has pointed, it is in some sense the beginning of life. Yet marriage itself is apparently beyond representation. Not only is the marriage of hero and heroine the end of the novel, but very often subsidiary characters are unmarried as well. In *The Crisis,* for example, both Stephen's father and Virginia's mother are deceased at the beginning of the novel. Thus, there is no marriage portrayed in this book. In the number one best-seller of 1899, Wescott's *David Harum,* the title character is married, but the marriage remains peripheral to his life and is at most a source of humor. In this sense, these novels seem to covertly assume the incompatibility of passionate love and marriage even as they depict their dependence on one another.

The restraint and leisureliness of *The Crisis* may make it hard to see the book as a novel of passionate love, but we need to understand that term as both more qualified and more general than it is in, for example, Rougemont. It is qualified in that it need not be understood as the experience of pain. While both Stephen and Virginia endure some painful moments, the novel is not mainly devoted to making us experience them. Since Virginia refuses to acknowledge her love for Stephen, she cannot fully experience the pain of his absence. Stephen does experience the pain of Virginia's repeated slights, but he has the great cause to divert his—and our—attention. Yet all romantic love is passionate in the more general sense that it is a love to which the subject submits. Love is an experience to be undergone rather than an act committed. And this experience may come to seem constitutive of what is most personal and internal about one's self, especially in the face of work and social life that seem increasingly impersonal and rationalized.

This less lurid, more normalized conception of passionate love is everywhere apparent in *The Crisis*. Like all love stories, this novel is devoted mainly to the obstacles that must be overcome for its hero and heroine to unite. We might classify those obstacles as being of three kinds. There are internal obstacles: in this case, Virginia's refusal to acknowledge her love for Stephen. There are the obstacles posed by the larger world: in *The Crisis,* sectional division and war are the major cause of these, and they are by far the most important to the plot. Finally, there is Clarence, who loves Virginia and with whom Virginia believes she is in love throughout most of the novel. Clarence, Stephen, and Virginia thus form a love triangle, a convention that is nearly indispensable to the romance and the novel. (Eliphalet is also posed as an obstacle, but he is never a possible love match for Virginia and so can't be regarded as an element in a love triangle.) If the triangles of medieval romances were usually adulterous, in the popular literature of turn-of-the-century America, they seldom are. In each case, however, the triangle serves similar functions. Not only does it, like the other obstacles, create narrative tension and help to defer the union of the lovers, but it also makes the object of the hero's desire more desirable.[23]

Although popular novels or stories are much less likely to make love triangles explicitly adulterous, the love triangle remains fundamental to popular fiction of the turn of the century, as *David Harum* illustrates. While the love story here is paired with an extended dialect sketch of small town life centered on the eponymous Harum, the courtship of Mary Blake and John Lenox is the novel's most extended plot line. This story is worthy of some further attention, for it is an almost perfect illustration of the prevalence of the romance discourse. John Lenox meets Mary Blake near the beginning of *David Harum,* on board a ship bringing them both back to New York from extended stays in Europe. They knew each other when she was a child and he a teenager. The first part of the novel is about what seems to be his failed courtship of her. As the result of the contrivance of lost correspondence, the two fall out of contact when John accepts a position with Harum, a banker in upstate New York. John's life in Homeville is lonely and boring, but he makes his fortune there, and, as a reward, he five years later finds himself on a ship to Europe, where he once again encounters Mary Blake, who is now called Mrs. Edward Ruggles. The two renew their acquaintance on shipboard, but John is unable to learn much of Mary's life since they parted. On the last night of the voyage, he recalls their earlier affection for each other. She admonishes him that he must never speak of this but then tells him that he may meet her in Naples. This plan is not explicitly proposed as a tryst, but the idea is clearly suggested by the mysterious arrangements for the meeting. Mary insists, for example, on the need for this meeting not to be followed by further encounters back in the States. We have what seems to be an adulterous meeting. When John arrives in Naples, he learns that Mary must leave the next day. But he also discovers that Mary Blake is not Mrs. Edward Ruggles but has merely been traveling on her ticket. That revelation leads to an immediate proposal, and the novel hastily concludes with John and Mary living happily ever after.

Now one can say of this episode that it is merely a hackneyed plot contrivance, a hook worthy of O. Henry. But though it is doubtless designed as such a hook, the fact that it is so effective a device depends on the power of the discourse of romance. It is because we as readers so readily become invested in the love story that a novelist can begin to tell it in the first hundred pages, leave off it for the next 250 or so, only to use it to bring the novel to a satisfying conclusion. Judging by narratives of all sorts, from fairy tales to Hollywood films, it is apparently the most satisfying of conclusions. Indeed, the conclusion of *David Harum* resembles nothing so much as the "happy endings" of classic Hollywood.

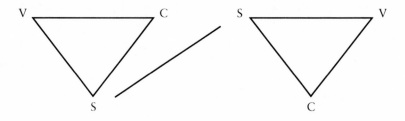

Narrative structure and succession in *The Crisis*.

But the triangle is more fundamental to the narrative of romance than the prevalence of the love triangle in the surface text can explain. The typical romance novel shares with the medieval romance a triadic narratological structure that features an included pair of subjects and an excluded third subject. In *The Crisis*, Stephen is the excluded party throughout the entire novel, while Clarence and Virginia most often form the inclusive pair. A detailed analysis would show moments in which different characters fill these subject positions, but figure 2 shows the novel's dominant structure. Since we are clearly asked to identify with Stephen, we experience his desire. The coincidence of narrative and figural desire is what makes romance so powerfully attractive in a narrative, and this doubtless in part explains why romance figures as an almost indispensable element of the novel.

An important innovation of the early romance narratives was the according of subjectivity to all parties in the triangle.[24] Women were no longer treated as mere objects of exchange, as they had typically been in older, dyadic narratives. In the discourse of romance, love is established through the subjectivity of the beloved, and thus a wife cannot be mere property. This emphasis on subjectivity helps explain how genres written in the discourse of romance may be distinguished from ancient Greek New Comedy, which also features a plot about overcoming obstacles to a couple's marriage. According to Frye,

> The theme of the comic is the integration of society. . . . New Comedy normally presents an erotic intrigue between a young man and young woman which is blocked by some kind of opposition, usually paternal, and resolved by a twist in the plot which is the comic form of Aristotle's "discovery." . . . At the beginning of the play the forces thwarting the hero are in control of the play's society, but after a discovery in which the hero becomes wealthy or the heroine respectable, a new society crystallizes on the stage around the hero and his bride.[25]

To recall the allegorical reading proposed earlier, *The Crisis* fits this model very well, the marriage of Stephen and Virginia being a much overdetermined figure of social integration. Moreover, Frye's account of the mythos of comedy, with its emphasis on "the obstacles to the hero's desire," seems to describe something very like what I have been calling the discourse of romance.[26]

Frye's conception, however, fails to take into account the changing historical context in which similar plot structures exist and derive their meaning. *The Crisis* can't be read simply as a latter-day example of New Comedy because the rise of subjectivity changed literary characters and the way that such characters were apprehended by audiences. The novel as a genre makes the lives of individuals the center of readers' attention. As Anthony Giddens argues, "The telling of a story is one of the meanings of 'romance,' but this story now became individualized, inserting self and other into a personal narrative which had no particular reference to wider social processes. The rise of romantic love more or less coincided with the emergence of the novel: the connection was one of newly discovered narrative form."[27] Like the bourgeois culture that produced it, the novel treats society as an epiphenomenon, the product of individual action rather than the reverse. According to Frye, the hero of New Comedy "is seldom a very interesting person."[28] The hero of a novel is almost by definition an interesting person, no matter how ordinary he may at first seem or how unreal he may turn out to be. For the novel to work, it must do what Maddox observed of earlier romances—that is, invest its characters with subjectivity. And unlike the audiences for ancient Greek drama, the readers of novels were being entertained in private. It makes sense to treat publicly staged and ritually performed theater as referring to society, which it embodies. It makes equal sense to regard a private entertainment, the novel, as referring mainly to the lives of individuals like the reader, lives that novels more or less richly represent.

It is no coincidence, then, that in novels written in the discourse of romance, the obstacles to love are not so predictably parental. In antiquity, not only did parents represent the social order, but they also were regarded as having the right and duty to govern their children's courtship. The discourse of romance, on the other hand, assumes the individual's right to choose his or her own mate. Clearly, this was a progressive aspect of the discourse in earlier periods. As late as the antebellum period in the South, for example, marriages within the ruling planter class were strictly controlled and were often arranged as economic alliances. In this context, fictional romances may have been a progressive challenge to limitations on women's freedom.[29] But in more thoroughly bourgeois cultures, such marriages of alliance were uncommon outside the small circle of the very rich. Social structure being no longer regarded as much at stake in marriage, society itself came to seem a mere obstacle.

The historical romance became the dominant popular genre of fiction at a time when the private, domestic sphere had come to displace the strong sense of a public, social sphere typical of pre–Civil War America. According to Stephanie Coontz, the Gilded Age was "the apex of the doctrine of private spheres" and represented the first episode of "family values" rhetoric in American history.[30] Previously the individual and the family were understood to exist within a web of social obligations and supports, and reformers assumed that change could be made through political and social action. Now middle-class Americans came to believe "that private morality and family life represented a higher and purer duty than did political or social activism."[31] The isolated nuclear family, not typical of antebellum America, now became the middle-class norm and a cultural ideal. Historical romances do not celebrate domesticity per se, however, as the sentimental fiction of the midcentury did. They assume the isolation of the individual and the couple; they are even less about the nuclear family than they are about marriage.

In the late nineteenth century, romances seem to be fighting the battle for spousal choice that has already been won.[32] They continue to pit the desire of the amorous couple against the opposition of some authority who represents the demands of family or state over those of the individual. The plot of Major's *When Knighthood Was in Flower* illustrates this. It is Henry VIII, here, who represents the third point of the triangle; he demands that his sister marry the King of France. Since arranged marriages were not a current custom, we should read this text not as challenging dominant marriage customs but rather as endorsing them and the reader's own freedom of choice. There is no evidence that parents routinely restricted their children's freedom to choose their own mates, much less arranged marriages for them. Rather than seeing these novels as responding to actual social restrictions on love matches, they should be understood as rendering society's very existence as an imposition on love. The romance thus expresses an individualism even more extreme than that represented by the privatized family of the period. The individual's desires and the amorous couple's union are what matter.

Understanding the cultural work of this fiction is made more complicated once we recognize its radical withdrawal from the social, for this move has both progressive and regressive effects. Feminists of the 1960s and 1970s tended to regard romance—the stories and the practice—as a fundamental element of male domination. Shulamith Firestone, for example, described romantic love as a corruption that results from the unequal balance of power between the sexes.[33] More recently, feminist theorists have looked at twentieth-century romance genres and have focused on what they see as certain utopian moments or feminist tendencies in such works.[34] I don't want to argue for or against those readings, which are mostly of contemporary women's romances, but I think there is a sense in which the romance has been liberatory.

That sense has little to do with the way gender is depicted in these books. Some historical romances seem to reinforce the most traditional conceptions of gender. In *Ben-Hur*, a novel that may reflect a more properly Victorian sensibility, gender roles are depicted in very conservative terms. Esther, the hero's eventual bride, is subservient to both him and her father. In fact, so passive is Esther that she can be only the most minimal object of desire. Ben-Hur's choice of her over Iras could be read as a rejection of marriage based on romantic attraction in favor of one based upon familial and tribal loyalties. While the latter are not to be discounted, the effect of the novel is not to reject romance but to try to put it in the service of such loyalties. Ben-Hur's marriage is not arranged—as it would have been if the story were to be historically accurate—but reflects the personal desires of both partners. Esther's wish is stronger, but it is Ben-Hur who must notice her if her wish is to be fulfilled.

This is not to say that most turn-of-the-century best-sellers depict women in the most conservative or traditional roles. Even Virginia in *The Crisis,* whose status as mid-nineteenth-century Southern belle makes her more passive than many other heroines of historical romances, is nonetheless depicted as desiring to escape the limitations of that role. In one of their early meetings, Stephen and Virginia have a conversation about sectional character. The narrator reports:

> This was a new kind of conversation to Virginia. Of all the young men she knew, not one had ever ventured into anything of this sort. They were either flippant, or sentimental, or both. She was at once flattered and annoyed. Flattered, because, as a woman, Stephen had conceded her a mind. Many of the young men she knew had minds, but deemed that these were wasted on women, whose language was generally supposed to be a kind of childish twaddle. . . . Virginia's annoyance came from the fact that she perceived in Stephen a natural and merciless logic.[35]

Virginia here both welcomes the intellectual equality she is accorded and protests the fact that such equality must take place on masculine terms. Mary Tudor, the heroine of *When Knighthood Was in Flower,* is willing to undertake all manner of risk in order to achieve marriage to Charles Brandon. While compared to Brandon, she is the more passive, her exploits were shocking to Victorian readers.

That turn-of-the-century romance narratives often indulged in bending the rules of gender construction suggests that such rules were somewhat less rigid than they have sometimes been depicted. Such rule bending, however, does not challenge the assumption that a woman's major role is to be a wife. Women in romances are accorded freedom, but such freedom is largely restricted to a choice among potential husbands. Although marriage is often portrayed as the deepest desire of both men and women, it is apparently women's only goal in life. Furthermore, since romance seeks to engage the reader's desire, it typically attributes to both hero and heroine those characteristics that are the strongest markers of desirability in each gender. One might say that in so far as particular gender rules are violated, it is because some minor violation of these is itself a marker of desirability. The romantic subject must be an individual and not a mere type.

The cultural work of these novels is less to make readers want to imitate their characters than to make them want what they want, love and marriage. By rendering that pairing entirely natural, these texts tend to prohibit thinking beyond them. Since marriage itself remains absent from the romance, it cannot be reimagined no matter how active or intelligent the heroine. But if marriage remains beyond analysis in this discourse, the romantic subject experiences the self in a new way. Giddens has argued that

> romantic love introduced the idea of a narrative into an individual's life—a formula which radically extended the reflexivity of sublime love. . . . The complex of ideas associated with romantic love for the first time associated love with freedom, both being seen as normatively desirable states. . . . Ideals of romantic love . . . inserted themselves directly into the emergent ties between freedom and self-realization.[36]

Romances didn't present a new picture of marriage, but they did allow people—especially women—to reimagine their lives as a narrative in which their choices and desires might be realized. Thus Giddens concludes, "The dreamlike, fantasy character of romance . . . drew scorn from rationalist critics, male and female, who saw in it an absurd or pathetic escapism. In the view suggested here, however, romance is the counterfactual thinking of the deprived—and in the nineteenth century and thereafter participated in a major reworking of the conditions of personal life."[37] This "reworking" will develop over the course of the twentieth century, and it will spawn the new discourse of intimacy that will address the actual character of marriage and other relationships. Readers of turn-of-the-century romances, however, did not have access to this discourse. These novels offered them a vision of a personal life that most had little hope of attaining. This reading renders the problem of the crisis of marriage a bit more complex than the simple thesis of increased expectations would have it. It is not just that people learned to expect more of marriage but that they also failed to learn how those expectations might be fulfilled. The fairy-tale romance vision of marriage suggested that marriage would automatically produce transcendent happiness.

American Tragedies

The relationship of the work of Edith Wharton and F. Scott Fitzgerald to popular expectations of fictional romance is worth noting. Wharton received numerous letters in response to *The House of Mirth* complaining that the novel should have ended with the wedding of Lily and Selden rather than with her suicide. Fitzgerald's "trade" stories, those he sold to magazines such as the *Saturday Evening Post* in order to support himself while trying to produce more serious work, often feature the happy endings that the serious work rarely exhibits. Yet the works I will deal with here either were popular in their own time or, like *The Great Gatsby,* have become so widely read that a certain, if perhaps not identical, popularity must be ascribed to them. I take these works, then, to express more than the author's idiosyncratic views of romantic love. Rather, they are expressions of something like a cultural unconscious, in which the repressed association of love with suffering and death returns. Moreover, they give voice to the more conscious sense that marriage—and romantic love itself—were not living up to the constantly repeated fictional models. My examination of the unhappy love of the novels and stories of Wharton and Fitzgerald will show that the dark side of romance—its obstacles, its pain, its ill fit with marriage—was not banished from North America, but it will also show just how powerful the fairy-tale version of romance has been here.

Unlike a number of other canonical American writers who dealt with unhappy marriages and failed courtships, Wharton and Fitzgerald wrote narratives in the discourse of romance—even if they also were able to comment on that discourse. Howells and Henry James often constructed plots that concerned romance, but from a remote, critical perspective. What distinguishes *The Age of Innocence* or *The Great Gatsby* from *A Modern Instance* or *The Golden Bowl* is that the former novels invite us to identify with the romance the characters experience. Howells and James do their best to prohibit that identification. While Howells's novel is a portrait of a marriage, the novels under discussion here are portraits of love outside marriage.

I am interested in the novels and stories of Wharton and Fitzgerald because they are examples of the discourse of romance even though we might be inclined not to regard them as generic romances. It has been argued of Wharton and Fitzgerald that their work embodies the development of the novel of manners in America from its origins in Henry James.[38] One can accept that argument and still recognize the elements of the romance novel that remain in *The Age of Innocence* and *The Great Gatsby*. Those elements are tightly contained in the former, where they consist mainly in the historical setting of the book, in the character of Ellen Olenska, and in the mind of Newland Archer. In the latter, the conventions of the romance novel are so mixed with those of the novel of manners that the work finally cannot be classified.[39] The finely drawn picture of a distinct social setting does, however, set these books apart from the historical romances discussed earlier.

The work of Wharton and Fitzgerald is preoccupied by love and courtship, and the discourse of romance figures significantly there. The mixing of genres in their work makes its use of that discourse unusual. Wharton and Fitzgerald give expression to the darker version of the discourse, but they do so in a distinctly American way. The lack of a tragic sense in American culture has long been observed by critics. Wharton and Fitzgerald both address romance as framed by innocence. In Wharton's case, the innocence is attributed to a particular cultural epoch, while in Fitzgerald it is a function of the age—whether literal or psychic—of his characters. As we will see, the state of innocence seems to protect both characters and readers from the degree of pain and suffering that would otherwise result in these situations.

Since the discourse of romance is focused on obstacles to union rather than on the union itself, it is not surprising that romantic narratives frequently concern lovers' frustrations. Traditionally the source of these frustrations is located in the imperfect world that cannot accommodate the transcendent love the lovers have for each other. This sense of a world inhospitable to love is certainly present in Wharton and Fitzgerald, but there is also in their work the sense that love's failure is the result of a failure in the loved being, and by implication, in all members of his or her gender. Both Wharton and Fitzgerald depict characters that fit Giddens's description of the "romantic" male as a "foppish dreamer."[40] But the two authors deal with this figure differently. Wharton's persistent theme is the failure of men like Selden and Archer to live up to their own romantic expectations of themselves. More important to Wharton, however, they also fail the women whom they love. Fitzgerald's male characters are more romantic than Wharton's men are, and their expectations of females are impossibly high. Fitzgerald's romantics are repeatedly surprised to discover that the women they love are not the pure and magical creatures that the culture makes them out to be.

Tony Tanner lists *The Age of Innocence* as one of the novels he might have discussed in *Adultery in the Novel*.[41] While this is certainly right, it is nevertheless so only in the odd sense that the adulterous relationship on which the novel centers is never consummated. *The Age of Innocence* is a novel of failed adultery. But if it is not quite a novel of adultery, still less is *The Age of Innocence* a novel of marriage. Tanner argues that "marriage is *the* central subject for the bourgeois novel."[42] I will argue with Tanner at some length in chapter 7, but it will suffice to say here that Mark Twain got the matter much more nearly right when he said, "When one writes a novel about grown people, he knows exactly where to stop— that is, with a marriage."[43] Twain's remark suggests that, even in the nineteenth century, when, according to Luhmann, "the end of the novel was [no longer] the end of life," marriage remained mainly a device by which a conclusion might be imposed. It was not then a situation fit for exploration in fiction. Of course, one assumes that Twain's remark was directed at the mass of popular fiction typically called "romances." Married people are, of course, depicted in many serious works of the nineteenth century. But that is not exactly the same thing as claiming that marriage is the subject of most of these works.

Marriage is a marginal topic of *The Age of Innocence*. Newland Archer's mother is a longtime widow as the story opens, so we get no sense of the marriage of Archer's parents. Several other marriages—of the Beauforts, the Leffertses, the van der Luydens, and the Wellands—are but briefly sketched. Archer's own marriage to May Welland is depicted only in sufficient detail to make it clear that the marriage is exactly what Archer feared it would be. Moreover, when we consider the more general way that marriages in this society are described, we hardly get the sense that this institution deserves reverence. In contemplating his own engagement, Archer "reviewed his friends' marriages—the supposedly happy ones—and saw none that answered, even remotely, to the passionate and tender comradeship which he pictured as his permanent relation with May Welland."[44] The novel's foremost defender of public morals—named "form" in this novel—is Lawrence Lefferts: "As became the high-priest of form, he had formed a wife so completely to his own convenience that, in the most conspicuous moments of his frequent love-affairs with other men's wives, she went about in smiling unconsciousness, saying that 'Lawrence was so frightfully strict.'"[45] Marriage in *The Age of Innocence* is depicted as a failed institution, but its major function in the novel is to serve as the condition for a would-be adulterous romance.

The central triangle in *The Age of Innocence* is established in the very first chapter, where May and Newland's engagement is revealed and Ellen Olenska's presence in America is observed. In one sense, this triangle never changes. May and Newland are always firmly coupled, Ellen Olenska always excluded. The action of the story revolves around the possibility that this state of affairs might change. It is hard to imagine a more successful formula for the construction of romantic love. Most such stories follow the model of *Tristan,* in which a love relationship is firmly established—often by sexual consummation—but is repeatedly troubled by obstacles of various kinds. In Wharton's novel, however, there is some sense in which we can say that no relationship exists between Archer and Ellen. In other words, this story is all obstacles, and the relationship is entirely a matter of what might have been. A relationship doomed never to start might be the ultimate instance of the discourse of romance.

I may seem to be playing a bit fast and loose with the facts here. Archer and Ellen do meet a number of times, and they actually touch each other once or twice. They encounter each other enough for the reader to believe that they belong together. Archer says to Ellen, "you are the woman I would have married had it been possible for either of us."[46] Because the story is told from Archer's perspective—the Jamesian management of point of view is strikingly similar to that of studio-era cinema, where the narration remains external but focused on a particular character so as to create audience identification—we as readers must feel his sense that he *should* have married her.[47] We are convinced of this more by Archer's thoughts about Ellen than by their very brief interactions. In fact, one repeated motif of their conversation is misunderstanding. Archer says of her that they do not speak the same language, and he even imagines that he can explain the obscurity of her messages to him as a result of her having translated them from French. Yet these moments actually reveal Archer's failure to understand her, or perhaps his refusal to admit his own feelings for her. It turns out that she knew perfectly well, whether she was escaping Beaufort's advances or the risk of a growing intimacy with Archer, what *escape* meant in English.

Paradoxically, however, the quality of their conversation does render Newland and Ellen as the more attractive couple. The conversations Wharton gives us between May and Newland are in the main pedestrian. Perhaps because they are already a couple when they are introduced, we get no sense of flirtation or excitement between them. In the serious conversations to which we are privy, such as the one in St. Augustine when Newland asks May to move up the date of their wedding, we get a sense of a business arrangement being shrewdly conducted. Archer is surprised by May's having guessed his motives in what will not be the last time he will underestimate her intelligence, and he is "disappointed," when she is so easily mollified, "at the vanishing of the new being who had cast that one deep look at him from her transparent eyes."[48] May is not the "innocent" that Newland makes her out to be, but her wisdom is of a more practical sort than he wishes or knows. What May is good at is playing the mating game by the rules of her society, something that requires the constant appearance of passivity. Ellen, by comparison, finds passivity almost impossible, even though gender codes demand it of her as well. In her conversations with Newland, she is aggressive even if at times also resigned, and she reveals herself also to be ahead of Archer in comprehending not merely the situation but him as well. The conflict in their conversation seems less a reflection of genuine misunderstanding than of their own conflicted desires and motives. And, whatever its source, the conflict gives to their interaction a sexual tension that is utterly absent between the betrothed couple. Like the verbal sparring between the stars of Hollywood's screwball comedies, Ellen and Newland's conflicts constitute a kind of mating dance that leads readers to want and expect their eventual union.

The critical writing on *The Age of Innocence* most often defines the chief obstacle to that union as "society." It is worth a bit of a digression to consider the double meaning that word has in the context of the novel. Its primary meaning is not the general "civil society" of New York or the United States but rather "high society," the little world unto itself in which these characters function. The distinction is worth making, since, while it is possible to read the latter as a metonymy for the former, it is not necessary to do so. The "form" demanded by high society is certainly one of the obstacles that impede the love of Newland and Ellen, but it is not clear that such form is to be regarded as having any relationship to some larger sense of society. Ultimately, the idea that this novel is about the conflict between the individual and society founders less on that weak link than on the fact that the obstacles to Newland's romance with Ellen are largely internal. The irony—perhaps too heavy-handed not to seem contrived—of the scene in which Newland finally gets around to declaring his love for Ellen is her observation that Newland has made their marriage impossible.

The critical issue is: How are we to take the "sacrifice" that Ellen makes of her own free will and that Newland seems to offer by default? The standard position—which comes out of the same problematic in which Tanner is working—is articulated by R. W. B. Lewis, who asserts that for Wharton "there was no . . . alternative to the social order . . . because society was the domain of the values that counted most. . . . To defy the social ethic was to disturb the foundations of society and to threaten those values."[49] I'm not interested in arguing with Lewis about Edith Wharton's own beliefs, about which, as her biographer, he has more information. My argument is about the impact or meaning of the narrative for its readers. Here, the context of the discourse of romance gives us grounds to question whether Wharton's beliefs (assuming Lewis has them right) actually come across in the novel. The disparity between the date of the novel's setting and the date of its publication is important in this context. If the book had been published in the 1870s, one imagines that most readers would simply have conceded the rightness of the outcome. Divorce was rare then, and it was not acceptable to undertake it merely to find a better relationship. But as Elaine Tyler May has shown, by the 1920s things had changed radically, and movie stars like Douglas Fairbanks and Mary Pickford could leave their respective spouses simply because they had fallen in love with each other. While the Fairbanks-Pickford wedding produced some scandal, it also served as a model for the less rich and famous.[50] Wharton's *Custom of the Country* and *Glimpses of the Moon,* set in more recent times, acknowledge this reality, and it is a stretch to read *The Age of Innocence* as a protest against the new morality. It is more likely that contemporary audiences would have read it as the opposite. Because of having internalized society's restrictions, Newland and Ellen fail to act to secure their own happiness. They are, by the conventions of the love story, made for each other; recognizing this, they nevertheless allow themselves to settle for less.

This "settling for less" is not tragic, however. Newland and Ellen apparently go on to live "normal" lives, but entailed in that normality is the diminishment that the failure of their relationship produces. In American stories, lost love results, not in murder, suicide, or even full-blown despair, but in mere quiet desperation. *The Age of Innocence,* however, should not be judged mainly by its outcome. What matters most is the evocation of spiritual connection and physical desire throughout the narrative. Unlike most fiction of the period, this novel does not link romance and marriage, but it recognizes the cultural acceptance of this linkage. Newland's courtship of May is described as a "romance," yet it turns out not to be one. Newland may have been in love with May, but that love lacks the transcendent and potentially transformative character of romantic love. Moreover, it lacks the transgressive element that romance has always featured. Every reader recognizes the real romance in this novel, and it is all the more recognizable because it does not end in marriage. Because Newland and Ellen will never have to negotiate the mundane details of life together, their love remains pure. It lives on because it is never consummated, much less prolonged as marriage. *The Age of Innocence* does not warn against basing marriage on romantic love but rather laments the failure of marriage to live up to the demands of romance. This makes the novel of a piece with the marital advice literature of its era, though unlike that literature it does not offer a vision of how marriage might be transformed. The opposition of marriage and romance remains powerful in this novel, as it does in American culture more generally, despite the wide acceptance of romantic love as the basis for marriage.

Like *The Age of Innocence, The Great Gatsby* depicts an extramarital adventure against the background of failed marriage. If anything, Fitzgerald's depiction of marriage is bleaker. Wharton tells us mainly of men who deceive their wives or of wives who look the other way in the face of their husbands' philandering. We do not see the Leffertses or the Beauforts from the inside, and while the little we get of Newland and May's marriage may be unromantic, it is civilized. *The Great Gatsby* opens with Nick's first visit to Tom and Daisy's East Egg mansion, and their marriage is immediately revealed to be a disaster. Daisy's first remark to Nick when they are alone is, "I've had a very bad time . . . and I'm pretty cynical about everything."[51] We see the everyday tawdriness of Tom and Daisy's life together. Tom has a mistress who calls at his home while Nick is dining with them. The call does not produce a major row, but it reveals to Nick and the reader the poisoned atmosphere of Tom and Daisy's marriage. Moreover, the "form" that hid the philandering of Larry Lefferts is nowhere to be found in Tom Buchanan, as the book's second chapter reveals. There, in the valley of ashes, Nick is introduced to Tom's mistress: "The fact that he had one was insisted upon wherever he was known. His acquaintances resented the fact that he turned up in popular restaurants with her and, leaving her table, sauntered about, chatting with whomsoever he knew."[52] So *Gatsby* begins not merely with a failed marriage but also with a terribly unromantic love triangle. And just as Newland continually compares his prospective affair with Ellen to Lefferts's behavior, Fitzgerald's novel invites us to see Daisy and Gatsby's relationship in the light of Tom and Myrtle's.

The world of the Buchanans might be understood as the adult world, while Gatsby's world appears to be the world of youth. Fitzgerald's writing has long been associated with adolescence, in part because his first novel, *This Side of Paradise*, and many of his short stories are about people of that age. But this association goes beyond mere subject matter. Leslie Fiedler claims that "for Fitzgerald, 'love' was essentially yearning and frustration; and there is consequently little consummated genital love in his novels. . . . The adolescent's 'kiss' is the only climax his imagination can really encompass."[53] Thus, Fitzgerald's work is a prime example of the failure of American novelists to deal with adult sexuality. Fiedler's critique of American fiction famously argues that it is chiefly about more or less repressed homoerotic desire, a condition that distinguishes it from British or European writing. Fiedler's argument is a plausible account of a number of American novelists, including Melville and Hemingway, but it misses the point when applied to Hawthorne or Fitzgerald, who are centrally concerned with adult heterosexual relationships. Moreover, Fiedler's broad thesis is based on an analysis of a few canonical texts. "The American novel" for him excludes the popular romances I discussed earlier in the book. Thus, the idea that American novels are primarily expressions of homoeroticism, though it is widely held, is based on an uncritical acceptance of Fiedler's hyperbolic claims. As a result of Fiedler's influence—which ironically has been augmented by the rise of gay and lesbian studies (Fiedler is clearly not *celebrating* the homoeroticism of the American novel)—it has become necessary to state what should be obvious: that while the homoerotic certainly is present in American fiction, heterosexual romance remains its dominant subject matter.

The implication of interpretations such as Fiedler's is that Fitzgerald himself never escaped an adolescent sensibility. More recently, biographers like Scott Donaldson have presented a more complex picture of

Fitzgerald's mental life, but the effect remains largely the same: his sensibility is not typical.[54] I want to suggest that, whatever Fitzgerald's personal problems, his fiction has captured the imagination of readers and critics because the discourse of romance remains a force in the lives of many adults. The association of romance with youth cuts both ways, making romance seem silly and ephemeral but also rendering it all the more attractive. Gatsby often acts like an adolescent and is described as inventing himself as "just the sort of Jay Gatsby that a seventeen-year-old boy would be likely to invent," but we prefer his immaturity to the sordid adulthood of the Buchanans.[55]

Fitzgerald told the story of the adolescent or young man smitten by a beautiful woman over and over. The situation is the background for most of the stories about Basil Duke Lee, though it is perhaps foregrounded only in "Basil and Cleopatra." These stories were ones Fitzgerald wrote for the *Saturday Evening Post,* and Basil usually emerges in them triumphant to some extent, though, since the stakes are much lower, the degree of happiness or sadness is moderate. Stories for the trade could not end unhappily, but a fourteen-year-old doesn't need to be married off either.

Fitzgerald's more highbrow stories—most of the stories collected in *Babylon Revisited* fit this description—usually recount the failure of the young romantic to win the woman of his dreams. We might think of these texts as "anticourtship stories," since they often take the courtship plot as their basis but depict a failed courtship. "Winter Dreams" and "The Rich Boy" tell the story in more or less the way Wharton tells *The Age of Innocence.* They end not in death but in the sadness of undying unrequited love. The effect of the woman differs from story to story, but it is always powerful. The young man may not always take advantage of the opportunities afforded him, making him, like Wharton's men, seem curiously passive. If he is not quite Giddens's "foppish dreamer," he may nevertheless seem feminized, as Roland Barthes suggests, by waiting for his beloved.[56]

The difference between *The Great Gatsby* and these stories is mainly one of degree rather than kind. Everything is more extreme in the novel than in the stories. The stories generally lack any equivalent to the Buchanans' world. That world functions in *The Great Gatsby* both to justify Daisy's involvement with Gatsby and as a contrast to Gatsby's behavior. The love triangle of Tom, Myrtle, and Daisy is tawdry, but it makes the triangle of Gatsby, Daisy, and Tom seem all the more beautiful. Newland Archer imagines that his affair with Ellen would be utterly different from Lefferts's liaisons, but he fears that it might not be. Gatsby, we may be sure, never doubted the rightness of his own quest. Gatsby is the male romantic in his pure form, something allowed by the presence of Nick, who embodies Fitzgerald's own reflexive understanding of the romantic, a reflexivity that somehow must find a place in the protagonists of the stories.

Nick imagines that there might have been a moment when Gatsby doubted the value of his prize:

> As I went over to say good-by, I saw that the expression of bewilderment had come back to Gatsby's face, as though a faint doubt had occurred to him as to the quality of his present happiness. Almost five years! There must have been moments even that afternoon when Daisy tumbled short of his dreams—not through her own fault, but because of the colossal vitality of his illusion.[57]

Of course, we have every reason to believe that Daisy, should Gatsby have managed to escape his fate and marry her, could not possibly have lived up to the image of her that he had constructed. Indeed, everything we know about Daisy suggests that she is not worthy of Gatsby's idealization. As Giddens notes, the romantic "is not really a participant in the emerging exploration of intimacy."[58] Gatsby doesn't want a relationship with Daisy; he wants her love to transform him, to make him truly Gatsby and not merely James Gatz in disguise. It is Nick who knows that Gatsby's Daisy is an illusion, that the romantic's love is always illusory.

But if Nick, and therefore Fitzgerald, knows this about the romantic, why does the novel read like a celebration of Gatsby rather than a critique? It is not merely the effect of Nick's judgment that "Gatsby turned out all right at the end."[59] The very fact of Gatsby's death immortalizes him and makes his love eternal. Instead of showing us the impossible "future" of his affair, the novel ends with it at its height. Gatsby will always love Daisy. He will never know what Nick knows about her—that she is careless (incapable of care) like Tom. Although we are told that Gatsby's love was illusory, that illusion is our only alternative to the Buchanans' cynicism. As the book's conclusion makes clear, Gatsby's belief in the green light at the end of Daisy's dock is meant to signify more than his love for a woman. Granting that, however, it is important to recognize that romantic love is not merely a metonymy but a synecdoche. If we cannot believe in love, then belief itself is impossible. *The Great Gatsby* is not, then, finally a novel that exposes the illusions of romance but one that praises the creator of such illusions. Just as Gatsby in death no longer seems the little boy he did in life, so romance in the end seems no longer a foolish illusion but a valuable achievement. I don't see this as a matter of Fitzgerald's own arrested development. It is rather an accurate representation of the role that romantic love plays in the society that produced him and about which he writes.

2

Romancing Marriage
Advice Books and the Crisis

Once upon a time Marriage was not considered a "problem."
—Elinor Glyn, *The Philosophy of Love*

Historical romances and many other novels depicted romantic love and marriage as if the second followed inevitably from the first. The connection was natural and did not need to be explained or justified. A marriage based on true love would, as the narrative pattern repeatedly insisted, produce wedded bliss. Yet many marriages in the era after World War I failed to realize even a modicum of happiness. As married people found themselves dissatisfied and their marriages in danger, a new genre of advice literature developed. It should be understood as a response to both these individual crises and the hue and cry about a crisis of marriage in the society at large. While these are obviously two aspects of the same phenomenon, they are experienced quite differently. The crisis of marriage is a social problem that seems to require a solution at the social level. Dissatisfaction in one's own marriage cannot usefully be attributed to social causes. If the marriage is to be made better or saved, it must be the result of changes that are under the control of the married couple. The new genre of marital advice was addressed to such couples, but demand for it was no doubt stimulated by the news of increasing divorce rates. As divorce became more common, it became a greater fear and a greater possibility.

Rethinking Marriage

The genre of marital advice that emerged in the 1920s has become one of the most profitable product lines in contemporary publishing. In almost any bookstore today there is a section devoted to books promising aid in improving intimate relationships. In one sense, such books could be understood to belong to a long established genre, one that goes back at least to *The Art of Courtly Love* and that would include various conduct books and seduction manuals of the seventeenth and eighteenth centuries and the guides to good health and moral hygiene of the Victorian era. In a stronger sense, however, contemporary advice literature on relationships has a much more recent origin, dating to the 1910s and becoming common in the 1920s and 1930s. What distinguishes contemporary advice literature is precisely its focus on a new object, what we have since come to call "the relationship." Earlier advice literature taught individuals how to achieve their desired ends—the avoidance of pain, successful seduction, healthy offspring, and so on. What such literature didn't seek to do was to teach people how to relate to each other. Relating was assumed to be natural but also unteachable, and what's more, not terribly important. The discourse of romance as expressed in fiction taught that love was something that one fell into; either it existed or it didn't. The advice books that will be my focus in this chapter seek to translate the discourse of romance into instructions about how to relate, how to "make" love within a marriage. They remain grounded in the discourse of romance rather than the discourse of intimacy, but they represent a step in the latter direction.

My leading examples are the books of two women whose writing in different ways reflects the beginning of the construction of the relationship as a therapeutic object. Though both women were British subjects, they were influential figures in America. Elinor Glyn first attained notoriety as the author of the salacious best-seller *Three Weeks* (1907), and by the 1920s she was well known to the American public as a writer of romantic novels and screenplays. She described herself as "a writer on psychological subjects which interest the average citizen" as well as a writer of romances.[1] Her book *The Philosophy of Love* (1923) collected essays she had previously published in popular magazines, and though it does not seem itself to have been a big seller, the original essays were available to a wide readership. Moreover, as we will see, *The Philosophy of Love* strongly reflects the ideology embodied in Glyn's popular fiction and screenplays. Marie Carmichael Stopes, a paleobotanist, sexologist, and birth control advocate, wrote advice books that were best-sellers, and she is far better remembered as an author of such books. *Married Love* (1920) and *Enduring Passion* (1931) were books that continued to sell into the 1950s, the former being the first book to successfully mediate sexology to a general audience.[2] For her trouble, Stopes was prosecuted for indecency. Glyn had also run afoul of English morals. The stage version of *Three Weeks* was refused permission for public performance, and the scandal caused the author to be socially blackballed. If both women were perceived as a threat to public morals, the character of their work differed greatly. Stopes's major concern was physical relations between the married couple, and the two books mentioned here were sex manuals. Glyn, on the other hand, never described sexual acts in her advice literature or in *Three Weeks*. Her offense was not explicit language but the supposed endorsement of an adulterous relationship.

While both authors were associated in the public mind with sex, their advice books are of interest for other reasons. What both authors have in common is the depiction of ideal marriage in terms taken from fictional romances, terms that were not explicitly applied to marriage in fiction but rather to courtship or to extramarital relations. This explicit endorsement of romantic marriage marks a shift from nineteenth-century advice literature, which regarded romantic love with suspicion. In Glyn and Stopes, romance is no longer merely presented as fantasy or diversion; rather, it is endorsed as an appropriate image of married life. The effect of continuing this discourse was to perpetuate the gender roles typical of the nineteenth century but also to make marriage as a relationship an object of discussion, and this discussion opened the door to the development of the discourse of intimacy.

This change in the conception of love is at least as significant as the more frequently observed phenomenon of the "sexualization" of marital advice, but one cannot entirely separate the two.[3] Steven Seidman titles his study of love in America *Romantic Longings,* but the major change he discusses in twentieth-century advice literature is that "sexual satisfaction . . . now assumes a primary role" in the foundation of a good marriage.[4] There is general agreement that the advice literature of this period represents an important shift from earlier, Victorian forms. These changes in advice about love and marriage correspond to changes in practice. The most frequently observed change is the increased importance of sex, which is seen as reflective of a "transformation in sexual mores . . . described as liberalization or modernization."[5] The main characteristic of this transformation is increased sexual activity on the part of women, especially middle-class women. The increased importance of sex in marriage doubtless had something to do with changes in courtship. As historian Beth Bailey has shown, between 1890 and 1925 there was a revolution in middle-class courtship conventions. In 1890,

> Conventional courtship centered on "calling," a term that could describe a range of activities. The young man from the neighboring farm who spent the evening sitting on the front porch with farmer's daughter was paying a call, and so was the "society" man who could judge his prospects by whether or not the card he presented at the front door found the lady of his choice "at home."[6]

The conventions of calling gave parents the ability to supervise their daughter's courtship and gave eligible young women the power to control their own contacts. But by the 1920s, "dating" had become the new convention. Now courtship took place in public, away from parental oversight, and money took on a new role. Since the man now paid for the costs of entertainment, he gained control over the process. Dating fit the new world of consumption in which entertainment was more likely to be purchased than not, and the date itself could be seen as a kind of purchase. As Bailey puts it, dating was an "exchange" in which the man contributed money and the woman only her company. "Men paid for everything, but often with the implication that women 'owed' sexual favors in return."[7] In the 1920s, such favors would typically have included, not intercourse, but rather "necking" or "petting."

The new world of dating and consumption is depicted in the film for which Glyn is best remembered, *It* (Clarence Badger, 1927). Glyn wrote a novella of the same title and adapted it for the screen, and she also had a walk-on part playing herself as a famous author who had discovered "it," a distinctive power of attraction innate in a happy few. Those who have "it" arouse powerful emotions in others, seemingly a special case of an ability Glyn attributed to anyone in love. *It* made Clara Bow a star— she was known as "The 'It' Girl" ever after—for her role as the quintessential flapper. Bow plays a poor shopgirl whose "it" powers enable her to attract both the department store's owner and his best friend. She gets them to take her to their usual haunts—fancy restaurants, yachting parties, etc.—while she takes them to working-class entertainments such as an amusement park. The character combines two of the traits most associated with the flapper, voracious consumption and a lack of feminine modesty and reserve. The idea of the mysterious "it" reflects the new importance that society gave to sex appeal, a quality that the dating system rendered much more valuable.

It is more radical in attitude than in action. Its most risqué moments involve bodies thrown together on amusement park rides. The movie leaves implicit the new behavior that was part of dating. The fact that dates occurred away from the home meant that there were more opportunities for physical contact than under the calling system.[8] According to historian John Spurlock, "The young middle-class women of the first decades of the twentieth century took some forms of sexual pleasure for granted, as the 'loving up' or 'spooning' of the generation born in the 1890s became the necking and petting of the generation born around 1900."[9] If sexual pleasure was assumed to be part of courtship, then it must also have been an expected part of marriage. Spurlock believes that, for women, these expectations were often disappointed, and, as we will see, marital advice books of the period seem to confirm this.[10]

Sexual pleasure was not the only new expectation of marriage. Indeed, as Francesca Cancian has observed, by the 1920s advice books assumed "'that the highest personal happiness comes from marriage based on romantic love.'"[11] Spurlock claims that a new model of marriage based on an ideal of mutuality and partnership became dominant among the middle class, reflecting the breakdown of separate spheres.[12] The new model was codified under the term *companionate marriage,* which was proposed in 1927 by Ben Lindsey, a Colorado juvenile court judge, as a prescription for the marriage crisis. According to Lindsey, "Companionate Marriage is legal marriage, with legalized Birth Control, and with the right to divorce by mutual consent for childless couples, usually without payment of alimony." He argues that while "Companionate Marriage is already an established social fact in this country," changes in law are needed to make it "openly available to all people."[13] According to D'Emilio and Freedman:

> As the concept was popularized, it redefined marriage in more egalitarian terms, consistent with the new freedoms that post-suffrage women seemed to possess. A successful relationship rested on the emotional compatibility of husband and wife, rather than the fulfillment of gender-prescribed duties and roles. Men and women sought happiness and personal satisfaction in their mates; an important component of their happiness was mutual sexual enjoyment. . . . Conservative critics attacked

companionate marriage as encouraging loose morals, supporters saw it as a flexible response to a new social reality.[14]

While advisors and social scientists propounded a vision of marriage that went beyond romantic passions, May attributes the spread of rising expectations in part to the image of love presented in movies and in stories about the offscreen lives of movie stars. She argues that movies and other popular media presented a superficial conception of an ideal marriage, one that was likely to occur after equally superficial rituals of courtship.[15] Contemporary observers such as the sociologists Ernest R. Mower and Ernest W. Burgess worried that romance did create unrealizable expectations of marriage.[16] But this was not the only cause to which the crisis was attributed. *The Marriage Crisis* (1928), by the sociologist Ernest Groves, argued that "marriage faces a crisis and birth control is largely responsible."[17] Marriage was in trouble because of "an attitude of mind and a code of behavior which may be justly described as a pleasure philosophy of life" and more reliable methods of birth control that permitted "marriage to be incorporated into the pleasure philosophy."[18] Groves observed that changes in the social role of marriage had contributed to the crisis. Economic factors no longer favored marital stability as strongly as they once had. As the home ceased to be a site of production, family life became an end itself. But with birth control, this end could be radically modified. Groves contrasted "orthodox marriage," defined by reproduction, and "companionate marriage," which he defined as "the union of husband and wife who from the beginning were determined not to have children."[19] He recognized that marriage had ceased to be regarded as a social necessity and had become a project undertaken to benefit the individual.

New Advice

The advice books I'm concerned with in this chapter are also a response to this new social reality. If they take the descriptive sense of *companionate marriage* largely for granted, what they prescribe goes beyond that ideal to what should be called "romantic marriage." Because of the absence of marriage itself from the fictional discourse of romance, those who sought to explain what romantic marriage might mean could not discover an answer in novels. But novels and other fictional forms were not all that modern lovers and their would-be advisers had to learn from. Nineteenth-century advice literature, however, seems to have conveyed mixed messages about romantic love. Many advice books claiming religious or medical authority, including the best-selling *Plain Facts for Young and Old,* by the cereal promoter Dr. J. H. Kellogg, reject romantic love entirely.[20] These books "rarely mention affection or companionship" and claim that "a sound marriage is based on being religious, industrious, and healthy, and sex is for the purpose of procreation only."[21] On the other hand, most Victorian advice books regard love as an essential element of a good marriage, and most assume that it will be the basis for the choice of a partner. Peter Stearns shows how the Victorians often extolled the virtues of passion, especially passionate love, but that they distinguished such "pure" love from "animal passion" or mere physical attraction. Victorian advisers often regarded love as a transcendent force that they understood in metaphysical terms: "'True love . . . appertains mainly to . . . this cohabitation of soul with a soul. . . . It is this spiritual affinity of the mental masculine and feminine for each other.' Religious-like intensity was love's hallmark."[22] Such intense love may seem to us "romantic," but, as Seidman argues, "The opposition between 'romantic' and 'true love' appeared prominently in middle class Victorian culture."[23] True love was spiritual, and, as a result, it was constant; romantic love was fickle. As one nineteenth-century lover described it, romantic love is "a golden vagary, a self-created illusion, a spring–dream full of the flutter of doves' wings."[24] As late as 1904, advisers could be heard asserting the need to "free the minds of young people from the romantic idea."[25] To avoid the illusions of romantic love required that "lovers had to know each other as thoroughly as possible," an injunction that in turn assumed "a norm of mutual self-disclosure."[26] This advice, of course, assumed the kind of reflective self-knowledge that would be seen in the twentieth century as blocked by the unconscious and compromised by power relations. In addition, such advice applied mainly to courtship; on how spouses were to maintain transcendent love, advisers were silent save for repeating familiar religious formulas. Nineteenth-century advice books, then, failed as much as novels to translate their vision of courtship into a model of marriage that told people how to fulfill that vision.

Twentieth-century advice givers were driven to offer their instruction because marriage seemed not to be living up to its billing. In a larger sense, they felt that marriage no longer could be left to nature. As Glyn put it in *The Philosophy of Love,* "Once upon a time Marriage was not considered a 'problem.' It was the natural course of events, and all in a day's work. But that was in the 'good old days' when a man was supreme master . . . and Woman was a chattel."[27] Like others during the period, Glyn saw that the changing social status of women meant inevitable changes in marriage. This corresponds to Luhmann's narrative, in which the rise of romantic love is said to occur at the same time as the decline of male domination within the family. Under the old model, the patriarch was morally enjoined to love all of his property, including wife, children, and servants. In the regime of romance, however, love is established through the subjectivity of the beloved, and therefore a wife cannot be mere property.[28] But as May points out, male dominance in society meant that "for women, finding and catching the right man was the key to personal fulfillment—the very essence of life."[29] Men had other sources of fulfillment, but they too were disappointed by wives who did not live up to the romantic allure. With many marriages failing and many more failing to satisfy, one can see why advice about marriage would become such a hot commodity.

Advice givers might have provided readers with lower or at least different expectations of marriage, but this tack was perhaps avoided because of the fear that marriage as an institution might disappear. If marriage were portrayed as less exciting or rewarding, readers might simply decide not to marry. The advice books under discussion here set very high expectations indeed. Some of these expectations derive from the Victorian advisers' spiritual conception of love with its religious intensity, but they also draw on romantic discourse about courtship and extramarital relations. *Married Love* depicts marriage as a "glorious unfolding" in which both partners are "transmuted," as in the chemical bonding of two elements to form a third.[30] Stopes's later book promises nothing less than *Enduring Passion*. Glyn envisions even more. *The Philosophy of Love* begins with a chapter titled "Ideal Love," which describes a "Perfect Love, . . . a love so infinite that on neither side is there a shadow of difference in intensity. A perfect understanding, a holy meeting upon the planes of the soul, the brain and the body. A complete trust, which is above outside influences. A physical satisfaction which sanctifies all material things. . . . Such love is pure Heaven on earth."[31] Later, ideal marriage is described as "the infinite bliss of the mating of the soul in peace and freedom from anxiety."[32] Glyn acknowledges that few marriages meet this ideal, but she offers it as a possibility, a goal. We can recognize in Glyn's quasi-religious language a vision of intimacy, but, as we will see, neither Stopes nor Glyn recognizes intimacy as the problem.

Stopes

Since Marie Stopes's books were mainly concerned with physical relations, one might be surprised by my claim that her work depends on the discourse of romantic love. Seidman, for example, thinks that Stopes simply confused "the language of love with the language of eroticism."[33] But as Lesley Hall has asserted, "In *Married Love* and its sequels [Stopes] was rewriting traditional narratives of marriage. . . . *Married Love* propounded that far from being the end of romance and adventure, marriage was only the beginning."[34] It is apparent that Stopes's new narrative was rooted in the discourse of romance. *Married Love* begins, "Every heart desires a mate. For some reason beyond our comprehension, nature has so created us that we are incomplete in ourselves." Thus does Stopes naturalize, not—or not merely—heterosexual desire, but monogamous marriage. The opening chapter of *Married Love* sounds very much like the vision of marriage at the end of romances like *The Crisis,* so that marriage is described not merely as a meeting of minds and bodies but as a supernatural connection: "the innermost spirit of one and all so yearns as for a sense of union with another soul."[35] The descriptions of love Stopes uses would be regarded as excessive in any romantic novel: bodily differences are "mystical, alluring, enchanting in their promise"; lovers are "conscious of entering on a new and glorious state . . . and see reflected in each other's eyes the beauty of the world . . . a celestial intoxication"; "From the body of the loved one . . . there springs . . . the enlargement of the horizon of human sympathy and the glow of spiritual understanding which a solitary soul could never have attained alone."[36]

But the romantic vision presented in the first chapter is, as the second chapter tells us, too often unrealized—which is, of course, why Stopes wrote the book. Her explanation for the unhappiness of so many marriages—"there are tragically few which approach even humanly attainable joy"—is that most married couples remain ignorant of how to satisfy one another sexually.[37] This affects both men and women, but differently:

In the early days of marriage the young man is often even more sensitive, more romantic . . . and he enters the marriage hoping for an even higher degree of spiritual and bodily unity than does the girl or woman. But the man is more quickly blunted, more swiftly rendered cynical. . . . On the other hand, the woman is slower to realise disappointment, and more often by the sex-life of marriage is of the two the more *profoundly* wounded.[38]

The "perfect happiness" envisioned in the first chapter and expected by betrothed couples is possible, Stopes implies, but sexual failure prevents it.

Stopes does seem to reduce the intimate relationship to a sexual one, but the questions of interest for my analysis are why she sees marriage in this way and why so many people seemed to find this picture of marriage helpful or enlightening. One obvious answer, *pace* Foucault, is that the Victorian era had repressed sexual knowledge. The traditional narrative of marriage had promised love, but it had not promised sexual satisfaction, which women were not even supposed to want and men were supposed to find elsewhere. As Stopes reports, "By the majority of 'nice' people woman is supposed to have no spontaneous sex-impulses."[39] Not only does Stopes provide practical knowledge about how to make sex more satisfying, but her new narrative depicts marriage as a relationship no longer dominated by men's needs. Creating a successful relationship is a matter of "mutual adjustment," as she titles one of her chapters. In Stopes's view, men and women have naturally different sexual needs to which each partner must adjust, but she also holds that each couple must discover how they in particular can best satisfy each other: "It often takes several years for eager and intelligent couples fully to probe themselves and to discover the extent and meaning of the immensely profound physiological and spiritual results of marriage."[40]

Stopes's books provided information that both men and women lacked and a new conception of the role of sex in marriage that spoke powerfully to women, whose pleasure and desire had previously been ignored. But Stopes's advice was offered, not merely in the service of greater pleasure or more equal relations, but rather in the quest to attain "marriage . . . as perfect, and hence as joyous, as possible."[41] Stopes's high expectations of marriage and the notion that they might be fulfilled by means of better knowledge about sex both derived from the discourse of romance. Marriage was now seen as the promise of romantic love, a transcendent conclusion to the passionate adventure of courtship. Stopes accepted all that the discourse of romance invested in marriage, but she recognized that most marriages did not pay off on that investment by living up to the promise of romance. In deciding that unsatisfactory sexual relations were the cause of this failure, Stopes located the problem where the discourse of romance told her to look for it. As Rougemont implies, romance has always been more about desire, or obstacles, than about its satisfaction. Romantic discourse originally denied the possibility of satisfaction, but during the nineteenth century it came to be located in marriage. This connection was not made explicit by Stopes, but it was implicit in at least two places. In *Married Love,* the chapter on "Modesty and Romance" urges couples not to become too familiar with each other and if possible to maintain separate bedrooms. This advice is meant to avoid the problem that "woman . . . has been so thoroughly 'domesticated' by man that she feels too readily that after marriage she is all his. And by her very docility to his perpetual demands she destroys for him the elation, the palpitating thrills and surprises, of the chase."[42] What this advice does is to bring the obstacle, which is indispensable to romance narratives, into marriage itself. As we will see, this tactic is central to Glyn's program.

The title of Stopes's later book, *Enduring Passion,* reveals its link to the discourse of romance, for passion is the characteristic state of the romantic subject, a state that was not previously understood to endure or even to exist in marriage. The book is "Dedicated to all who are, might be, or should be *married lovers,*" a name that crystallizes marriage understood on the model of romance.[43] Typical of her reductionism, Stopes relates the belief in the inevitable decline of marriage to a more fundamental but mistaken belief in the proverb "Post coitum omne triste."[44] The purpose of the book is "not only to challenge the desolating" proverb, "but to show in detail how it is wrong, and how that wrong may be righted."[45] The proverb in her view is the result of "various physical faults commonly practiced," such that changing what happens in individual sex acts can change marriage itself. Stopes claims that "where the acts of coitus are rightly performed, the pair can disagree, can hold opposite views about every conceivable subject under the sun without any ruffling or disturbance of the temper, without any angry scenes or desire to separate."[46] But despite the mechanical explanation of passion's endurance or lack thereof, Stopes continues to understand passion itself as far more than physical desire. She coins a new term, *erogamic,* to name "the mating and relation together of man and woman in all three planes—physical, mental and spiritual."[47] It is the discourse of romance that explains why it is "passion" that Stopes thinks must endure, and thus why sexual excitement becomes the guarantor of true love.

Glyn

Stopes was a scientist, and it is plausible that her reductionism stemmed from habits of mind ingrained during her professional training. The very different form that Glyn gave to her advice also seems to have stemmed from her work, writing romantic novels and screenplays. This experience explains why Glyn's advice much more explicitly reveals its connections to the discourse of romance. Glyn herself seems to be the perfect case study of the effects of that discourse on nineteenth-century women and girls. We know that Glyn was someone on whom romantic fictions had an early and lasting impact. Joan Hardwick titled her biography of Glyn *Addicted to Romance,* and she traces her subject's addiction all the way back to stories told by a grandmother in early childhood. Romance for the young Glyn came to be associated with marriage, and when she lived in France as a young woman, she resisted the notion pervasive there that romance was to be found outside marriage. Her own courtship and marriage, however, failed to live up to her hopes for romance, and as Hardwick notes, her novels do not depict fairy-tale marriages: "Not all of Elinor's fictional marriages are depicted in [a] negative way, but the novels in which the couples do find sexual joy are those in which a union is achieved only after great difficulty and misunderstanding."[48]

The book for which Glyn was most famous was *Three Weeks,* a novel she wrote in response to an unconsummated affair with a younger man some twelve years after her marriage. The young man served as the model for the book's hero, Paul, an innocent who leaves England for a tour of the Continent and there becomes involved passionately, but only for the eponymous three weeks, with a mysterious older woman going by the name of Mme. Zalenska. Paul later learns that she is apparently the wife of an eastern European monarch, and she is most often referred to by the narrator as Paul's "lady." The novel is the quintessential romance of the older model in which love and marriage are opposed rather than linked. Paul leaves behind in England Isabella, for whom he is "perfectly certain his passion . . . would last."[49] Isabella soon recedes far into the background, and Zalenska's husband is never more than a threatening but distant shadow. *Three Weeks,* then, makes much less of the triangular pattern than most romances, but it still depicts an adulterous relationship. It is hard to miss the connection to medieval romances and lyrics: Paul's lover is "his lady," and his attitude toward her is appropriately worshipful. Perhaps in imitation of courtly love, the affair itself begins with the lady's prolonged teasing of Paul, delaying sexual consummation in spite of increasingly provocative gestures and poses on her part. The reader is also teased, since all he or she actually experiences are the preliminaries. After the affair is consummated, Paul quickly learns of the potential violence that his lady's husband might do to both of them. The plot provides the typical range of obstacles to the lovers' happiness. Moreover, while the three weeks of the affair are experienced by both lovers as blissful, the brevity of the relationship is a cause of great pain to Paul, and Mme. Zalenska is described as suffering greatly during the year after their affair; she is murdered by her husband before she and Paul can meet again. Love and death are here linked, even if not so directly as in *Tristan*.

Although *Three Weeks* produced a scandal in England, its depiction of love is remarkable only in that an adulterous affair is not explicitly condemned—though, as Glyn was wont to point out, the lovers suffer greatly. The novel is of interest here because it exemplifies the romantic vision that *The Philosophy of Love* explicitly grafts onto a conception of marriage. Indeed, a great deal of Glyn's philosophy is already present in *Three Weeks*. Paul's lady is constantly teaching him, and she can be seen as a quite explicit example of that European institution, the older woman who initiates young men into sexual experience. Paul is explicitly a neophyte, as his lady's favorite term of endearment for him, "baby," emphasizes. But it is not just that Paul is young and inexperienced; his lack of wisdom is also at least implicitly a function of his gender. It would be hard to imagine the gender roles reversed, and not only because it would be unremarkable for a young woman to become passionately involved with an older man. What is taught in *Three Weeks* is not sexual technique— which a man might plausibly teach a younger woman—but lessons about the character of passionate love that would seem quite out of place expressed by a man. The lady provides not an *ars erotica* but a philosophy of love. For example, his lady tells Paul that "the duration of love in a being always depends upon the loved one. I create an emotion in you, as you create one in me. You do not create it in yourself," a point that Glyn restates virtually verbatim in her *Philosophy*.[50] In creating the character of the lady, Glyn presents us with a vision of the role she herself will later take on in her essays, a woman who has authoritative knowledge about love that men—and most women—lack.

The brevity and extramarital character of the romance in *Three Weeks* mean that the issue of preserving love in a long-term relationship need not be addressed. Indeed, the lady's philosophy seems to imply that love is not likely to last very long. Glyn herself believed in the possibility of romantic marriage, but she lived in a social milieu where marriages continued to be formed as alliances and where romance took place principally outside marriage. According to Hardwick, *Three Weeks* sprang from an "urgent need to put together on paper all the frustrated emotions of the last few years which had been suddenly set free by the love of Alistair Innes Ker."[51] Glyn said that "the book meant everything to me; it was the outpouring of my whole nature, romantic, proud, and passionate."[52] The paradox that marriage is supposed to be the goal and fulfillment of romance but that romance is identified with brief, intense affairs is not merely a problem for Glyn; it is the legacy of the discourse of romance to Western culture. *The Philosophy of Love* should be understood as Glyn's attempt to resolve the paradox by explaining how marriage can be romantic.

It is worth recalling that *The Philosophy of Love* and Stopes's marriage manuals emerged in a culture that had been recently taught all manner of new and improved methods for doing things that had previously been thought to entail their own natural or inevitable processes. Frederick Taylor, for example, showed employers how workers' productivity might be greatly increased using methods of "scientific management." Advertising, which had become culturally pervasive only since the 1890s, constantly explained to the readers of magazines and newspapers how new products could make life easier or more pleasant.[53] May notes that advertisements for products such as Pears' Soap claimed to be the means to youth, beauty, and finding a mate.[54] It is as part of this regime of rationalization that the advice books under discussion here should be understood. *The Philosophy of Love* is an attempt to rationalize the basic assumptions of romantic love in order to make possible happy marriage. As Glyn explains, "Whether or no there is logic in love, we certainly cannot be so idiotic as to pretend that logic cannot be used in the management of it!"[55] Like those of Taylor and the advertisers, Glyn's method is primarily one of manipulation.

Manipulation is necessary because one of the fundamental assumptions of romance is that love is passionate in the sense that it is something to which the subject submits. Love is an experience to be undergone, rather than an act committed. My own love is always beyond my control, or, as Glyn puts it, "*No one can love or unlove at will.*"[56] In earlier times, the idea that love befell one led to the widespread association of passionate love with madness. But for Glyn, to understand that the other produces love in me gives me the opportunity to control the love of the other:

> Thus, realise that it is in yourself that the responsibility lies of keeping love. You ought to be very careful to use the right methods to accomplish this.
>
> When once two people feel certain that they love, their whole intelligence should be used to see if they can manage to remain in this blissful state. Every art of pleasing should be exercised by both, and every attraction polished. Selfishness should be curbed, and all habits likely to disillusionise the other.[57]

The love Glyn is describing and trying to teach her readers to preserve is not companionship but a "blissful state." Such a description certainly goes along with May's notion of rising expectations of marriage, but its extremity reveals that these expectations are at least partly derived from a conception of love that was considered antithetical to marriage. Glyn herself seems aware of this contradiction and therefore makes avoiding "disillusionising the other" the central tenet of her advice. One wonders whether she ever thought about the idea, implicit in her position, that long-term lovers must be "illusionised," or, to put it more plainly, deluded. Producing love in the other seems on this reading like a magician's trick, and perhaps precisely so, since the other is moved in spite of his or her awareness that an illusion is being produced. We may seem close here to the cynicism German philosopher Peter Sloterdijk calls "enlightened false consciousness," but this clearly is not what Glyn intends.[58] That she remains a true believer in love's transcendence is revealed in the quotation above (it is asserted often enough elsewhere in the book) by her phrase "when once two people feel certain that they love," since this postulates an authentic, primary condition that the lovers will seek to perpetuate by the maintenance of mystery. Glyn's belief in the need for illusions, which corresponds to Stopes's advice about avoiding "domestication," is typical of other advice literature of the period. Newspaper columnist Dix, for example, explicitly urged married couples to "preserve illusions" by not being overly frank or inquiring too deeply.[59] Here, the Victorian norm of "mutual self-disclosure" is trumped by the need to preserve mystery and sustain a sense of difference.

If the argument for the origins of this vision of marriage in the discourse of romance needs any more support, we may find it in her discussion of love outside marriage, which is focused on the figure of the mistress. Glyn's familiarity with the mistress stems from her own experience of Europe's ruling classes—she had by this time already played the role—but her privileging of it follows from the romantic ideology already apparent in *Three Weeks*. Glyn asserts that "often illicit unions are very happy, much happier while they last, than married ones. Why? Because both parties are showing the best side to the other, and the very knowledge that there is no tie, and that either can slip off if wearied, makes both take pains to be agreeable."[60] The relationship unbound by law exists at the pleasure of the parties involved, and it is the model for Glyn's conception of marriage. She remarks that "the wife can learn a great deal from the mistress: Continual attention to physical attraction; reviewing calmly what will be the best line to go upon with the particular man in case; and never nagging him, or wearying him."[61] Mistresses, in other words, are experts at avoiding disillusionising. Though wives have security that mistresses do not, wives must continually fight against the ill effects of this state.

Gender and the "Pure Relationship"

Glyn's views of marriage take for granted the gender roles of her day, but Glyn clearly sees herself as contributing to women's continuing emancipation. Her discussion of male and female roles in marriage demands a degree of equality unusual for her time. She urges both male and female partners to take responsibility for managing each other's love, where most authorities of this period regarded it as a woman's task to keep up illusions for love's sake. Glyn's conceptions of gender serve as the grounds for much of her marital advice. Gender for Glyn is rooted in biology, which has given each sex a "fundamental nature," men being dominant and women subservient, men hunters and women mothers and wives. This biologism leads her to endorse the double standard. She counsels women involved with men in their twenties to "well past thirty" to tolerate some infidelity, while proclaiming that "for a woman married to a man and *living with him as his wife,* to deceive him, and give herself to another, sharing herself with them both, is a *supreme degradation,* a greater one for physiological and psychological reasons than for a man in like case."[62] Yet Glyn's biological notions of gender turn out not to be essentialist, and women are depicted as having changed significantly after having lived under "conditions of restraint and coercion . . . for thousands of years."[63] Women, in Glyn's view, now recognize their own rights and intelligence, and she predicts that in the future women may, like many men, regard love "as an ephemeral emotion, which comes and goes according to the physical attraction of the man calling it forth. The further emancipation goes . . . the more it is possible that women will look upon life more and more as men interpret it."[64] In an explicit rejection of essentialism, she asserts that "the woman of to-morrow will be in the melting-pot, where she will be reformed for the best use which evolution can make of her."[65] Stopes also believed, as *Enduring Passion* tells us, that human nature was in a constant process of change.[66] Both authors, however, mainly take for granted the contemporary "fundamental natures" of men and women and do not challenge the contemporary construction of gender.

These books' conceptions of gender doubtless contributed to the continuing emotional differentiation of men and women, but we also should observe that such emotional differentiation may account for their approach. Male advisers tended to present a more rational or scientific attitude.[67] It would be a mistake, then, to read the advice books by Glyn and Stopes as simply perpetuating traditional gender roles. While the degree to which twentieth-century advice literature continues the discourse of romance has often been misrecognized, the effects of this literature beyond sexualization have also not been well understood. This advice literature used the discourse of romance to conceive of marriage itself, imagining a new ideal, romantic marriage.[68] In their attempts to imagine such a marriage, Glyn and Stopes offer, I would argue, early instances of what Giddens calls the "pure relationship . . . a situation where a social relation is entered into for its own sake, for what can be derived by each person from sustained association with another; and which is continued only in so far as it is thought by both parties to deliver enough satisfactions for each individual to stay within it."[69] *The Philosophy of Love* and *Married Love,* typical of advice books of the period, regard marriage not as a religious or social obligation but as a source of personal fulfillment. Moreover, they imagine the emotional life of marriage as more or less the equal responsibility of men and women.[70] Though neither Glyn nor Stopes is ready to abandon the privileging of marriage over other sexual relationships, they both define the ideal conception of marriage in terms drawn from relationships outside marriage. If Giddens is right, books such as these need to be understood as participating in the continuing transformation of intimacy. While perpetuating the discourse of romance, such books paved the way for intimacy itself to become an object of inquiry and as such to be denaturalized.

It would be a mistake, however, to understand the emergence of this new discourse as evolving directly from books like those of Glyn and Stopes. In fact, the success of Stopes's books led most directly to the publication of even more explicit sex manuals like Theodore Van de Velde's *Ideal Marriage* (1930). This genre in the main did not perpetuate the spirituality with which Stopes inflected sex. Another response to the marriage crisis was the development of a pedagogy of marriage. Ernest Groves, who "pioneered in integrating courses on marriage and the family into the college curriculum," saw better formal training as one solution to the marriage crisis.[71] As Groves put it:

> Education itself has been notoriously neglectful in its attitude toward marriage and family. At a time when we have come to realize that everything which is to flourish as a social experience must have preparation of an instructional character, it is amazing that we have been so slow to take over in our educational program any specific and practical effort to conserve family welfare.[72]

This view became increasingly influential, and by the 1950s, courses in marriage and the family had become commonplace on American campuses. While the textbooks that these courses used took the companionate model as their norm and typically accepted romantic love as the basis for marriage, their focus was "adjustment" rather than communication. They mainly taught "appropriate" gender roles even though they often counseled the need for flexibility in those roles. Moreover, perhaps because of the official, public way in which these books were used, they distanced the reader from their object. They provided a different sort of instruction than did advice books written for private consumption. It would require a new genre of advice writing before intimacy would emerge at the center of a new conception of marriage.

3

Marriage as Adultery

Hollywood Romance and the Screwball Comedy

It is the premise of farce that marriage kills romance. It is the project of the genre of remarriage to refuse to draw a conclusion from this premise but rather to turn the tables on farce, to turn marriage itself into romance, into adventure, . . . to preserve within it something of the illicit, to find as it were a moral equivalent of the immoral. —Stanley Cavell, *The Pursuits of Happiness*

The real world is a place that I've never felt comfortable in. I think that my generation grew up with a value system heavily marked by films. . . . My ideas of romance came from the movies.
—Woody Allen, *Rolling Stone*, Sept. 93

The marriage manuals of the 1920s presented a vision of the romantic marriage, a vision that had been absent from the fictional versions of the discourse of romance. Romantic fiction, whether in print or on screen, typically ended with marriage. In the 1930s, a new Hollywood genre emerged in which the action very often takes place after the central couple have already been married. The name that this genre acquired at that time was the "screwball comedy."[1] It was defined by fast talk, zany situations, and a romantic plot.[2] As Stanley Cavell has demonstrated in *Pursuits of Happiness*, there is a significant group of screwball comedies that can be called "comedies of remarriage." Cavell argues that the comedy of remarriage shifts "emphasis away from the normal question of comedy, whether a young pair will get married, onto the question whether the pair will get and stay divorced, thus prompting philosophical discussions on the nature of marriage."[3] But Cavell's neglect of feminist film studies causes him to misunderstand the cultural work of the genre. Cavell thinks that the screwball comedies he discusses succeed in enlightening us about marriage itself. My argument is that they do just the opposite: they mystify marriage by treating marriage as if it were an adulterous affair. The major cultural work of these films is not the stimulation of thought about marriage but the affirmation of marriage in the face of the threat of a growing divorce rate and liberalized divorce laws.

In the story I'm telling in *Modern Love,* screwball comedies represent an innovation in the discourse of romance. They take the familiar elements—the obstacles, the love triangle, courtship, adultery—and combine them in a new way. Like historical romances, screwball comedies typically position the viewer as the subject of their romance so that he or she must feel marriage as the thing desired. Like the advice books discussed in the last chapter, these films seem to be a response to an immediate social problem, the crisis in marriage, but unlike them, they are a disguised response. Yet in the screwball comedies there is a curious disjunction in the way the discourse of romance functions. On the one hand, romance functions in them more as an ideology than it did in the previous genres I have discussed. Romance here is much more directly used to mystify marriage, to make it seem to be what it cannot be, an affair. On the other hand, romance sometimes seems to be *revealed* as a mystification or ideology by the very implausibility or "screwiness" of these films. I will argue that this seeming critique is actually itself an aspect of the discourse of romance and does not therefore represent a genuine move beyond its limits. But if these films don't represent a successful critique of romance, they do in another way carry the seeds of an alternative. Because screwball comedies typically focus on the interaction and conversation of the central couple—and often a pair who seem to know each other all too well—these films represent a step toward the discourse of intimacy. Moreover, certain elements in the genre do suggest a critique of both romance and contemporary marriage. The former is reflected in many of Preston Sturges's films, including *The Lady Eve* (1941) and *Unfaithfully Yours* (1948), while the latter elements become dominant in such films as *Adam's Rib* (George Cukor, 1949) and in some revivals of the genre such as *Desperately Seeking Susan* (Susan Seidelman, 1985). However, the cultural power of the screwball formula was demonstrated by more or less faithful revivals beginning in the 1980s, and by even more conservative transformations of it in the 1990s.

Hollywood Romance

Cavell says of *The Lady Eve* that "Preston Sturges is trying to tell us that tales of romance are inherently feats of cony catching, of conning, making gulls or suckers of their audience."[4] I'm not sure what Preston Sturges is trying to tell us in *The Lady Eve,* but I am sure that the movie depends upon our both recognizing this characterization of romance and our not finally accepting it. The film involves a woman (Barbara Stanwyck) and her father (Charles Coburn), a pair of cardsharps on a cruise ship, who pick the heir to a brewing fortune (Henry Fonda) as their mark. Fonda falls for Stanwyck as planned, but in the process of setting him up, Stanwyck falls in love herself. The two are to be married, but just before the ship is to dock, Fonda is informed of Stanwyck's true identity and calls things off. Stanwyck, seeking revenge, arranges an invitation to Fonda's family estate as the Lady Eve Sedgewick. Though she attempts no physical disguise—her rationale: only if she does not try to hide the resemblance will he fall for her story—Fonda does not recognize her but falls— the film underscores this point with numerous pratfalls that Fonda takes—in love with this "new" woman, using on her the same, apparently heartfelt lines he used the first time. They depart on a honeymoon trip during which the Lady Eve "reveals" a sordid past that causes Fonda to leave the train marriage unconsummated. A divorce is arranged (Stanwyck, to the chagrin of her con artist cohort, does not take advantage of Fonda), and Fonda takes a cruise on the same ship to get away from it all. He there meets Barbara Stanwyck for the third time, believing her to be the first woman, and falls for her again. The film concludes with this reunion, the couple together, a happy ending.

Clearly, this is not a story that ought to inspire confidence in romantic love. The film focuses on romance as false consciousness. Sturges even gives William Demarest—who has been an opponent of Stanwyck all along—the last word, "It's the same dame," perhaps undermining the otherwise transcendent happy ending. Yet none of the film's self-reflection, none of its satire undermines the naturalness of romance. Romance already undermines itself; making lovers look like suckers just makes them look all the more like lovers. As a piece of Hollywood entertainment, *The Lady Eve* works because it can trust that the audience will see through the false consciousness that afflicts the character Fonda plays but that it will also forget this glimpse of reality and believe in the film's ending as an affirmation of romance that the rest of the film has denied.

In one way that *romance* is used, it and *ideology* are synonyms in that both mean illusion or false consciousness. Cavell sees Sturges as offering a critique of romance in this sense, a critique Cavell himself cannot in the main accept.[5] Romance, however, is also a kind of ideology, a particular lived relation to or imagination of intimate relationships and the emotions they produce. What I have been calling the discourse of romance at least sometimes functions in this way. The group of related genres that constitute this discourse function ideologically to greater or lesser degrees. Romance, then, is curious in that it seems to call attention to its own work of mystification.

Understanding *romance* as a name for illusion or false consciousness has been common to its association with both love and narratives. The idea that lovers are typically deluded by their love is a long-standing convention of both literature and folklore. As we saw in chapter 1, the opposition of the genres of romance and novel in literary criticism has usually been constructed on epistemological grounds, the novel being identified with realism and truth and the romance with idealism, fantasy, and falsehood. In terms of this opposition, the vast majority of fiction films are romances. Even filmic adaptations of realist novels—for example, the typical Merchant-Ivory productions—tend to be rendered historical romances on the screen by their period settings.

However, in the film theory of the 1970s and 1980s, the term *realism* was used predominantly to designate the illusion of realism.[6] This illusion was seen largely as an effect of what has been called Hollywood's "invisible style"—that is, a style of filmmaking that disguises the fact of filmic mediation.[7] Among the elements usually attributed to this style besides "invisible editing" are shot/reverse shot sequences, the elision of mundane time, and even—perhaps preeminently—narrative itself. Here, the opposite of realism is not romance but avant-gardism in which the medium is what is being represented. Realism in this sense is an ideology. Only by eschewing the illusion of reality can a filmmaker avoid perpetuating not only the realist ideology itself but also ideology *tout court*. Seen in this way, realism is not merely an ideology but, like romance, ideology itself.

There is a difference, however, in conceiving of Hollywood films as romantic or realist. I take it that the claim of the critique of the realist illusion is that the audience is regularly made to believe in the truth, the reality, of the events on the screen. While all illusions or mystifications entail some acceptance of the unreal as real, the mechanisms of cinematic realism have about the same effect on the audience as the machinery used by magicians—or illusionists. In other words, the audience knows that what it is watching is unreal, but it appreciates being temporarily fooled, mystified, conned. There is doubtless a minority who don't get it, who think that the illusionists of Hollywood are actual conjurers, but we can disregard their social significance. If one takes Hollywood films to function as romances, however, one captures the complicated relationship of this cinema to the real. The viewer knows that he or she is watching what is unreal—and, in fact, is likely to have chosen the film for its unreality, for its value as an escape from what is reality to the viewer. The "realism" of the cinematic machinery allows for the escape to take place; to make that escape enjoyable, however, the film must take the viewer somewhere he or she wants to go. As Bordwell, Staiger, and Thompson have demonstrated, heterosexual romance figured as a major or minor plot line in 90 percent of Hollywood films during the studio era.[8] We have to assume that the studios favored romance because the vast majority of the audience could be counted on to be already invested in romantic narratives about themselves. Such narratives may be unreal even to those who are invested in them, but they are nevertheless representations of "real" desires. Hollywood films thus might be said to appeal to what Sloterdijk has called "enlightened false consciousness," or, in the Slovenian psychoanalyst Slovoj Žižek's gloss, "They know very well what they are doing, but still, they are doing it."[9] "Enlightened false consciousness" seems to describe perfectly the state to which a film like *The Lady Eve* brings its viewers.

The discourse of romance was, as I have argued, also very important to the entire history of the novel, but even its prominence in prose fiction does not come close to rivaling the role it has played in Hollywood. It seems likely that the conditions and relations of production of films forced Hollywood narratives to resort frequently to romance and to its triadic structure in which female subjectivity is given a place. Movies of this era, like the fiction of the previous one, typically follow the mythos of comedy, an erotic intrigue between a young man and young woman that is blocked by some kind of opposition, usually paternal, and resolved by a twist in the plot.[10] This is true of films in most genres, and of the major ones is atypical only of the women's film and the western. Hollywood films specialized in telling romantic stories, not only because they were already popular commodities, but also because the studio system of production strongly favored such stories. The studios' contract system kept stables of male and female actors, and simple economics dictated that they should be working as often as possible. Hollywood assumed that most of its products (westerns perhaps excepted) would include a male and a female star. The star system, predicated as it was on sex appeal to secure the attraction and identification of the audience, both reinforced the predilection for romance and was in turn reinforced by it. Female stars were not mere sex objects but subjects with whom the film audience developed continuing imaginary relationships.[11] Furthermore, that audience was presumed to be as much female as male. Major budget films could not appeal only to men as, say, hardboiled novels might. These considerations together with ideological ones meant that Hollywood films would be far more dependent than novels on heterosexual romance. The movies, then, can be regarded as the broadest reaching and most intensive dissemination of the discourse of romance. This suggests that Woody Allen was speaking for several generations when he said, "My ideas of romance came from the movies."[12]

The importance of romance to Hollywood films is illustrated by the transformations typically wrought on stories adapted from other media. Consider, for example, the hard-boiled detective novel, a genre that has been frequently adapted for the screen. The historical development of these novels in the 1930s has been understood as a response to threats to patriarchal dominance.[13] In them women are typically the source of the evil that the detective must discover and eliminate. In this sort of narrative, female characters need not be subjects and may be mere functions. Such novels may be considered dyadic narratives in which women are objects of exchange among men. Though some Hollywood narratives may follow this pattern, most do not. Hollywood versions of hard-boiled stories make women much more prominent as characters, and they typically are the subject of a romance with the detective hero. Howard Hawks's *The Big Sleep* (1946) is an extreme example, but its extremity can help us see the typical pattern. The film was made as a vehicle to reprise the screen romance of Humphrey Bogart and Lauren Bacall in *To Have and Have Not* (Howard Hawks, 1945) and was marketed on the basis of the couple's off-screen romance. A radical departure from Raymond Chandler's novel, where the detective hero is lonely, celibate, and misogynist, the film makes the love story its focal point. The locus of evil in Hawks's film is not a female betrayer but the gangster Eddie Mars. Virginia Wexman reads *The Big Sleep* "as a study in the creation of the companionate couple," something that might also be said about many screwball comedies.[14]

But how can we account for the development of a new comic genre? Why did *re*marriage suddenly become a more important issue than marriage? The crisis of marriage seems an obvious answer, although it is true that the comedy of remarriage would be a somewhat belated response. The first screwball comedy is usually said to be *It Happened One Night* (Frank Capra, 1934), more than ten years after the marriage crisis first made headlines and during the Depression when divorce rates were, for the moment, on the decline.[15] The genre is usually thought to have peaked in the late 1930s, and its first cycle to have run its course by the early 1950s. Thus, it corresponds to the period in which patterns of marriage might be seen as returning to normal. It is my argument, however, that remarriage became the leading plot of screwball comedy because divorce had become a common—but still threatening—feature of American life. So even if the rhetoric of crisis receded during the 1930s and 1940s, the rise in divorce in the 1920s and the change in attitudes that accompanied it represented a point of rupture in the way marriage was practiced in the United States. Screwball comedies respond not so much to the fears of social collapse articulated by moralists as to the fears of individuals about the fate of their own current or future marriages. The project of the comedies of remarriage is to reaffirm the romantic view of marriage in the face of its failure. Hollywood films take up this cultural work not only out of patriarchal interest and ideology but also for the coincident reason that films that participated in this ideology were popular. A majority of the film audience doubtless found it pleasurable to be reassured about the possibilities of marriage. The movies were the obvious place for such reassurance to be offered. During the 1920s, the popularity of feature films had left that of best-selling books in the dust. In 1930s, movies became a genuine mass medium, reaching audiences of almost all classes and regions.

If the mythos of comedy was the standard plot structure of Hollywood films, it exists unusually close to the surface of screwball comedy. These are films that are explicitly devoted to "erotic intrigue" where the obstacles to the couple's marriage are typically so powerful that the marriage happens only at the very last minute, the result of a major reversal. This "twist" ending, however, does lead to marriage, which often is depicted—rather than merely being implied as in many Hollywood films. Cavell observes that these films typically feature the "green world," usually located in Connecticut, "a setting . . . in which the pair have the leisure to be together."[16] As in New Comedy, the green world serves as a symbol of rebirth, "the triumph of life and love over the waste land" and of the couple's reconciliation.[17] Yet nowhere is the transformation of the mythos of comedy from the social to the personal so apparent as in these films. Unlike Shakespeare's comedies, for example, which typically end with scenes of multiple weddings celebrated as festivals, screwball comedies typically reject a planned festival, the wedding that does not happen, in favor of a much more private celebration.

Another innovation of the screwball comedy was its intensification of the erotic. We noted that the historical romances of the turn of the century were in general quite tame in their treatment of sex. The romances did not merely fail to depict physical relations; they didn't seem even to present sexual desire in disguise. In the meantime, fiction had become much more explicit, and the films of the precode era sometimes included nudity and often what are now called in the language of film ratings "sexual situations." The screwball comedy emerged on the cusp of the newly restrictive production code of 1934, which forced films to become much less explicit. *It Happened One Night* was made and released before the new code's advent in June of that year, but its formula would prove useful afterward. Screwball comedies typically depict a sexual relationship without literally showing one. The developing relationship on which these films focus is meant to be experienced as growing sexual desire.

To some extent, narratives in the discourse of romance have always used this strategy. Because romance seeks by almost any means it can to heighten desire, there must be obstacles to the couples' union. But in the older, typically tragic, version of romance, desire waxes and wanes as the couple's desire is first frustrated by their separation and then temporarily satisfied when they are briefly reunited. In the screwball comedy, desire builds until the wedding that ends the film: "the delayed fuck," as Harvey calls it.[18] Furthermore, other desired objects become associated with the couple such that we are enticed into not only sexual but other material kinds of desire. One reason that screwball comedies almost always involve the rich is that their world is a metaphor for the reward romance promises of love. In this version of romance, "the bliss of genitality" is the *end* of desire.[19] When the right man or woman is found, and returns one's love, the subject will be satisfied and desire no more. But romance does not focus its energy on describing this bliss, which exists in the film only as the release of tension provided by the ending.

The specific illusion that the screwball comedy constructs is that one can have both complete desire and complete satisfaction and that the name for this state of affairs is marriage. But the unacknowledged flip side of the romantic economy is that satisfaction is the death of desire. Romantic tragedies such as *Tristan and Isolde* allegorize this in the literal deaths of the lovers. According to Juliet Mitchell, romance seeks an idealized object, and when that object is attained, love ceases to be romantic.[20] Marriage must be the death of romance between the couple, who, if they are to continue to participate in romance, must find other partners. Hence, for the project of the screwball comedy to work, romance must occur outside of marriage, and marriage must be the end of the movie.[21]

Mystifying Marriage

It is Cavell's failure to recognize the contradiction about marriage in the discourse of romance that causes him to contradict himself. In his view, comedies of remarriage tell us that romance is illusion and depict marriage romantically, but they can still tell us the truth about marriage. His claim that the comedy of remarriage prompts "philosophical discussions on the nature of marriage" is undermined by his own remarks about romance.[22] We already noted his interpretation of *The Lady Eve* ("Preston Sturges is trying to tell us that tales of romance are inherently feats of cony catching"), but Cavell also argues that "the project of the genre of remarriage . . . [is] to turn marriage itself into romance, into adventure."[23] Perhaps most important, we are entitled to wonder why, if these films are intended to prompt "philosophical discussions of the nature of marriage," they typically deal with characters who are *not* married to each other. Only two of the seven comedies deal with characters whom we actually see interacting as husband and wife for any length of time, and, as I will argue below, one of these, *Adam's Rib,* is entirely atypical. That leaves *The Awful Truth* (Leo McCarey, 1937), which Cavell calls "the best, or deepest, of the comedies of remarriage" and of which he says, "It is the only member of the genre in which the topic of divorce . . . [is] not displaced," as the only pure example of the type.[24] In the other comedies, remarriage is presented only metaphorically, or, in *His Girl Friday* (Howard Hawks, 1940) or *The Philadelphia Story* (George Cukor, 1940), as the conclusion to a story that takes place after the couple has been divorced. Like other narratives of the discourse of romance, screwball comedies typically deal with courtship, not marriage.

Like the print romances discussed in chapter 1, the screwball comedies are built on a triadic narrative structure in which one party is excluded by the pairing of the two other parties. What distinguishes screwball comedy is the degree to which this structure is brought to the surface and emphasized. In *The Crisis,* the entire novel is needed for Stephen to replace Clarence in Virginia's affections, and the love triangle remains virtual since Virginia's virtue is not in question. In *The Philadelphia Story,* not only has Tracy Lord been divorced and thus previously paired, but she is currently engaged. Nevertheless, she spends the film in the proximity of a reporter she has just met, McCauley Connor (James Stewart), and her ex-husband, C. K. Dexter Haven (Cary Grant). It is the actual or potential transgressiveness of this behavior that makes the triangle significant. Adultery here is not literal, but neither is it vestigial.

It Happened One Night and *The Philadelphia Story* are the two films I take to represent the paradigm of screwball comedy. In *It Happened One Night,* the triadic structure is closer to the surface and less complicated by intersecting subplots. The film begins with both Ellen Andrews (Claudette Colbert) and Peter Warne (Clark Gable) excluded, but not involuntarily, from something: Ellen from her father and home, Peter from his boss and the newspaper. Their exile places them on the road together trying to return, Ellen to her husband, and Peter to his home and presumably a job. The resulting relationship makes Ellen and her husband, King Wesley, a pair and excludes Peter, while paradoxically also constituting Ellen and Peter as a pair and excluding King. But it is Peter, not King, who is the male subject of desire in the film. Peter's desire for Ellen, in fact, his claim on her, is announced in an outrageous double entendre, his first words to her when she has taken the bus seat he has fought for: "That upon which you sit is mine." The camera makes Ellen the object of Peter's desire and ours by giving us the first tight close-up of Colbert's face. The first part of the narrative is the story of Peter's attempting to displace King Wesley, not as Ellen's husband, but in her affections. It is irrelevant, of course, that Peter may not be conscious of this desire, for the audience is aware of it.

Just when the triangle shifts is necessarily ambiguous, as it is in all adulterous situations. Of course, Peter and Ellen do not become lovers until the end of the film—when it is still not entirely clear that they are legally married—but they have already spent several nights together in motel rooms separated by blankets hung from a clothesline strung between twin beds. We are meant to read their "sleeping together" sepa-

It Happened One Night: The walls of Jericho separate Ellen Andrews
(Claudette Colbert) and Peter Warne (Clarke Gable).

rated by these "walls of Jericho" as an adulterous adventure even if the
night is literally chaste. A more extreme version occurs in *The Philadelphia Story*, when Tracy and Connor go for a drunken, and implicitly
nude, midnight swim together. As Cavell argues, Tracy can be said
metaphorically to lose her virginity with McCauley Connor, even though
she was not literally a virgin and he did not actually take advantage of
her.[25] The walls of Jericho are *It Happened One Night*'s equivalent of the
sword of chastity that voluntarily separated Tristan and Isolde. In fact,
the paradox of adultery without sex, having been codified in the rules for
courtly love, might be said to be one of the central conventions of narratives of romantic love.[26] The transgression of the marriage bond without
sex serves to create adventure and intensify desire. Officially, King Wesley is excluded for the first time when Ellen trespasses to the other side of
the walls to tell Peter that she loves him. When Ellen is awakened by the

owners of the auto court and discovers that Peter is gone, she calls her father, and Peter is once again excluded. The final reversal occurs when Ellen flees for the second time in the film, here from King Wesley and knowingly to Peter.

The other screwball comedies I discuss here can be understood to fit the triadic pattern also, although it is least descriptive of *Adam's Rib*, the film most about marriage and least romantic. As I alluded earlier, the significance of the triangular or triadic structure is its figuring of the structure of desire. Not only is the viewing subject positioned in this structure, but also his or her desire is mirrored by at least one other desirer. The films present a desiring subject whose desire is confirmed by the gaze of another gazer, even as his or her gaze threatens the prospect of our satisfaction. The viewer these films position is undoubtedly heterosexual but is not gendered. What distinguishes screwball comedies and other romances from dyadic narrative forms is that the woman is never merely an item of exchange between two men but is also presented as a desiring subject. Though women in screwball comedies, as in other Hollywood films, are more often the object of the camera's gaze, more often presented as the object of the gaze of a male character than vice versa, men are also gazed upon. This is a formal equivalent of increased independence and importance, of the status of subject that women have in these films. While this is doubtless a progressive element of these films, it is also a necessity for films whose topic is marriage and divorce. The belief that a woman is free to choose a mate and, if necessary, to divorce him is an important part of the ideology of marriage these films assume. If it is the primary cultural work of comedies of remarriage to ease anxieties about divorce, then they must portray women as capable of desiring. The issue cannot be put merely in terms of a woman's presence; she must want to remarry, and her decision must be based on her attraction to as well as love for her partner. Thus, it is not a coincidence that Clark Gable begins a striptease for Claudette Colbert or that it is she who first breaches the walls. But even if women are in screwball comedy free subjects capable of choice, their choices are limited to the option of whether to marry one man or another.

The investment of the viewer in the romance of screwball comedies involves more than the use of the triadic deep structure. The power of these films depends upon their ability to get us to invest our selves in the hope that a certain couple will achieve the bliss discussed earlier. In screwball comedies, this is done in part by casting. We cannot imagine Rosalind

The Philadelphia Story: Tracy Lord (Katharine Hepburn) after losing her metaphorical virginity with McCauley Conner (Jimmy Stewart).

Russell in love with Ralph Bellamy in *His Girl Friday,* or Irene Dunne with him in *The Awful Truth.* We want each actress to be with Cary Grant from the moment we first see the two of them together. These films always tell us early on whom we are supposed to root for. There is no need, for example, for *The Philadelphia Story* to open with the prologue of Dexter getting thrown out of Tracy Lord's house except to plant the seed of a wish that Cary Grant and Katharine Hepburn will get back together again.

In addition to our attraction to a Grant or a Hepburn, we are invited to participate in the growth of a verbal relationship between the two. Verbal exchanges function mainly to create a sense of attraction, an "electricity" that stems first from the claim made by the man on the woman and her resistance to it. The claim may be stated as in Warne's double entendre, or implicit as in *The Philadelphia Story,* where, on the day before Tracy is to be married to Kittredge, Dexter returns to the Lord mansion

His Girl Friday: Casting tells us to root for the right pair, Hildy (Rosalind Russell) and Walter (Cary Grant), not Bruce (Ralph Bellamy).

and more or less stays there until she marries him instead. In *His Girl Friday,* the scheming of Walter Burns (Cary Grant) to keep Hildy Johnson (Rosalind Russell) in town and at work for the newspaper serves the same purpose, as the final scene, in which her breaking down in tears when she believes he is going to let her leave, demonstrates. The woman's response to this claim is to resist but not reject it. Tracy could, for example, simply have Dexter thrown out. The resistance by the woman to the man's claim upon her produces dialogue that is the verbal equivalent of foreplay—that is to say, teasing. I say *foreplay* rather than *seduction* because the result of the conversations is to increase desire on all sides without making the woman seem like a mere conquest. The male side of the dialogue, however, is an odd form of foreplay. Rather then speaking seductively, the males in screwball comedies typically scold, lecture, admonish, or preach. In the codes of the screwball comedy, what this tells us is that the man cares, but it also mimics rational persuasion, something that corresponds to the presumption that the woman must choose her mate.

The dialogue of screwball comedy in Cavell's view is illustrative of marital relationships. Other critics have found the films to depict "greater gender equality" than typical Hollywood products and to reflect a contemporary endorsement of "companionable" marriage.[27] These readings ignore the absence of marriage itself from the films, and they don't take account of the particular character of the dialogue—which is not only argumentative but also highly crafted, witty stage talk. It is very different from the perhaps equally unrealistic self-analysis we will get in the relationship stories that emerge in the 1970s. But unlike earlier romance narratives, screwball comedies identify conversation with love, so that we actually see the courting couple's love develop. The man and woman still "fall" for each other, but the film tells us why they should. Love at first sight is not a convention typical of this genre. The depicting of the development of affection between a couple may reflect changes in courtship patterns that began after the turn of the century. Where chaperoned courting had been the norm before the emergence of dating, courting couples now got to know each other on their own. Moreover, the social networks that had protected young men and women from marrying outside their class and caste were losing some of their power. Most screwball comedies acknowledge this relatively new reality, although *It Happened One Night* and *The Lady Eve* are unusual in creating a couple from different classes.

In addition to its expression in verbal fireworks, romance is projected in a pastoral vision of a place where the constraints and sins of civilization may be shed and innocence renewed. It may be the island of Peter Warne's dreams, the landscape of the Lord estate, or the honeymoon place to which Walter and Hildy are bound at the end of *His Girl Friday*. Romance demands not just desire and affection but also isolation from the claims of everyday life. It is on this point that these romantic comedies come closest to fitting the usual definition of the romance novel, with its setting distant from everyday life. Yet in the Hollywood comedies I am discussing, most of the action takes place well within everyday settings. It is the purpose of each of these films to do what Cavell asserts only of *His Girl Friday*: to romanticize being at home, in the everyday or even the "black world," the dingy, competitive, and immoral realm in which this film's story is set.[28] We are given a vision of a world elsewhere but not the actual experience of such a locale, since the purpose of the vision is to make us see the everyday in rose-colored hue. What distinguishes the suburbs, whether they are near Philadelphia or in Connecticut, is not their exotica, their isolation—though the latter is part of their attraction—but rather the luxury, the wealth, they represent.

Luxury and the appeal of upper-class privilege are yet another means by which desire is heightened. As Cavell himself notes, luxury is "essentially an expression of eroticism."[29] Film historian Thomas Schatz has misunderstood this when he argues that the screwball comedy, beginning with *It Happened One Night,* is fundamentally about the overcoming of class differences. Thus, according to Schatz, if a "working-class stiff" (Peter Warne) and a "spoiled heiress" (Ellen Andrews) "can overcome their ideological disparity and finally embrace, then we should not lose faith in the traditional American ideal of a classless utopian society."[30] His definition of the genre leads Schatz to go so far as to include in it populist melodramas like *Meet John Doe.* While it seems to me that one of the ideological activities of the screwball comedy was to paper over the reality of class difference, this can hardly be seen as a "prosocial thematics," for reconciliation in these films never occurs at the expense of the power and privilege of the rich.[31] To call Peter Warne a "working-class stiff" is misleading, since he works for a newspaper. Like the Horatio Alger hero, Warne is middle class—in education, income, and employment, if not entirely in manners—and his solid middle-class values make him appealing to Ellen's father. Yet even this degree of interclass marriage makes *It Happened One Night* an exception. More typical is *The Philadelphia Story,* which proposes and rejects intermarriage when Mike Connor proposes and is rejected by Tracy. Hildy and Walter of *His Girl Friday* are both professionals, and they are distinguished, not from each other, but from various less "classy" of their journalistic cohorts. *My Man Godfrey* (Gregory LaCava, 1936), one of Schatz's major examples, involves a marriage between an heiress and a "forgotten man," in fact a renegade heir, so properly bred that he can instantly succeed as her family's butler, a position that he holds until his identity is revealed. Only then is he fit material for the inevitable marriage at the film's end. Like all narratives of manners, screwball comedies depend upon class differences to create, on the one hand, comedy in the form of jokes at inappropriate behavior and, on the other, romance by enhancing the appeal of the hero and heroine. Of the two, it is far more important to the demands of romance that she be rich. Working-class women do not fit well on pedestals.

The creation of desire and the process of courtship are then what consume—and produce—most of the energy of screwball comedies. But do these films tell us anything about marriage? They tell us, in spite of themselves, that marriage remains a patriarchal institution. An element of dyadic narrative persists in many screwball comedies, expressed in the frequent importance of the bride's father in spite of his extraneousness to the basic narrative structure. As artifacts of the patriarchal organization of culture, these films cannot abandon the daughter as an object of exchange between the father and husband. In both *It Happened One Night* and *The Philadelphia Story,* the father has been betrayed or rejected by the daughter: in the former by Ellen's marriage to King Wesley and in the latter by Tracy's specific refusal to invite her father to her wedding and her more general refusal to be father's girl, a substitute for the mistress she has forced him to seek. In each film, the concluding marriage results in a state of affairs acceptable to the father. Such approval is necessary so that the ending can be unambiguously happy.

Both *It Happened One Night* and *The Philadelphia Story* make it clear that married women must become little girls. Men, on the other hand, spend a lot of time being parental in these films.[32] The representation of this "parenting" in *It Happened One Night* includes not only "nurturing"—or preparing breakfast and offering carrots—but also the repeated reference to Ellen as a child or "brat," and protecting her, not only from external threats (the detectives, Roscoe Karns's salesman), but also most importantly from her own incompetence. The one exception, Ellen's success at hitchhiking, depends entirely on her sexual attraction and not her skill. What the journey proves to us and perhaps to Ellen herself is her own helplessness, her need for a protector like Peter. Peter Warne may be both Ellen Andrews's mother and father, but she is only his child, and not a parent to him of either gender. In *The Philadelphia Story,* Tracy Lord's metaphorical journey from Lord of her household to safe Haven as Dexter's wife parallels Ellen's, for Tracy also learns to lose her self-confidence and habit of thinking for herself. She is accused by each of the significant men in the film of being unapproachable—a virgin, a goddess, one who belongs in an ivory tower—but what they are really charging is that she behaves like a man. Her high standards would be a mark of character in a man, but they make a woman "a prig" or "a spinster." Near the end of the film when they will remarry, she says, "I don't know what to think anymore," and Dexter gives his approval of this lack of certainty. In another comedy of remarriage, *My Favorite Wife* (Leo McCarey, 1940),

Irene Dunne declares to both her husband, Cary Grant, and the man she spent seven years with on a desert isle, Joel McCrea, that she can do fine without either of them, and promptly falls into a swimming pool. Actually, however, it is less important that the woman take on any particular characteristics than that she submit to the man who will become her husband. Rosalind Russell's Hildy certainly demonstrates ability and intelligence—even a kind of professional independence—but she must finally submit to Walter Burns. The women give unmistakable signs of their submission. Just before her confession of love, Ellen finally does eat the carrot Peter has been trying to feed her. Tracy Lord says exactly what Dexter tells her to, just before they will remarry, and Rosalind Russell's Hildy, following Walter Burns's orders, allows all sorts of nasty things to happen to her fiancé and his mother.

I want to emphasize, however, that I don't believe that the major point of these films is to tell us that wives should be submissive if marriages are to work, because I don't believe that the films are mainly about marriage. In fact, they suggest that spunky, strong women are attractive but that their submission is required for the romance to be consummated, for marriage to take place. In this sense, they are comedies of conquest, the woman being not like one more bird taken in the hunt but like the duchy one wishes to annex. But for the marriage to occur, these films often ask us to believe that their heroines are changed utterly as a result of experiences described in the narrative. This change is often represented in a sudden reversal of the woman's repeatedly stated position or attitude, the most striking example of which, in this genre, is Tracy Lord's last-minute acceptance of Dexter. We accept the happy ending in part because we are positioned as the subjects of erotic tension seeking to be relieved in orgasm. In this sense, the ending functions as a consummation of our desire as well.

In most of the films, the endings are metaphors for sexual consummation, but the ending of *The Awful Truth* is quite explicit about this. While it is true that *It Happened One Night* ends with "the walls of Jericho" being blown down, that is merely a coda. *The Awful Truth* gives us a picture of the couple's reattraction to each other and ends with Jerry and Lucy Warriner (Cary Grant and Irene Dunne) in bed together (or so it is implied; we don't actually see this). This occurs only after an extended series of contrivances, first by her and then by them both. Lucy has disrupted Jerry's visit with the family of the woman he plans to marry after their divorce becomes final—at midnight that night—and has then taken him off to her Aunt Patsy's cottage in Connecticut. On the way, she disables the car so that Jerry must spend the night, and when they arrive, we find Lucy pretending to be surprised that Aunt Patsy is not there. This obvious setting of the scene for a seduction turns out to be a negotiation as well. Lucy and Jerry retire to separate but adjoining bedrooms, and Jerry first finds and then looks for reasons to cross over to her room. If we witness, as Cavell describes it, Lucy's "all but open sexual arousal, under the bedsheet," we also experience Jerry's response, his own desire to be in her bed.[33] Their negotiation is an all but nonsensical exchange on the paradox of sameness and difference, but it leads to Jerry's promise that he will no longer doubt her. The film ends with an actual if underdeveloped reconciliation. Yet even in this film the ending radically reverses the course of events that were expected at the beginning of the same day. When he woke up, Jerry was planning to marry someone else, but when he goes to sleep that night, he finds himself remarried to Lucy.

Such reversals may seem to treat marriage ironically, as an absurd social convention. A case could be made that *The Lady Eve* does render marriage in just such terms because the couple's first marriage is an absurdity, the result of a con game. But even in this film, the final reuniting of the couple wipes out the earlier failure, in this case because the man doesn't recognize her as the same woman and because the audience has been made to believe in their love by their first, aborted courtship. The endings of these films differ from those of New Comedy in the enormous burden that they must bear. All comic endings are resolutions, but the screwball comedies I have been discussing typically end with a complete reversal for which no plausible explanation is offered. In traditional and screwball comedy, the end is achieved after obstacles are overcome. But the obstacles that lovers in traditional comedy must overcome are externally imposed, while in most screwball comedies they are primarily a function of the couple's own actions. And since these are thoroughly bourgeois comedies, there is no sense of festival accompanying the marriage. Marriage is a private matter, a fact that the invasive camera of *Spy* magazine recording Tracy and Dexter's wedding only serves to underline. The ending leaves the couple isolated in their own bliss; the troubles of the temporary partners they jettison never trouble them or us. As film scholar Dana Polan has argued, the Hollywood happy ending is an "absolute point," an eternal moment "in which all contradictions are resolved under the force of a force that allows no difference, no excess."[34] In other words, there is no possibility of post coitum triste, but rather the

The Philadelphia Story: *Spy* magazine makes the private wedding public.

explicit denial of the temporality of satisfaction. It is in this illusory eternity that marriage is rendered mystical, in spite of whichever of its realities the film has indulged earlier.

Reversals

What I think I have shown so far is that while these "comedies of remarriage" can be made to reveal many of the conventions of marriage under patriarchy, they seek to hide these realities by constructing a romantic mystification of marriage. Marriage is presented as the natural end toward which love must inevitably tend. In this section, I want to look at *Adam's Rib* and the recent *Desperately Seeking Susan* as films that suggest a critique of marriage and the ideology of romance in their reversal of some of the conventions of the screwball genre.

Cavell observes of *Adam's Rib* that it is with one minor exception the only comedy of remarriage where we see the pair at home, but he finds this merely an interesting variation and has more trouble explaining why he considers this a comedy of remarriage at all, since Adam and Amanda Bonner (Spencer Tracy and Katherine Hepburn) never get divorced.[35] I believe these are both significant differences that demand that we treat *Adam's Rib* as a member of a different subgenre. Like another Tracy/Hepburn film, *Woman of the Year* (George Stevens, 1942), *Adam's Rib* is a screwball comedy, but it is about marriage in ways the paradigmatic films I have been discussing are not. This film is explicitly concerned with feminist issues, something that is true about the others only in the sense that they seek to defuse the threat posed by women who reject the roles imposed by patriarchy. Amanda Bonner initiates the action of *Adam's Rib* by taking the case of a woman who has wounded her husband after following him to his lover's apartment and shooting the lock off the door. Her defense of this woman is explicitly a defense of women as a class and a protest against the double standard of sexual morality that generally excuses male philandering (something that the father in *The Philadelphia Story* did explicitly). In taking the case, Amanda knows that she will have her husband as an opponent; in fact, it is his call to tell her that he has been assigned to prosecute the case that motivates Amanda to seek out and offer to defend the woman. In so doing, she is challenging not only gender privilege in the society at large but also her husband's authority publicly in court. By winning her case, she proves both her superiority to her husband as a professional and—although not unambiguously—the right of women to resist male domination.

As a result of having taken the case, Amanda and Adam quarrel, and he finally leaves her. His accusation that she has no respect for the law, as it pertains to either attempted murder or marriage, makes it explicit that she has challenged patriarchy. Before this occurs, we have seen a marriage portrayed in which sexuality is clearly acknowledged, but we also see them prepare dinner on the cook's night off. That is, we see a couple who are sexually related and attracted to each other but who live lives that are not dominated by sex. We cannot mistake their relationship as one of absolute bliss. As a result, the romantic element of this film remains on the margins until the end. In spite of its romantic elements, the film represents a critique of romance at several levels. For not only does the film show us the difficulties of married life, but the only real love triangle in the film, shown as a kind of prologue, is the tawdry one that results in the assault and the trial. That we do not find this triangle in the least appealing suggests that class is a decisive factor in the discourse of romance.

There is, however, another triangle, that formed by the Bonners and their neighbor Kip. Kip is completely extraneous to the major narrative action of the film. His only purpose can be to build romance by making Amanda seem desired. Like the spurned, would-be husbands in most screwball comedies, Kip is completely unsuitable as a mate—there are some fairly strong hints that he is supposed to be gay—and we cannot believe him as a threat. Nevertheless, he does attempt to woo Amanda after Adam leaves her. A second romantic element is the house in Connecticut. The romance of this location is treated ironically earlier in the film by means of home movies for which Kip provides a running commentary. At the end, however, Adam and Amanda go there to reconcile, and it is hard not to understand the place as an unambiguous retreat from the world of courts and competition. Like the other films, *Adam's Rib* ends with an unexplained change of sentiment, but this time it is the man whose feelings suddenly shift. The issue here is not that we cannot believe that Adam Bonner would change his mind and decide to stay married but rather that the problems the film raises about the difficulties of two genuinely adult professionals living together as equals get papered over. The narrative displaces the social conflict onto the drama of a single marriage. Furthermore, the patriarchal status quo is restored by Adam's impending election to a judgeship—where he will represent, rather than merely practice, the law. The ending makes us happy that the two are reunited, forgetful of the problems that caused the conflict in the first place and unworried by any significant change in the patriarchal order.

Adam's Rib alters some of the conventions of the screwball comedy to produce an examination of conflict in a marriage that seems ideal, but the film nonetheless affirms marriage. This film was produced during a period when a single marriage remained the expectation of most men and women. After World War II, divorce became so common that some observers began to describe the marriage system of our culture as "serial monogamy." Hollywood films could no longer treat divorce merely as something to be avoided. Too many members of the film audience had already failed to avoid it. While it took some time before Hollywood could ratify this social fact, in the 1970s and 1980s a series of films appeared that might be called comedies of remarriage in an altogether different sense, since they take as their situation the plight of the postmarried and repeatedly married. Among these films are *Choose Me* (Alan Rudolf,

1984), *Annie Hall* (Woody Allen, 1977), *Manhattan* (Woody Allen, 1979), *Something Wild* (Jonathan Demme, 1986), *Desperately Seeking Susan,* and *When Harry Met Sally* (Rob Reiner, 1989).

Some of these films will be discussed in detail in chapter 7 as "relationship stories," a new genre of romantic comedy. Some others remain closer to screwball comedy, borrowing and modifying its conventions and putting them to use in radically new contexts. *Choose Me* and *Something Wild,* for example, combine the screwball and thriller genres. *Desperately Seeking Susan* is the film that most explicitly and systematically reverses screwball conventions, and, as a result, it can shed the most light on the genre. It is also most explicit in affirming independence and divorce as potentially positive choices. Since this film was made more than forty years after the others I have discussed here, we can assume that its director, Susan Seidelman, would have greater distance on the genre than earlier directors of screwball comedies and that she used genre conventions not (or not only) as a blueprint for the production of a popular commodity but as a historical form to be self-consciously used as needed: transformed, parodied, played off against. However, it would be ludicrous to leave the impression that a Howard Hawks or a Preston Sturges was incapable of transforming or reversing genre conventions. In fact, these directors incorporate some significant reversals of gender roles into their screwball comedies *Bringing up Baby* (Howard Hawks, 1938) and *The Lady Eve,* where we find examples of weak, bumbling men being pursued by strong, competent women.[36] Likewise but to greater effect, *Adam's Rib* alters the conventions of the genre by beginning with a strong woman but allowing her to remain strong, to defeat her husband and make him submit—if only in a charade—by crying. It is not the director's genius to which I appeal in trying to account for *Desperately Seeking Susan*'s reversals. Obviously, changes in American culture contributed to the possibility of these reversals. However, the director's *gender* is also a reasonable explanation for her having been able to revise the conventions of screwball comedy in a way that male directors had not.

Desperately Seeking Susan picks up some potentially oppositional moments in screwball comedies and explores them further. The first of these is the possibility of life and sex outside marriage, for although the screwball comedies set out to affirm marriage through romance, they must present an alternative to marriage in the representation of a threat to it. In other words, in representing the situation these films seek to resolve, they must acknowledge that marriage is not inevitable. In depicting women who at first are not helpless or housebound, they make these possibilities available to the viewer. Second, as I argued earlier, women in screwball comedies tend to be less the object of the camera's gaze and even occasionally the gazing subject. Thus, *Desperately Seeking Susan* is not an "anti–screwball comedy" but one that acknowledges its debt to the classical films. It does this by means of several striking allusions. One is its beginning in a beauty parlor recalling *The Women* (George Cukor, 1939), a comedy about divorce that featured an all-female cast. A more significant allusion is to *It Happened One Night*: Roberta (Rosanna Arquette) and Des (Aidan Quinn) spend the night together in his nearly empty apartment separated by a makeshift room divider apparently constructed of old doors. These rickety "walls of Jericho" serve the same function as the blankets did in the earlier film, but we now are able to see what it barely suggested: both man and woman sexually aroused and frustrated by the arrangement.

These references to particular screwball comedies are just the tip of the iceberg. The film may be seen as systematically reversing most of the conventions of the genre. For example, instead of beginning with an investment in marriage lost, we begin with an interest in adventure to be found. The first dialogue we hear tells us that Roberta has been following a series of personal ads that feature as a headline the title of the film and that have been placed by Jim (Robert Jog). Roberta, a bored suburban New Jersey housewife whose husband, we learn later, is having an affair, finds this desperation romantic: the film thus begins with its heroine explicitly seeking the kind of fantasy that screwball comedies typically present. What happens to Roberta eventually is that she gets amnesia and finds herself mistaken for Susan (Madonna) and living Susan's life. During this period, Roberta learns that she can rely on herself and that she does not want to go back to her husband. The film ends with her involved with— not married to—Des and also paired with Susan as heroes who have recovered stolen antiquities.

By using the device of amnesia and mistaken identity, the film greatly complicates the typical narrative structure by proliferating the triangular relationships. In fact, one could understand this film as "coupling" almost everyone with almost everyone else at least for a brief moment. This constitutes, of course, the particular zaniness of *Desperately Seeking Susan,* but it also serves to create erotic tension by thrusting various characters together and then keeping them apart. This eroticism is sustained by visual rather than verbal pyrotechnics: the repeated use of match cuts, for example, to link Roberta's and Susan's stories. When Des and Roberta have sex for the first time—on the second night she has spent in his apartment—it serves the same function as the concluding wedding of other films, the release of erotic tension, but it is not the end of the movie. There remains a tension between Roberta's desire for Des and her identification with Susan. The final scene of the film, like that of *The Philadelphia Story* recorded in a still photograph, shows Roberta and Susan together receiving an award for the recovery of the earrings. Thus, the end of the film suggests three triangles, though it is ambiguous who is excluded by the pair of Roberta and Susan, since the other triangles include Des and Jim respectively.

If the end is ambiguous on this point, the film as a whole strongly suggests that the relationship between Roberta and Susan is its primary focus. This is represented by the match cuts that, by replacing one woman with the other who is not in the scene, disrupt expected shot/reverse shot sequences. These match cuts are the visual representation of the two characters' identification with each other. The narrative is structured as a romance—though not literally a sexual relationship—of Roberta's about Susan, a romance of identification. It is, after all, Susan about whom Roberta is daydreaming as the film opens, and it is *as* Susan that her adventures, her romance, begins. Given the lack of female identification by women in screwball comedies or other Hollywood films, Roberta's identification with Susan must be regarded as a politically significant reversal of convention.

Let me summarize *Desperately Seeking Susan*'s other major reversals of genre conventions. The film begins with marriage and ends with divorce. It opens in the suburbs, but its zone of adventure and pleasure is the city. Rather than being claimed by her lover, Roberta chooses Des. While most screwball comedies split identification between the leading man and woman, this film asks us to identify with Roberta, or, less often, Susan, but rarely with the male characters. Rather than affirming the values of the middle class, the film endorses bohemian or countercultural values by Roberta's willingness to leave New Jersey and comfort for New York and excitement but relative poverty. The film deals with adultery, but this convention is also reversed because it is here explicit and undertaken by Roberta in full knowledge of what she is doing, since she has by this point regained her memory. Romance in the film, whether its object is Des or Susan, is used not to mystify marriage but to critique it, to show that marriage fails to live up to its billing. *Desperately Seeking Susan* ends

Desperately Seeking Susan: Roberta (Rosanna Arquette) and Susan (Madonna), honored as crime stoppers, are the most important "couple" in this film.

with a vision of a kind of personal liberation—one undermined, to be sure, by its status as a film fantasy but also made more significant by its tenuousness and ambiguity. It is a happy ending but not one that claims a happily ever after.

In its reversal of the conventions of romantic comedy, however, *Desperately Seeking Susan* reminds us of some of the problems that come with what Giddens has called the "everyday social experiments" of contemporary interpersonal existence.[37] In affirming divorce, the film affirms individual freedom over social solidarity. If marriage is no longer understood as the foundation of society, then it is possible for films like this one to exist without seeming subversive to the average viewer. While critique of marriage is prohibited when marriage and society are identified, we need new ways of envisioning society that do not assume the naturalness of marriage. The best *Desperately Seeking Susan* can do is offer Roberta and Susan's relationship as a hint at such a vision. While this is a decided limitation, to dismiss Roberta's liberation because of it would be to forget that the personal is the political.

What films like *Adam's Rib* and *Desperately Seeking Susan* show us is that the discourse of romance is neither a simple apologetics for male dominance nor a mere synonym for false consciousness. We are entitled to speak of Roberta's relationship with Susan as both a romance and an antipatriarchal statement, and of romance itself as having a utopian character in this film. This is not to deny feminist Shulamith Firestone's contention that there is an intimate connection between male culture and romance but rather to argue that the discourse of romance is not entirely defined by this connection.[38] Screwball comedies typically present marriage mystified by romance, but in films such as *Desperately Seeking Susan,* romance returns to the work it may have performed in medieval culture, the suggestion of alternatives to patriarchal social practices and structures.

Back to the Future

After the first cycle of screwball comedies ended in the late 1940s, the genre seemed largely to disappear until the 1980s. The 1950s and 1960s were relatively weak decades for film comedy. The Doris Day vehicles of this era apparently owed something to screwball comedies, but the adventure of the illicit had become a mere vestige. No one really believed that Doris Day was capable of adultery, regardless of the predicaments in which the plot might put her. It might be argued that the most successful version of screwball comedy to be made in the 1950s was Alfred Hitchcock's thriller *North by Northwest* (1958). Of the significant films of the 1960s, only *The Graduate* (Mike Nichols, 1967) is a romantic comedy, and, although it contains the irreverence of the screwball, it explicitly opposes adultery—Benjamin Braddock's affair with Mrs. Robinson—to romance—his pursuit of Elaine. As we will observe in some detail later, Woody Allen's *Annie Hall* (1977) reinvented romantic comedy in the form of the relationship story. But by proving that romantic comedy could command both critical and box office success, Allen's film also opened the doors for a new cycle of the screwball formula. Some of these films simply recycle, but several of them revise the formula in a direction opposite that of *Desperately Seeking Susan*, thereby seeming to endorse the form of marriage at the expense of the personal fulfillment promised by romance.

Perhaps the most successful and popular recycling of the screwball comedy was *Moonstruck* (Norman Jewison, 1987). The plot involves the familiar triangulation of a woman planning to marry one man but falling for another, adultery continuing to be the operative conception of marriage. Where the film might be said to break new ground is in its gender and class identification. As Kathleen Rowe has shown, *Moonstruck* is told from a woman's perspective, incorporating elements of an apparently antithetical genre, the melodrama or women's picture.[39] The competing men in the film, Danny Aiello and Nicholas Cage, play characters who are weak and hysterical respectively. It is Cher's Loretta who is the film's locus of strength and sanity. Moreover, while none of these characters is poor, none is haute bourgeois, as characters in the films of the original cycle typically were. The Italian American ambience of the film may lead us to read the characters as more working class than their economic status would permit. Still, Cage's Ronny is a baker, and Loretta's father is a plumber, traditionally working-class jobs, however lucrative they may be.

For luxury, *Moonstruck* substitutes moonlight and opera to create the proper setting for romance, in effect creating a kind of "Connecticut" in New York City. Yet the supposed power of the moon named in the title represents another modification of screwball conventions, and this one takes us back to older versions of the discourse of romance. Loretta and Ronny fall immediately for each other, and they are very quickly shown in bed making passionate love. After the sexual revolution of the 1960s, audiences came to expect sex as a part of courtship. But in ratifying this cultural reality, *Moonstruck* sacrifices the development of the relationship, a distinguishing feature of the comedies of the first cycle. Instead, it returns to the mystery of love at first sight, of falling—rather than growing—in love. *Moonstruck* thus reflects significant changes in American culture but not in the discourse of romance.

Moonstruck, at least, was not a simple recycling of the old formula but an interesting recontextualization of it. Several films from the period are much more literal recyclings, being remakes of 1930s and 1940s screwball comedies. The first of these, *What's Up Doc* (Peter Bogdanovich, 1972), an uncredited version of *Bringing up Baby*, was a box office success, but it didn't start a trend. After *Annie Hall* brought romantic comedy back, there was a trend of remaking studio-era screwball comedies, including *Unfaithfully Yours* (Howard Zieff, 1984), and *His Girl Friday* as *Switching Channels* (Ted Kotcheff, 1988). *Runaway Bride* (Garry Marshall, 1999) is not a remake of *It Happened One Night,* but its title comes from a newspaper headline that describes the abortive wedding near that film's end. Julia Roberts plays a woman who keeps leaving prospective husbands alone at the altar, and Richard Gere is the reporter who becomes the last of these and the one she finally does marry. First Gere has to win her away from the man she is currently engaged to, making much of the film's focus on a love triangle. The bride's escapes provide opportunities for plenty of zaniness, and Gere's job gives him a reasonable excuse to spend enough time with Roberts for their relationship to develop. What distinguishes this film is that, after a narrative that fits perfectly within the discourse of romance, the couple's marriage is explained in the discourse of intimacy. In a scene that plays something like a detective's explanation of a murder at the end of a mystery, Roberts explains to Gere why they are right for each other. By ending the film with a justifying conversation before the usual wedding, the film is able to satisfy the desire it has constructed in the most persuasive form possible. The resources of both discourses of love support the rightness of this match.

As I will argue in the conclusion, the revival of the screwball formula is by no means the most conservative trend in recent filmmaking. What it shows, however, is the continued power of the discourse of romance. In films like *Runaway Bride*, romance manages to contain and make use of the discourse of intimacy, and even in those works in which intimacy prevails, romance almost always has a place.

4

Power Struggles
Casablanca and Gone with the Wind

Historically, the discourse of absence is carried on by the Woman: Woman is sedentary, Man hunts, journeys; Woman is faithful (she waits), man is fickle (he sails away, he cruises). . . . It follows that in any man who utters the other's absence *something feminine* is declared: this man who waits and who suffers from his waiting is miraculously feminized.

To make someone wait: the constant prerogative of all power. . . .
—Roland Barthes, *A Lover's Discourse*

Screwball comedies take the struggle for power within courtship as a comic premise. The arguments between the central couple produce not only laughs but also a significant measure of the erotic tension that will be resolved in their finally wedding. Screwball comedies treat women as independent thinking, feeling beings, but they typically assume male dominance even if that dominance is comically brought into question. Moreover, since power in its full, political sense is regarded as antithetical to romance, as something from which romance is an escape, romance typically treats the power dynamics of relationships as entirely isolated from politics. Thus, in the screwball comedy, as in most versions of Hollywood romance, power cannot be dealt with as a serious issue. The two films I'm concerned with here do take power seriously, though even they must do so only covertly. And part of why they do take power seriously is that these films are concerned with politics in a much more overt way than most Hollywood products.

It's Still the Same Old Story

Casablanca (Michael Curtiz, 1942) and *Gone with the Wind* (Victor Fleming, 1939), two of the most enduringly popular films made in the studio era, are often taken to epitomize romance. The American Film Institute and several recent magazine articles have ranked each of them as among the most romantic films of all time.[1] Yet both films are unusual in that they end neither in the wedded bliss of most Hollywood romances nor in the tragedy typical of European love stories.[2] Rather, they are stories of romantic suffering that end, not in death or even defeat, but in some kind of hope or triumph. As such, these films have something in common with American novels such as *The Great Gatsby* and *The Age of Innocence,* discussed in chapter 1. Moreover, these films are themselves similar enough that one can argue that they tell the same story from different perspectives. *Casablanca* tells it from the man's side but also from the shared perspective of a nation united by war. *Gone with the Wind* presents the reverse of each of these, the woman's perspective and that of the losing side in a war that divided the nation.[3] While these films are heavily invested in questions of nation and region, my concern with those issues will be principally the way they enable the films' love stories, the reversal of the usual way in which these two elements of narrative are discussed. My argument is that, by telling more or less the same story from different subject positions, these films reveal the way men and women are differently written by the discourse of romance.

Since it may not be immediately obvious that *Casablanca* and *Gone with the Wind* tell the same story, let me outline my case for their similarities. Both films involve a love triangle of three figures, an "official hero," an "outlaw hero," and a woman who is involved with both of them.[4] The story of the love triangle is in each case set against the background of a war that is depicted as justly demanding sacrifice by ordinary citizens and unjustly causing hardship to them. Both films prominently display the passion or suffering of their protagonists, Rick (Humphrey Bogart) and Scarlett (Vivian Leigh), in the face of lost love. Both stories feature the transformation of the outlaw hero, a process that each renders as a kind of "growing up." The films end with the outlaw hero rejecting the woman, but, as we will see, to at least partially different effect.

Moreover, the narratives of both films are romances in the generic sense that romance novels are. The novel *Gone with the Wind* is a latter-day variant of the historical romances that dominated American best-seller lists around the turn of century. The equivalent Hollywood genre would be something like the "costume picture" or "period picture," a genre to which the film *Gone with the Wind* belongs. *Casablanca*'s temporal setting is contemporary with its date of production, but it uses its geographical setting to the same effect that historical romances used temporal ones. Like romance novels, these films take place in a world removed from mundane social life. Casablanca and especially Rick's Café are as much removed from World War II America as Civil War Atlanta and especially Tara are from the United States of the Depression. Both films insist on the remoteness of their settings. *Casablanca* opens with a globe that is replaced by a map showing the difficult, circuitous route by which refugees found themselves in Casablanca waiting to be able to take the penultimate trip (to Lisbon) in their journey to America. The Casablanca of the film is a place where the usual rules of war and of peace are suspended. Rick's Café represents another entire level of unreality where American habits of leisure and rules of sportsmanship allow the antagonists of the larger war to interact in relative civility. The title *Gone with the Wind* itself signals the unreality of the world the film evokes, an unreality that Ashley Wilkes (Leslie Howard) both recognizes and symbolizes. Tara also is another level of remove from social reality. Unlike Rick's, it is not a place at odds with its environment; Tara is rather a synecdoche for the film's larger setting, the lost civilization of the old South, and as such it intensifies the same unreality. If "everybody comes to Rick's," Scarlett always returns to Tara. The distancing achieved by these settings does not sever all connections between the films and their social contexts but rather simplifies them. And, as we all know, long ago and/or far away are the most appropriate settings for romantic love, which is characteristically defined against all other social ties, obligations, and restrictions.

History functions in these films to put the love story in relief, to give it a context or background. Feminist film theorist Mary Ann Doane notes that *Gone with the Wind* and other films that have been called "great love stories" are "narratives which are usually buttressed by the weight of History," while ordinary love stories, such as those told by women's pictures, render history "an accumulation of memories of the loved one." Her point is that we experience these latter films as manipulative or excessively emotional, while in the former History gives meaning to affect. Doane also observes that the love story is considered "a feminine discourse" and points out that little boys turn away from love scenes.[5] She perhaps thought it unnecessary to add that history, especially the history of war, is understood as a masculine discourse. "Great love stories" are "great" in part because they give male viewers an alibi for enjoying them, but the historical setting would seem to broaden the emotional appeal for both men and women by raising the stakes beyond the personal.

It is curious that these most American of love stories are films that lack that staple of the film factories, the happy ending. So why is it that films about unhappy love, films where the obstacles finally cannot be overcome, would be considered the most romantic? I have been arguing that we as a culture have identified romance with the "fairy-tale" version, in which the link between romantic love and marriage is assumed. The complications and inconsistencies of the romance discourse are as a result suppressed and ignored. This version of the romantic discourse, however, depends on the very same conception of love—an older variant that linked love not with happy marriage but with suffering and death. According to Luhmann, when "passionate love [was proclaimed] to be the very principle upon which the *choice* of a spouse should be based," "the old thesis of the incompatibility of love and marriage had to be covered up."[6] When something is covered up or repressed, it must make itself known in one way or another. The darker side of romance that I discussed in chapter 1 has continued to be expressed in a number of significant narratives in print, and it also is present in the lyrics of many popular songs of Tin Pan Alley writers such as Cole Porter. Not only are these stories and songs often perceived to be among the most romantic of their kind, but stories of unhappy love are also much more often regarded as great works of art. These positive evaluations of unhappy love stories suggest a covert awareness of the problems of romance that the culture in general ignores. They deal with problems that most people who have lived the romantic discourse have experienced, and, by at least seeming to offer insight into these problems, they may seem more profound.

Screwball comedy and other studio-era Hollywood films affirm monogamous marriage by depicting romantic love outside marriage. What is explicitly borrowed from extramarital love in these stories is the adventure and excitement of transgression. But the pain and suffering that was traditionally said to follow as night from day in these relationships are missing. Rougemont claims that romance concerns "not the satisfaction of love, but its *passion*. And passion means suffering."[7] What distinguishes *Casablanca* from most versions of Hollywood romance is that passion is not displaced. While passion or suffering is typical of the genre known as women's films, a genre to which *Gone with the Wind* is strongly related, other genres in Hollywood cover up the oppositions that have historically structured romantic discourse: love and happiness, romance and marriage. In women's films, it is invariably women who suffer. *Casablanca* provides an unusual glimpse at a male in the throes of romantic suffering. *Gone with the Wind* gives us an equally unusual picture of a woman who suffers but who refuses to accept suffering as her lot in life.

Rick's Revenge

Casablanca is recognized by just about everybody as a romantic movie. Producer Hal Wallis, director Michael Curtiz, and the raft of writers who contributed to the screenplay all understood that the love story was central to the film. Aljean Harmetz suggests that Wallis's favorite writer, Casey Robinson, was assigned to the film mainly to fix what he regarded as the deficiencies in the screenplay's love story.[8] Curiously, however, film scholars have almost entirely ignored the film's romance, usually treating it as a mere surface text to be stripped away in order to get at some deeper meaning. Indeed, one of the most persuasive and influential readings of *Casablanca,* Robert Ray's in *A Certain Tendency in Hollywood Cinema,* holds that the film is a "disguised western" that reflects a male wish to escape from heterosexual love.[9] According to Ray, "The outlaw hero's distrust of civilization [is] typically represented by women and marriage."[10] In reading through the romance in *Casablanca,* Ray leaves the woman behind in order to describe the film as if it depicted an all-male group characteristic of real westerns.[11] I propose to attend to what has been taken to be the obvious.

Early scenes in *Casablanca* define what we might call the conundrum of Rick's character. He gives the appearance of being a hard, cynical individualist, but Louis Renault (Claude Rains) asserts that that is merely a disguise and that Rick is "at heart a sentimentalist." Everyone but a few film critics probably believes that Renault is telling us something important, but nothing he says quite prepares us for what happens to Rick after Ilsa Lundt (Ingrid Bergman) turns up in his café. Rick reveals his feelings indirectly when he first greets Victor Lazlo (Paul Henreid) and Ilsa, but the key scene for my analysis occurs later, after the saloon has closed. We find Rick, already drunk, sitting in the darkened café, when Sam (Dooley

Casablanca: Sam (Dooley Wilson) tries to get Rick (Humphrey Bogart) to go fishing, but he is "waiting for a lady."

Wilson) tries to persuade him to leave. Rick responds, "No sir, I am waiting for a lady." Though we will learn that Rick once waited for Ilsa before, he has not expected to see her again. Though in emotional pain, he has been playing the hypermasculine role of the loner. By proclaiming that he is the one who waits, Rick is, as Barthes would have it, feminized and disempowered.[12] Like the waiting lover Barthes describes, Rick does not know that Ilsa will be coming. The utter agony that Rick's face expresses is remarkable in the context of Hollywood representations of men. While his suffering further disempowers Rick, its style may not be exactly feminizing. Getting drunk is one culturally acceptable way for a man to deal with emotional pain, as is anger, which Rick expresses a number of times during the scene. But Rick is more than drunk and angry; he is hurt and in some way defeated.

The fact that this scene frames the flashback sequence of Rick and Ilsa's days in Paris makes it all the more powerful. There we see Rick offer himself to Ilsa. He suggests twice that they get married after they leave Paris, offers to which Ilsa is unable to respond. Rick's face on the platform betrays the hurt he feels at Ilsa's rejection, and he has to be walked to the train by Sam in order that he not fail to escape the Nazis. This weakness is carried over into the resumption of the previous scene when the flashback concludes. This portion of the film opens with a shot/reverse shot sequence that renders Rick a disempowered *subject*. The first shot reestablishes Rick as our locus of identification, but the shot in which Ilsa appears defines her as something other than the object of a voyeuristic gaze. She is here an object of Rick's imagination. We experience her through our identification with Rick, an identification that the film has previously worked very hard to establish.[13] She is imaged almost as a goddess—she has been called the most beautiful woman in Casablanca—backlit and glowing in the distance. After a reverse shot close-up of Rick, we return to a radiant Ilsa still backlit, still goddesslike. It is as if we were seeing Rick's fantasy of Ilsa. But when Ilsa approaches Rick, she no longer enacts his fantasy. Whatever Rick was waiting for Ilsa to do or say, he certainly does not expect the businesslike request to help her and Victor Lazlo. The scene concludes with Rick burying his head in his hands. Hollywood's codes of masculinity perhaps did not allow us to see tears in Humphrey Bogart's eyes, but we know that Rick is crying and that his pain is far deeper than that which we saw in Ilsa's face earlier.

The pain and suffering that we see Rick experience are what Rougemont thinks define romantic love. I have argued that Rougemont's claim that "happy love has no history" is contradicted by the prevalence of narratives in which happy love—while it may not be given a history—is projected into the future. Yet even in these narratives, love is depicted as involving pain and loss. "Boy loses girl" is an indispensable element of the formula. Narratives that dwell on this element may seem the most romantic because the discourse of romance defines love as an experience—happy or sad—that one undergoes. One might contract a marriage, but one falls in love. Thus, in one sense of the term, romantic love is always "suffered." Rougemont believes that we worship passion because of a historical accident. My treatment of romance as a discourse accepts that historical contingency has played a role. But our cultural construction of romance as suffering also doubtless has roots in childhood patterns that provide the frame in which later intimate relationships are understood. None of us escapes the drama of loss and recovery of our earliest love objects.[14] The culture writes the drama differently, however, for men and women: women are allowed—perhaps expected—to suffer and express their suffering; men, on the other hand, must recover from their suffering on the pain of losing their power over women and over other men.

Rick's humiliation by Ilsa represents a nadir from which he as the film's hero must recover. Far from being the "isolationist" that he seems, Rick is shown to have a powerful emotional connection to Ilsa and to have suffered greatly as a result. Rick's experience of passion is disempowering, and the film must find a way to right the balance of power so that it is once again in his favor. The rest of the film might be seen as Rick's gradual return to power. The film casts this story as Rick's growing up. Rick often acts like a child; his facial expressions and his tone of voice betray emotions that adult males are supposed to disguise. Lazlo would have to have been a fool not to recognize that Rick was acting like a spurned lover. When Ilsa visits Rick in the scene described above, she expects him to behave as an adult—to repress his feelings and do his duty to her and the cause. When she finds Rick incapable of that, in spite of her attempts to explain that she did not mean to hurt him, she walks out. The next day in the market, Ilsa treats him, appropriately enough, like a child. She scolds him: "The Rick I knew in Paris, I could tell him. He would understand." Later she will explicitly accuse him of self-pity and self-absorption: "One woman has hurt you and you take it out on the whole world."

Several scenes later, a Bulgarian woman (Joy Page) asks to speak to Rick at the café. She has come to get Renault's references. Will Renault keep his word if she sleeps with him in order to get visas for her and her husband? Rick says he always has, but the woman worries that her husband would not understand if he found out. "If someone loved you very much so that your happiness was the only thing she wanted in the world, and she did a bad thing to make certain of it. . . ." Rick's response is another expression of his pain: "Nobody ever loved me that much." The woman continues, "Jan is such a boy. In many ways I am so much older than he is." This response suggests that Rick is also "such a boy." Like the woman's husband, Rick has trouble understanding the compromises of adult life. Indeed, Rick's not understanding Ilsa is really the same response the woman fears. Rick's growing up, however, will be marked by his renunciation of his love, for that is what the adult male must do.

Yet *Casablanca* does not simply reject Rick's attitude toward marriage as juvenile. It also endorses that attitude as an element of a cultural bias reflected in Rick's character. We notice that Renault, Lazlo, and Ilsa all have less rigid conceptions of love and loyalty. Lazlo and Ilsa can live knowing the other's imperfections and betrayals. Rick, on the other hand, stands for a strict conception of monogamy and for honesty. I have already noted Werner Sollors's observation that "American culture has in an exceptionally intense way emphasized . . . romantic love as the basis for marriage."[15] Rick is explicitly portrayed as the defender of this association. When Renault asks him why he interferes with his "little romances" by letting the Bulgarian woman's husband win at roulette, Rick responds, "Put it down as a gesture to love." In protecting that marriage, Rick enacts the position that the film will finally endorse. But like most romances, *Casablanca* endorses marriage by depicting mainly extramarital relationships. The one marriage the movie depicts in any detail—Lazlo's and Ilsa's—is antiromantic.

In the market, Rick tells Ilsa that one day she will lie to Lazlo and come to see him. We suspect that that prediction will come true, and it does, with the help of the film's McGuffin, the letters of transit. Holding them gives Rick the literal power of life and death over Lazlo. The letters bring Ilsa to his apartment, and there Rick wins her back, thus partially righting his loss of power. As in the earlier scene, Ilsa appears here as if out of nowhere, but this time she emerges only partially from the shadows. She is now not a goddess, but something more like a ghost. She at first tries to reason with Rick, but he refuses to listen. Then, in what seems like a complete shift in character, she pulls a gun and threatens to shoot if he doesn't give her the letters. Rick calls her bluff—he has, after all, nothing to live for—and, astonishingly, she breaks down and confesses that she is still in love with him. This scene works only because we do not know who Ilsa is or what she feels. She now becomes, however, what Rick (and we) wants her to be. They kiss, and a Hollywood fade gives us a shot of a light tower out of the window. Rick and Ilsa began the scene as adversaries, but they are now, by Hollywood convention, lovers. Now subservient, Ilsa tells Rick that he "will have to do the thinking for both of us."

But regaining Ilsa and patriarchal dominance over her is not enough. The status quo has been regained, but as it stands, Ilsa has not suffered, so the score between her and Rick is not yet evened. We are, of course, meant to see the famous airport scene not as a continuation of Rick's aggression against Ilsa but rather as an heroic sacrifice. But we can see it this way only because we have been excluded from Ilsa's perspective. Yet in thinking about Ilsa's feelings, one may observe a rupture of the film's ideological project. Once we violate the film's semiotic instructions and imagine what Ilsa must feel—and believe that she has told the truth in her

Casablanca: Rick (Humphrey Bogart) and Ilsa (Ingrid Bergman) and the audience will always have Paris.

confession of love—then we must recognize the violence that Rick's send-off does to her. Ilsa is entirely disempowered and virtually silenced. The scene reverses the earlier one at the train station, except that Rick's abandoning of Ilsa is justified by the cause. His sending her off with Lazlo is in this film's logic a sort of revenge that confirms male authority. Moreover, this logic is not inconsistent with the scene's overt message about the need for wartime sacrifice. While Rick is giving up Ilsa for the good of the cause, she and other women must give up their loved ones to a war that is the expression of the very logic that informs this scene.

Yet, contrary to Ray, Rick does not leave because he prefers Renault's company or seeks a world without women and their "entanglements." If Rick were giving up what he really didn't want, the film could not so effectively evoke the need for wartime sacrifice. The power of the film's conclusion lies in its combination of sadness and triumph. The end of the film is just as effective in presenting the ideology of romance as it is in providing a boost for the war effort. Rick's gesture affirms male dominance and monogamous marriage, the latter, however, rendered in the glow of "Paris," the film's word for love outside marriage. We are thus allowed to have our cake and eat it too, to have both official monogamy and illicit romance without recognizing their conflict.

Scarlett's Perspective

Probably the most significant difference between *Casablanca* and *Gone with the Wind* is that the latter is the woman's story. The opening scene, where we are introduced to Scarlett on the porch at Tara, firmly establishes the audience's identification with her. Her refusal to talk about the war controls the behavior of the two boys in the scene, and their report that Ashley Wilkes will marry Melanie (Olivia de Havilland) yields the revelation of Scarlett's desire for him. It is her subjectivity that matters. *Gone with the Wind* acknowledges the meaning of the male gaze even as the events unfold through Scarlett's eyes. When she first sees Rhett Butler (Clark Gable), she says, "He looks as if he knew what I looked like without my shimmy." But the shot/reverse shot sequence—in which the film cuts from a shot of Scarlett near the top of a staircase to track in on Rhett at the bottom staring up at her, and then back to Scarlett—makes him the object of her gaze. Moreover, he is explicitly the object of her fantasy, as revealed in her whispered conversation about Rhett's previous romantic adventures. The scene perfectly encapsulates the ambivalence Scarlett feels in her attraction to Rhett, making clear that she is both drawn to him sexually and frightened by that fact.

Told from the point of view of a woman and made to appeal to women, *Gone with the Wind* might seem to fit the genre known as the women's picture. Although it incorporates many of the features that define that genre, also known as "weepies" or "tearjerkers," this film is not contained by the genre's conventions. Women's pictures are fundamentally about loss. As such, this was the one genre that was defined by its unhappy ending, thus violating the standard Hollywood formula that called for a film's leading couple to be together at the end. In such films as *Camille* (George Cukor, 1937), *Now, Voyager* (Irving Rapper, 1942), and *Letter from an Unknown Woman* (Max Ophüls, 1948), the couple are separated by insurmountable external obstacles. Thus, Greta Garbo's

Camille does not end up with her lover, Armand (Robert Taylor), because social propriety forbids their marrying and, ultimately, because she dies. The women's picture almost always ends with the woman's resignation to the failure of her romantic dreams, a failure that is not her fault. As Doane observes, "The woman almost always gives up everything, including other marriage proposals, for the sake of her love."[16] This passive renunciation is often accompanied by long periods of waiting for the loved man, as in *Letter from an Unknown Woman*, where such waiting constitutes virtually the entire plot of the film. As these films illustrate, women's passion in Hollywood usually consists in suffering in silence.

The romantic character of these films is expressed most powerfully in the sense of tragically missed opportunity. It is the precise opposite of the marriage at the end of the fairy-tale romance. Here a match made in heaven is prohibited by earthly circumstance. Such melodramas lack some of the attributes usually associated with tragedy: the heroine lacks blame; the milieu is often mundane or worse, and thus the narrative lacks heroic stature. These are *minor* tragedies that represent loss not as an extraordinary event but as definitive of women's lives. There is little in the way of hope and nothing like triumph offered by their conclusions. The best they can do is offer solace or a vision of courage in the face of pain. The moral of these stories is almost always that "you can't have it all," or, to put it as Bette Davis does at the end of *Now, Voyager*, "Don't let's ask for the moon. We have the stars."

Gone with the Wind is about loss of numerous kinds, not excluding the loss of the "civilization" Ashley laments and the loss of the war. While these events themselves are not emotionally significant to Scarlett, they cause the loss of material comfort and emotional connections. Scarlett loses three husbands, a mother, a father, a daughter, a sister-in-law, and Ashley, the great love of her life, though she never really had him. While her reactions to these losses range from nil to quite powerful, none of them define her in the way, say, Bette Davis is defined by her loss of Paul Henreid in *Now, Voyager*. Unlike the heroines of women's pictures, Scarlett does not suffer in silence. Like Ilsa, the heroines of women's pictures lack agency; Scarlett, on the contrary, is the principal agent of her story. Scarlett does, like Rick, spend a great deal of the film waiting, in her case for Ashley. But if Rick is feminized in his waiting, Scarlett is masculinized by her refusal to be passive in her waiting. She doesn't much sit around crying over Ashley but rather takes action to pursue her own interests. It is unremarkable that Rick becomes the proprietor of a nightclub, an activity that is portrayed as relatively passive, a taking of refuge, as it were. Scarlett's entrepreneurialism, on the other hand, is a part of her refusal to play the role of the lady. Neither Scarlett, nor Rhett—at least through most of the story—gives a damn about social conventions. In this sense, they are both "outlaw heroes." Their status as outlaws allows them to pursue their emotional goals unencumbered by what others might think. This freedom renders Scarlett culpable for her loss, but in being worthy of blame she is also rendered capable of action.

It is clear that part of the great appeal of *Gone with the Wind* to female viewers is their identification with Scarlett the resister. In her study of women's responses to the film, Helen Taylor reports that "again and again, women described to me their identification with and admiration of the strong, resourceful Scarlett." Taylor's subjects often envied Scarlett's "rebelliousness, which many women found her most exciting characteristic."[17] The film's qualifications of Scarlett's resistance apparently mean little to these viewers, who see Scarlett as a model. *Gone with the Wind* is a love story especially attractive to women because the heroine, like Rick and the heroes of most Hollywood films, is not merely a lover, much less a love object, but an individual with other, sometimes more important, desires and interests.

The more important interest in *Casablanca* is winning the war against the fascists. *Gone with the Wind* also should be read as a response to a contemporary social crisis, the Depression of the 1930s, an era when capitalism was under overt threat in the United States. The Civil War and Reconstruction may seem to have little in common with the Depression, but in fact, they mark the moment in history when the American South was forced out of its feudal plantation economy and into capitalism. Yet in another sense, the South remained on the periphery of capitalism, continuing to supply mainly raw materials to industry elsewhere. *Gone with the Wind* praises the culture of the Old South, but it fully recognizes its outmoded economic status. Ashley says if it weren't for the war, he would have been happily "buried" in the unreality of his familial plantation, Twelve Oaks.

Scarlett and Rhett, on the other hand, are defined by their capitalist initiatives. As Jan Cohn argues, Rhett is "the representative man of the new economic order."[18] A war profiteer and a collaborator during Reconstruction, he is a social outcast with a talent for self-enrichment. But Scarlett also reflects this new economy, as she "demonstrates an amazing and unimpeded precocity in the calculations and manipulations of the brisk capitalist economy brought to Georgia by Reconstruction."[19] In over-coming material obstacles, Scarlett is fantastically successful. Imitating Rhett, she profits by taking advantage of the opportunities Reconstruction presents her. Though both characters are regarded as infra dig for their capitalist activities, they are the ones who survive and succeed. Indeed, one could argue that *Gone with the Wind* is as much a parable of capitalist individualism and self-reliance as it is a love story. Scarlett's most passionate speech has as its object neither Ashley nor Rhett, but food. As the first half of the film closes, she vows, "As God is my witness, I will never be hungry again."

Scarlett's initial attempts to fulfill this vow and to hang on to Tara involve using her sexual appeal to con men into helping her. Where Ilsa is incapable of using her feminine wiles to get the letters of transit from Rick, Scarlett has no such scruples. Her love for Ashley remains pure only because he has nothing to give her. She does find a sucker in Frank Kennedy (Carroll Nye), who becomes her second husband, bringing her not only money but power, since he is one of the few Southerners who has money during Reconstruction. Her marriage to Rhett brings her even greater wealth. I want to insist on the importance of these marriages of economic convenience—or alliance—because they place the events of the film on terrain familiar since the Middle Ages: marriage as an economic or political institution is opposed to romantic love, which coexists with marriage but outside it. As a woman in the old South, Scarlett finds marriage her only means to her economic ends. This puts Scarlett in the contradictory position of having to contract marriages of convenience when she deeply wants to marry for love. Yet these marriages are initiated by her, and they are relatively minor obstacles in her relationship to Rhett.

Gone with the Wind clearly does not mean to endorse such marriages of convenience. On the contrary, the view of marriage that both book and film seem to endorse coincides with the "companionate" model, discussed in chapter 2, that emerged in the 1920s and that historians take to be increasingly dominant during the period when these works were produced.[20] The narrative insists that Melanie and Ashley, and Scarlett and Rhett, are suited for each other by their similar values, interests, and temperaments. Ashley says of himself and Melanie: "She's like me. She's part of my blood. We understand each other." His feelings for Scarlet are powerful, but "that kind of love is not enough to make a successful marriage for two people who are as different as we are." The film thus acknowledges the attraction of opposites but rejects it as the basis of marriage.

Rhett is Scarlett's appropriate mate. He tells her, "I love you because we're alike. Bad lots, both of us. Selfish and shrewd, but able to look things in the eye as we call them by their right names." These kinds of statements, entirely absent from *Casablanca,* also reflect a woman's perspective on romance, one more practical than the man's view as reflected in the mysterious power that love holds over Rick and Ilsa. Given their lack of power, women needed to be more calculating and analytic in their approach to love.

In its analytic attitude, *Gone with the Wind* presents glimmers of what will become the discourse of intimacy. Unlike most romantic narratives, *Gone with the Wind* does actually portray several marriages—or it seems to, at any rate. Melanie and Ashley *are* happily married, though the film can hardly be said to dwell on their relationship, which serves mainly as an obstacle to Scarlett. Moreover, Ashley spends most of the film off-screen, so we see only brief moments of his marriage. Scarlett's marriage to Rhett is a disaster in spite of their oft-proclaimed similarities, and one might go so far as to question whether they were really married at all. Legally, of course, a marriage did exist, since a child was conceived. But after the birth of Bonnie, Scarlett bars Rhett from her bed, a bed he finds his way back into only once more—in what is often referred to as the rape scene. The narrative thus undermines its own stated idea of the ideal grounds for marriage. True to the structures of the discourse of romance, *Gone with the Wind* continues to oppose romantic love and marriage in spite of itself.

This may be most clearly illustrated by the timing of the story's key event: Scarlett spends the entire narrative waiting for Ashley Wilkes, only to discover, exactly at the moment when he becomes theoretically available, that she loves, not him, but her husband, Rhett, who at this point famously doesn't "give a damn." Given this plot synopsis, it is entirely plausible for Catherine Belsey to read the story as the perfect illustration of Lacan's doctrine of desire, finding the novel "more revealing for my purposes than most canonical literary texts of the twentieth century."[21] The discourse of romance has its own internal logic to explain why Scarlett seems to want only the man she cannot have. It opposes true love to all considerations of practicality, economics, power, or convenience. Love is not something you may achieve, by either scheming or legitimate effort, but something that befalls you. The suffering lover may often utter lines like Ilsa's "I wish I didn't love you so much." Scarlett tells Rhett, just before he walks out for the last time, "I must have loved you for a long time and not even known it." True love is unwilled, but it is all the truer if it is made difficult, by, say, the inconvenience of marriage to another or even overt rejection by the love object.

Gone with the Wind features not one but multiple triangulations. The two most significant are the marriage of Ashley and Melanie, which excludes Scarlett, and the relationship of Rhett and Scarlett, in which Ashley is the third party. But unlike *Casablanca,* it is a story of failed adultery. Like Edith Wharton's Newland Archer, Ashley Wilkes is just not up to the deed. As Rhett puts it, "Ashley can't be faithful to his wife mentally, but is incapable of being unfaithful technically." The story of failed adultery is the woman's story, a response to the contradictory conceptions of masculinity offered by the discourse of romance. An official hero like Lazlo, Ashley is the good soldier who reluctantly does his duty in a war that he does not relish. This makes him the perfect prince for a fairy tale, an appropriate love object for an adolescent. As numerous commentators have pointed out, Ashley's androgynous name denotes his mixture of masculinity and femininity. While such a combination renders Ashley a safe love object for the young Scarlett, it makes him an unsuitable mate for her in the eyes of the audience. Rhett's masculinity is defined by his refusal to obey the rules. He has been thrown out of West Point, he is not received in society for "ruining" a girl's reputation, and he profits from rather than sacrifices for the war. *Gone with the Wind* makes this opposition of official and outlaw hero much more extreme than does *Casablanca.* Unlike the westerns that Ray takes to be paradigmatic of this opposition, *Gone with the Wind* treats its two heroes as sexual objects. Ashley is lovable, but Rhett is exciting. The former will make a reliable husband and provider, but he is not strong enough to be the lover Scarlett desires; the latter is unfaithful and undependable, but he personifies the strength and will to match and to master her own. But if Ashley's traits would in the end bore Scarlett, Rhett's frighten as well as attract her. She both wants and does not want to be mastered.

According to the discourse of romance, men may be either faithful, good, weak, and boring, or unfaithful, bad, strong, and exciting. In many romances, the former type is the cuckolded husband while the latter is the adulterous lover. As long as romance remains antithetical to marriage, these ideals can be safely kept separate. Once romance comes to define marriage, they no longer can. The ideal man must be the outlaw hero during courtship but become the official hero in marriage. This is the formula of the women's romance, in which the sexy but threatening lover is transformed into a loving and nurturing husband.[22] But this story of transformation is merely a subplot of *Gone with the Wind*. Rhett is transformed, not so much by marriage as by fatherhood, but Scarlett doesn't see it and probably wouldn't care even if she did. The transformation makes Rhett a truly eligible husband in the minds of the audience, and it thereby renders the failure of the marriage all the more tragic. The audience sees clearly that Rhett is Mr. Right, and we are sad that Scarlett can't recognize this in time.

The overt reason why Scarlett isn't moved by Rhett's new character is that she is too immature to appreciate it. Just as *Casablanca* is a story about a man coming to accept the realities and responsibilities that go with maturity, *Gone with the Wind* is about a woman's failure to do so. Ideally, just as Rhett becomes a bit more like Ashley, Scarlett should become more like Melanie. That she does not defines her all the more as the subject of romance. Romance is by definition irresponsible; lovers are always immature regardless of how old they are. Men and women, however, are not free to be irresponsible in the same ways. The imbalance of power between the genders entails the fiction that men become fully adult while women remain to some extent childlike. But the reverse of this fiction is the fact that women usually are forced by their primary role in child rearing to mature faster and thus to be less romantic in their behavior. Because marriage and family are less important to men in the current gendered division of labor, men are freer to indulge romance. Once again, in these terms, Scarlett represents a gender reversal. Scarlett's immaturity is never that which is usually associated with women—the need for protection, for example—but precisely the same immaturity that Rick and the men he represents typically manifest: self-absorption. We are not ever convinced, I think, that Scarlett loves anyone but herself. Rhett clearly loves their daughter, but Scarlett sees her mainly as a burden. Even in the end, after deciding that she loves Rhett, Scarlett still speaks of "getting" him, as if he were a piece of property. While Rhett has always seemed to understand Scarlett, it is never clear that Scarlett understands Rhett. Scarlett's conception of love thus seems to be purely romantic, lacking the care and empathy that we expect of love, especially from women.

Just as there is a combination of triumph and tragedy in the ending of *Casablanca*, so too *Gone with the Wind* is not a story that ends simply in love's victory or defeat. The ending of *Gone with the Wind* is, on the surface at least, much more ambiguous. Some critics describe the narrative as having a happy ending, while other critics and the film's producers saw its ending as unhappy. As is well known, producer and auteur David O. Selznick fought with Louis B. Mayer to preserve what they both saw as its unhappy ending, and he won his point when preview audiences accepted his version without reservation. In terms of Hollywood's conventions, the film ends unhappily because the leading man and woman are not united. The film ends, however, not with Rhett's famous exit line but with Scarlett's statement of faith: "Tomorrow, I'll think of some way to get him back. After all, tomorrow is another day." The ending confirms that Rhett's departure will not defeat her any more than the Yankees could.

Moreover, the ending lacks the complete closure typical of most Hollywood narratives. As Belsey notes, this ending continues to "tease, elude and frustrate . . . sustaining the desire of its central character and of the audience simultaneously."[23] But "desire" in Lacan's sense can be sustained by the most final of unhappy endings, since all desire requires is lack. What the ending of *Gone with the Wind* allows is the hope of future satisfaction. Belsey believes that this "end-lessness" is satisfying to the audience and that the usual happy endings are not. While I think it clear, given the overwhelming popularity of the narrative, that the ending of *Gone with the Wind* is in some way satisfying, happy endings are also satisfying to movie audiences and readers of formula romances among others, who often object to endings that either are unhappy or lack closure. *Gone with the Wind*'s ending works because it allows the viewer to impose the closure he or she wishes. The lack of closure of *Gone with the Wind* is thus only partly like that which feminist critics have observed of soap operas, which also continue to tease and elude their viewers. That lack of closure depends on the quite literal lack of an ending, since soap operas typically run for years. But both the novel and the film versions of *Gone with the Wind* do end, and it is reported that Margaret Mitchell laughed at the possibility of a sequel.

Mitchell's laughter, one imagines, must have had something to do with her quite reasonable inability to want to imagine this narrative being any longer. But there is a sense, especially strong in the film, that the original already contains a sequel. The pre- and postintermission halves of the film tell two stories that are themselves virtually complete. So there is a sense in which *Gone with the Wind* ends not once, but twice, and the endings are similar. In each case, Rhett abandons Scarlett. After he does so the first time, we see her go to Tara where the episode ends with her vow not to be hungry. After the second time, she announces that she will go to Tara and get Rhett back. Rhett's taking leave of Scarlett at the end of part 1 might have been the model for the conclusion of *Casablanca*. Like Rick, Rhett leaves Scarlett to go off to war. Just as Rick proclaims that "the problems of two people don't amount to a hill of beans in this crazy world," Rhett proclaims his love for Scarlett in spite of "the whole silly world going to pieces around us." And, although Scarlett puts up much more of a fight, she, like Ilsa, is unable to prevent her man from leaving. But because this is Scarlett's story, it is her we see going on to Tara to re-build her life alone. The second ending repeats this pattern, with the important difference that Rhett's leaving is now because of Scarlett rather than in spite of her.

If *Gone with the Wind* were Rhett's story, we would almost certainly feel a powerful sense of justice in his leaving Scarlett. In that case, the ending might exactly parallel *Casablanca* in that Rhett's not giving a damn would seem a fair punishment of Scarlett. Since this is the woman's story, however, we are not encouraged to feel this as a triumph. But the ending of *Gone with the Wind* also fictionally resolves a set of contradictory claims for the discourse of romance. Again as in *Casablanca,* the conflict is at root a result of the imbalance of power between the genders. As the man's story, *Casablanca* had to reassert male dominance that had been threatened by passion. The woman's story must express continued resis-tance to that domination. Where *Casablanca* ends with Ilsa silenced, *Gone with the Wind* ends with a statement of Scarlett's agency. She vows not to wait but to act. Rhett's leaving paradoxically frees Scarlett to main-tain both her power and her vision of romance, both of which would be lost in marriage.

How could a mainstream film and cultural icon endorse such a posi-tion? Scarlett's rebellion is enabled by the fact that the entire story is set in the context of the rebellion that was the Civil War. At one level, this is perhaps to state the familiar point that war frequently forces people to take on roles or tasks that they typically would not or could not do dur-ing peacetime. Scarlett is thus "free" to pick cotton, an activity that would have previously been "prohibited" by racial, gender, and class re-strictions. But in a larger sense, the film isolates its story from any gov-erning set of social conventions. In identifying itself with the Confeder-acy, it rejects the culture of postwar America. But this identification is with a "civilization," as Ashley calls it, "gone with the wind," a utopia, a no-place. The result is that no social order is at stake in Scarlett's story.

Gone with the Wind: The war makes Scarlett (Vivien Leigh) "free" to do manual labor.

Where *Casablanca* asks its audience to agree that the fate of the world hangs in the balance of Rick's decision about Victor Lazlo, the fate of the world of *Gone with the Wind* was decided long ago. *Gone with the Wind* is free to tell a woman's story of resistance because the order she resists is depicted as if it no longer existed. Like the Southerners who lost the civil war, Scarlett will forever be a rebel and never a revolutionary. *Gone with the Wind* does not advocate overturning the balance of power between the genders any more than it advocates overturning the results of the Civil War. Rhett's not giving a damn means that he leaves unbowed, and, as Barthes would have it, his leaving itself puts him in the traditional masculine role. Moreover, Scarlett's resistance seems as futile as Rhett's was when he at last adopted the Southern cause.

It might be argued that *Casablanca* and *Gone with the Wind* are experienced as "most romantic" because they exploit the possibilities of the discourse of romance so fully. Both films leave us with a powerful sense of missed opportunity, a powerful sense of a love lost that should have flourished. Yet they also leave us with an undying love, a "Paris" Rick and Ilsa will always have, a "tomorrow" in which Scarlet will get Rhett back. This contradiction is at the heart of the current meaning of romance in American culture. These films are quintessentially romantic because they manage to embrace both of the conflicting narrative patterns that the discourse of romance has produced. On the one hand, the films depict romantic love as something that flourishes only outside marriage. On the other hand, because these films are products of a culture in which romance and marriage have become powerfully linked, they cannot reject marriage as the goal of romance. Indeed, with the crisis of marriage as part their historical context, these films needed to affirm that institution. They therefore can't follow the traditional model that links love and death. Rather, they tell stories in which the lack of resolution in happy marriage is rendered as a triumph for the protagonists, who will continue their love forever even if they are separated from the objects of their affection. This may be the most powerful of romantic situations, since, unlike in death, both subjects remain conscious of their love and of their suffering.

PART II

Intimacy

5

Talking Cures
The Discourse of Intimacy

It really shows you how love works.
> —Larry King, quoted in a cover blurb of De Angelis's
> *How to Make Love All the Time*

"Just what *is* intimacy?" asks the recent manual *Heterosexuality,* to which one feels the need to add, "and why is everybody talking about it all of a sudden?"[1] My argument is that all of this intimacy talk represents a newly emerging discourse that has come to complement and compete with the older discourse of romance. The critique of romance has a history that is probably as old as the discourse itself, people having been long warned to be wary of the illusions of romantic love. Indeed, as I suggested in chapter 3, *romance* has become virtually a synonym for *illusion.* At present in the United States, constant exposure to romance narratives from print, film, and television, to romantic lament and celebration in popular songs, and to romantic images and vignettes in advertising has tended to make us all at least a little suspicious of romance.[2] The discourse of intimacy is another matter; it represents itself as the truth about love and relationships, and so far this claim has been little examined. I believe that this discourse has come to be for many today the most important paradigm for understanding love, courtship, marriage, and other relationships, not so much by displacing romance as by coexisting with it and, to a great extent, incorporating it. In this chapter, I will show how and why this discourse emerged, and I will describe its key words, its structuring oppositions, and its dominant rhetorical modes. While I won't offer a judgment about the truth of this discourse, I will show that the intimacy it assumes to be the goal of relationships is necessarily elusive.

A New Discourse

As a distinct discourse, intimacy doesn't exist until at least the 1960s, and it is only in the 1970s and later that a significant body of it appears. But this discourse does not emerge out of nowhere. The conception of marriage that social scientists began in the 1920s to call "companionate" already entailed expectations of closeness and friendship that the discourse intimacy would develop and expand. The even greater expectations of the romantic marriage, advocated by Elinor Glyn and Marie Carmichael Stopes and suggested by screwball comedies, also helped pave the way. Perhaps most important, however, were two broader changes in cultural beliefs and behavior. First, at the turn of the twentieth century, books that gave advice on choosing a mate most often dealt with the soundness of physique and character. Psychology played no significant role. The idea of psychological compatibility would develop over the course of the century as human psychology came to seem increasingly deep and diverse. Second, the separate gender spheres of the Victorian world would increasingly break down, and women's roles would become increasingly diverse. As a result, marriage no longer could be taken for granted as following a "natural" pattern. We will see how both of these changes were expressed in two movements that directly presaged intimacy discourse: family therapy and second-wave feminism.

Like the advice literature of the 1920s and the screwball comedies of the 1930s and 1940s, the emergence of the discourse of intimacy should be understood as a response to the crisis in marriage. This crisis received less attention in the 1940s and 1950s, as the divorce rate fell at the end of World War II and then leveled off until the mid-1960s. Divorce continued to be more common than it had been in the 1930s, but so did marriage. "Those who came of age during and after World War II were the most marrying generation on record: 96.4 percent of women and 94.1 percent of men. . . . [N]ot only did the average age at marriage drop; almost everyone was married by his or her mid-twenties. And not only did the average family size increase, most couples had two to four children, born sooner after marriage and spaced closer together than in previous years."[3] Thus, Elaine Tyler May concludes that we should understand the 1950s not as a return to normalcy but as an aberration, "a temporary disruption of long-term trends. . . . In many ways the youths of the sixties resembled their grandparents, who came of age in the first decades of the twentieth century."[4]

The marriage and family boom of the 1950s reflects an ideological reversion to conceptions of marriage and family that were challenged in the 1920s. Since the publication of Betty Friedan's *The Feminine Mystique* in 1963, we have been aware that the 1950s were dominated by an ideology of domesticity that sought to reverse changes in gender roles in progress since the turn of the century and accelerated by the need for women's labor during the war. Women's magazines, television situation comedies, and other media were important in disseminating this ideology, but it was also represented in the advice writing of the period. Marriage manuals did continue to include the sexual instruction that Stopes had initiated, but they also typically instructed men and women on what roles to play. Moreover, in the 1950s, college courses in marriage and family had become common. While textbooks for these courses suggest that they took an objective, sociological approach as the frame for their subject, they also continued to depict marriage and the family as under threat. In describing the empirical norms of marriage and family, the marriage and family courses treated them as normative. For example, here is how one text describes "the homemaker role": "The constant presence of the wife in the home and her management of most of its functions make her a unique 'center' of family life."[5] The teachers and advisers of the 1950s assumed the value of distinct roles for men and women even if they acknowledged the need for some flexibility in them, and "adjustment" to those roles was held to be the key to a successful marriage.[6]

If the marriage crisis was relegated to textbooks during the 1950s, it reappeared in public again all the more sensationally in the 1960s as the divorce rate again jumped dramatically and as the "sexual revolution" was making headlines. By the 1970s, social commentators were claiming that serial monogamy had become the norm. Whether this was the case, the divorce rate of 50 percent meant that very many people would come to think of marriage as something other than a lifelong bond. One response, of course, was the moralistic one, which urged couples to obey their vows and decried the liberalization of divorce laws. Another response, the one that concerns me here, was to attempt to figure out how to fix what seemed to be broken in individual marriages. The assumption of this response was that people wanted to make their marriages succeed but didn't know how. Psychoanalysis and the other "talking cures" that developed out of it enabled the problem to be defined in this way and provided the terms in which a solution could be formulated. While therapy or counseling became the solution of choice under this model, it was more often than not in practice the solution of last resort. For the less desperate, there developed an enormous body of self-help writing, material that I take to be the new discourse's most characteristic expression.[7]

The books in this category range from sophisticated analyses such as Maggie Scarf's *Intimate Partners* to simplistic and prescriptive tracts like Barbara De Angelis's *How to Make Love All the Time*.[8] Such books are clearly heirs to a tradition of advice giving that goes back to Dorothy Dix, Stopes, and Glyn, but this new self-help literature also represents a fundamental break with that tradition. These earlier advisers wrote in the discourse of romance, and they took romantic marriage to be the goal of their readers. The post-1960s self-help books are written in a new language of love, the discourse of intimacy. Instead of focusing on the drama of the chase and taking love and marriage as a natural sequence, intimacy focuses on a new object, "the relationship" both in and out of marriage. Where romance depicts the always-rocky path to true love, intimacy describes the way "actually existing" relationships function. Based on such knowledge, advice books promise to help repair broken relationships or explain how to build solid new ones. Many of these texts focus on communication and the language that couples use, so this chapter will concern both talking that cures and cures for (sick) talk.

While the rising divorce rate and the sexual revolution explain the felt need for a new way of thinking and talking about love and marriage, they don't much help us to understand how the discourse of intimacy developed as it did or why it arose when it did. The key event was the emergence of new theories and practices of psychoanalysis during the 1950s. While few self-help books say much about the theories they assume or invoke, Maggie Scarf, an author and journalist who is a contributing editor at the *New Republic,* offers a brief account of the development of family therapy out of psychoanalysis and psychiatry in general that previously treated only individuals. While Scarf's account is directed to explaining her own particular approach, it reveals a more general history that pertains to the discourse as a whole. Scarf notes that "all the way up until the mid-1950s, most clinicians tended to think of emotional distress as problems going on *within an individual's own head.* . . . Those people who were closest to the person in distress were, said Freud, 'a positive danger, one which we do not know how to deal with.'"[9] Freud observed that mates and other family members often seemed to want to keep the patient ill. But this practical difficulty was only one reason why families weren't regarded as fit objects of clinical practice. As psychoanalyst Jessica Benjamin has argued, Freud's theory treated "the human subject as a monadic energy system."[10] In this view, other significant humans, such as parents and siblings, were treated, not as interacting subjects, but as objects within the psychic system of the individual. Moreover, the most important American branch of psychoanalysis, ego psychology, described the infant as developing through a "gradual separation and individuation from an initial symbiotic unity with the mother." This theory assumed "that we grow *out of* relationships rather than becoming more active and sovereign *within* them."[11] In this view, healthy adults were defined by their successful separation from their parents and not by their success in forming relationships. What Benjamin labels the bias of psychoanalysis in "overvaluing of separation" corresponds, as she notes, to the same bias elsewhere in the culture, from Hegel's philosophy to the ideology of individualism.[12]

The discourse of intimacy emerges out of theories that rejected Freud's view of the isolated human subject and a clinical practice that took families rather than individuals as its object of treatment, but it also needs to be understood as a reaction against the individualism of the larger culture and the overvaluing of autonomy it fosters. Family therapy provided the models, terms, and methods on which intimacy advice books are based. It gave therapists a paradigm under which, as Scarf puts it, "the marital unit—not the wife alone or the husband alone, but the particular relationship that they have, in combination, created together . . . will be viewed as 'the patient.'"[13] This approach has not only enabled the couple to become an object of diagnosis and treatment, however, for it also has contributed its own bias to the discourse, one that author Francine Klagsbrun names in her advice book "a bias toward marriage."[14] The (often unstated) assumption of intimacy discourse is not only that monogamous and usually heterosexual relationships are normative but that they represent the only form in which intimacy can be achieved. Like the discourse of romance, intimacy discourse naturalizes the connection between love and marriage even though it depicts both of these in quite different terms. Most intimacy writing assumes that relationships follow predictable cycles and that they exist to fulfill the natural needs of individuals. It thus tends to define—at least by implication—states other than coupledom as unnatural.

Family therapy only partially explains the emergence of the discourse of intimacy. Among other things, it doesn't explain the particular kind of marriage or relationship that the discourse takes as its ideal. The other significant condition required for the emergence of intimacy discourse was second-wave feminism and its intellectual offshoots. This is not to say that most intimacy writing is overtly feminist. Indeed, one of the frustrations of reading this material is its strong tendency to ignore the context of societal gender inequality in its discussion of patterns in relations between individual men and women. But if these books do not feel the need to argue against male dominance, they usually take it for granted that an intimate relationship can exist only between equals. They all to some degree recognize that power is an issue in any relationship, something that both partners will struggle to attain. Prior discussions of marriage tended to assume male dominance within the relationship and thus saw power struggles as an aberration caused either by the man's unusual weakness or the woman's unnatural ambition. The ideal within the discourse of intimacy is what Pepper Schwartz, a professor of sociology and advice columnist for *Glamour,* calls "peer marriage," in which neither partner dominates emotionally, financially, or in the division of household labor.[15] Moreover, they typically diagnose failing relationships by their unequal distribution of emotional tasks and unceasing struggle for control of the relationship, the latter an area in which a woman even in an outwardly traditional marriage may well covertly have the upper hand. If intimacy writing doesn't overtly treat the personal as the political, it does offer a politics of relationships.

Feminism also contributed to the reaction against individualism and the privileging of psychic autonomy. Feminists characterized these cultural biases as male or as serving the interests of men. Feminist psychoanalysts Nancy Chodorow and Dorothy Dinnerstein argued that the different ways in which male and female children were parented led men to overvalue autonomy and to devalue relatedness.[16] They believed that this problem might be solved if fathers became actively involved in child rearing and established greater intimacy with their children. Psychologist Carol Gilligan observed the different ways that boys and girls related to each other in play, the former tending to construct and contest hierarchies and the latter seeking to build mutually beneficial relations of equals.[17] Feminists not only observed these gendered differences but also held that the male-dominated culture had devalued attachment and relationship. They argued the need to recognize the importance of these qualities in general and to try to encourage their growth in men in particular. However influential these particular arguments have been, probably more significant has been the more general demand that the patterns of domestic relationships not be taken for granted. The perception that such relationships could be different is a primary condition for the development of intimacy discourse. And, by making the kitchen and the bedroom sites of struggle, feminists made both men and women attend to their modes of relating.

For all feminism's influence on people's thinking, however, it was its success in changing the way many people actually behaved that may have been its most important contribution to the emergence of the discourse of intimacy. In this sense, we might say that feminism changed intimacy itself. Feminism has been a major factor in what Anthony Giddens calls "the transformation of intimacy," a major shift in human practice that has occurred for the most part during the twentieth century. Giddens's basic argument is that the character of intimate relations, once more or less fixed by law, custom, and morals, now has become fluid: "Personal life has become an open project, creating new demands and anxieties. Our interpersonal existence is being thoroughly transfigured, involving us all in what I shall call *everyday social experiments,* with which wider social changes more or less oblige us to engage."[18] Giddens describes one of the fundamental changes with which he is concerned as the emergence of the "pure relationship":

> The term "relationship," meaning a close and continuing emotional tie to another, has only come into general usage relatively recently. To be clear what is at stake here, we can introduce the term *pure relationship* to refer to this phenomenon. . . . It refers to a situation where a social relation is entered into for its own sake, for what can be derived by each person from a sustained association with another; and which is continued only in so far as it is thought by both parties to deliver enough satisfactions for each individual to stay within it. Love used to be tied to sexuality, for most of the sexually "normal" population, through marriage; but now the two are connected more and more via the pure relationship. Marriage—for many, but by no means all groups in the population—has veered increasingly towards the form of a pure relationship, with many ensuing consequences. The pure relationship, to repeat, is part of a generic restructuring of intimacy.[19]

It can be argued that Giddens overstates his case and that many, if not most, marriages continue to be strongly regulated by external imperatives, especially those stemming from male dominance and the economic inequalities of capitalism. Nevertheless, the restructuring of personal relationships he observes has been significant, and it is both an explanation and a partial result of intimacy discourse. Giddens notes that in this transformed world "new terminologies of 'commitment' and 'intimacy' have come to the fore."[20] His emphasis is on changed behavior, and he does not explore these new "terminologies" in themselves. Giddens's formulation, however, of the "pure relationship" is a useful one for my purposes because, regardless of how often such relationships actually occur, the pure relationship is the principal object of intimacy discourse. Since marriage remains the preferred form for such relationships to take—it is worth noting here the demands that gays and lesbians have made for their relationships to be legally recognizable as marriages—intimacy writing still tends to treat marriage as the privileged sort of relationship. But marriage in this writing is almost always cast as a pure relationship and seldom as defined by social, religious, or moral obligations.

Intimacy Itself: An Elusive Goal

Advice and self-help books are a response to and manifestation of the transformation of intimacy Giddens describes, and they seldom if ever take explicit account of it. Such books use the word *intimacy* not, or not merely, to mean the condition of particular kinds of relationships—friendly, familial, or romantic. *Intimacy* has long been a term with multiple meanings: it has ranged from being a euphemism for a sexual relationship to describing all relations that are especially close and are typically considered to be private rather than public. *Intimacy*, of course, hasn't lost these meanings, which continue to exist in the new discourse. As a result, the word itself is no more a definite signifier that the speaker is using the new language I'm discussing here than the word *romantic* guarantees that the perspective is that of romance. Moreover, just as romance names a number of variant narratives that cast love in quite different lights, so intimacy can't be understood as a single, coherent set of prescriptions. Like romance, it consists of differing narratives and conflicting visions. Also like romance, these differences are seldom argued out or even acknowledged, so that intimacy discourse seems to be more or less unified.

Intimacy seems to me to be the proper name for this discourse because of the enormous value and weight the term is given in these advice books.

What is distinctive about the meaning of the term in this discourse is that it now designates both a process and a goal, the particular kinds of interaction that typify marital relationships and the closeness that successful interaction is said to produce. I take up intimacy as a process at some length below, but here I want to discuss its meaning as the goal, perhaps even an entitlement, of relationships. Klagsbrun claims that "of all the components of marriage, intimacy is probably the quality most longed for, and often the most elusive." She explains the longing for intimacy by claiming that "without it, inside as well as outside marriage, there is loneliness."[21] The assumption here is that everyone needs intimacy—and not merely friendship or companionship—to avoid feeling bad. While most intimacy discourse does not lay the matter out quite this plainly, I think Klagsbrun's statement explains the longing for intimacy: it is imagined precisely as the absence of loneliness. In his self-described "manual" *Soul Mates,* Thomas Moore, a former Roman Catholic monk, begins his discussion of "intimacy" with etymology: "The word *intimacy* means 'profoundly interior.' It comes from the superlative form of the Latin word *inter,* meaning 'within.' It could be translated 'within-est,' or 'most-within.'"[22] Putting Klagsbrun's and Moore's points together, it would seem that intimate relationships are valued because they cross the presumed boundary that separates self from others, allowing an other to be "most-within." The problem with this formulation is not only that it assumes the alienated individual as its norm but also that the proposed antidote to this state is nothing more than its formal opposite. We still don't know in what having intimacy actually consists.

One approach to this question might be to try to distinguish the term *intimacy* from others like it. This is difficult because the terms are not used consistently by different writers and because *intimacy* tends to expand to include more and more. But careful reading does yield some fairly consistent distinctions. Scarf explicitly distinguishes intimacy from one sense of romance, "candlelight, a table for two in a small bistro, a violinist playing gypsy melodies as the absorbed couple engages in mutually fascinating, intensely romantic conversation."[23] Intimacy is also distinguished from romantic love as passion, a term that is virtually absent from intimacy discourse. As Klagsbrun describes romance, it is "the excitement of love . . . , the sexual thrills and the haze of rosiness" that she associates with the beginning of a marriage.[24] Nor is intimacy the same as companionship or friendship, though it seems to entail both of these. According to cognitive therapist Aaron Beck, companionship simply means doing things or spending time together. In this regard, we might keep in mind that one term for pets such as dogs and cats is "companion animals." Their function for their human owners is simply to be company, and, however much people love their pets, they don't typically describe their relations with them as intimate. Friendship, as Beck distinguishes it, is "the genuine interest you take in your mate as a person," and he notes an observation much repeated in these advice books, that a man is much more likely to regard his wife as his best friend than a woman is to name her husband as such.[25] Linguist Deborah Tannen explains why this is the case when she describes the way women's conversations with each other are characterized by the sharing of personal secrets, while men tend to talk either about topics of shared interest, like business or sports, or about the political relationships in which they are involved. If they do share secrets, it is likely to be with their mate. According to Tannen, the "intimate" talk of telling secrets is not only "evidence of friendship; it *creates* a friendship, when the listener responds in the expected way."[26]

For Tannen, intimacy is a condition of friendship, but her own account of the way women talk to each other reveals why intimacy is often imagined as "friendship plus." Women want to be able to have with their partners the kind of talk that they have with their friends. The category of "best friend" gets us close to the state of intimacy that this discourse extols. Personal advertisements are now often in search of a partner who will be a "best friend" or "soul mate." This aspect of intimacy is expressed by family therapist Augustus Y. Napier when he asserts that "our potential mate . . . is often a cleverly disguised emotional twin. This person offers us some purchase on life's terrible loneliness; he or she may have some chance of knowing what it is like to be us."[27] Intimacy sometimes seems to be mainly a kind of talk, as in Tannen or Beck, who describes intimacy as ranging from "discussing everyday details of your life, to confiding the most private feelings that you would not share with anybody else, to your sexual relationship."[28] But more often, it seems to entail a kind of deep communication, one that requires talk but is not exhausted by it. Scarf appears to define intimacy as the condition of openness or freedom of self-expression, "an individual's ability to talk about *who he really is,* and *to say what he wants and needs,* and *to be heard by the intimate partner.*"[29] Klagsbrun exemplifies intimacy by an emotional situation in which nothing needs to be said because the partners know each other so well and trust so deeply.[30]

Notice that these accounts individually and as a group circle around a definition of intimacy. It is necessary to the project of the discourse that the state of intimacy not be pinned down. In the discourse of romance, the mystery of attraction and the fall into love that it causes serve the same function. Intimacy discourse seeks to demystify attraction and love itself, but it needs to be able to leave a space that exists beyond its explanations, exercises, strategies, and therapies. While a writer of a certain religious background, like Moore, might be willing to call this dimension a mystery, most simply leave the idea vague enough to accommodate the reader's hope for transcendence. Intimacy thus exists between isolation and fusion, between talk and the conditions for talk, as interest, caring, and understanding and as a product of these. Intimacy must continue to seem, as Klagsbrun put it, "longed for and elusive" because the discourse itself would be otherwise devalued. There would be no market for all of the books explaining how to achieve intimacy. The elusiveness of intimacy is structural to the discourse and deeply bound up with the allure it holds. In Scarf's model, the most fully intimate marriage type, the "integrated," "is relational heaven itself, . . . less an interpersonal reality than it is an ideal." At this level intimacy itself is transcended: "autonomy and intimacy are experienced as integrated aspects of each partner's personhood and of the relationship that the two of them share."[31]

Commitment is another key word in the discourse of intimacy. Usually it is represented as a requirement for intimacy to develop, but Klagsbrun collapses it into intimacy itself. She quotes Eric Erikson, who "defines intimacy as the [individual's] 'capacity to commit himself to concrete affiliations and partnerships and to develop the ethical strength to abide by such commitments, even though they may call for significant sacrifices and compromises.'"[32] This gives *intimacy* a strongly moral or ethical cast that is at least not part of the surface text in the discourse in general. Those who see intimacy as possible only with commitment would also point to a frequent lack of intimacy even in committed relationships. Commitment is usually defined as a matter of will, while intimacy is something that everyone wants but that many are prohibited from achieving by factors beyond their conscious control. But *commitment* is a term proper to the discourse of intimacy. Romance never made love a matter of will, but precisely as something into which one "fell." There remained a gap between this conception of love and the contractual obligation undertaken in marriage. The latter didn't require commitment; it required only simple obedience to law. Commitment becomes an issue only when marriage comes to be understood as a "pure relationship," one that exists for the good of the parties involved. Conversely, love under romance was a justification for transgressing the laws of marriage. Falling for someone outside the marriage might result in a breach of the contract, but it was not understood as a failure of commitment.

Romance as a discourse takes extramarital relations as its model. The discourse of intimacy, on the contrary, assumes a monogamous relationship as its paradigm. As a result, intimacy deals with the love triangle very differently than does romance. Instead of taking the triangular relation to incite desire, create suspense, and provide the occasion for adventure, intimacy writing treats adulterous relationships and desires as pathologies of the marital relationship. Scarf goes so far as to claim that they are undertaken in the attempt to preserve the original relationship, however unconscious and misguided this attempt might be. Moreover, adultery is in her view not an act committed by one of the partners but an event produced by their relationship:

> An affair is . . . not something that happens *to* somebody; it is something that happens *between two people*. And often it is the weaker spouse who acts first; he or she makes a strengthening move by getting into a coalition with the extramarital partner. Becoming involved in an outside relationship is, for this person, an adaptive maneuver—a way of dealing with the problems in the relationship. The affair itself is a symptom, the symptom of a global marital disturbance; it is not the disturbance itself.[33]

An affair, in Scarf's view, "indicate[s] that the intimacy in a couple's emotional system is out of balance."[34] The affair is undertaken either to gain intimacy lacking in the marriage or to escape the demands for intimacy the partner is perceived to be making. In the former case, the third party will at least seem to provide the attention and communication that the marital partner does not. In the latter, the affair is safer because its inherent limitations protect the adulterer from becoming closer than he or she desires. The idea that the third party is what the wayward spouse really desires, that this person might make a better mate than the current one, is not even considered as a possibility. Not all intimacy writing is quite this limited in its assumption of the primacy of the original, monogamous dyad. Barbara De Angelis, for example, allows that "your relationship may not be working" because "you are with the *wrong person*," and she even provides a *Cosmopolitan* style self-test to help you determine if this is so.[35] Intimacy allows that a different dyad might be the solution to relationship woes, but it can't conceive, even covertly, that some people might not find happiness in monogamy rightly practiced.

Intimacy discourse doesn't assume that intimacy is the only need that individuals experience in relationships. They also experience the need for autonomy. The basic conflict with which this discourse is concerned is between these two needs. According to Scarf, the most typical condition is that of a man who cannot accept his own need for intimacy and his mate who cannot accept her need for autonomy. The pattern that this condition produces is an unconscious collusion in which the partners agree that one of them, the pursuer, will express the intimacy needs of both, while the other, the distancer, expresses their needs for autonomy. But the problem is more difficult than just the failure of each partner to be able to articulate one need. Rather, each partner is internally conflicted about his or her desires for intimacy and autonomy, but the conflict is, by means of "projective identification," shifted from the internal to the interpersonal, so that it is continuously fought out between the couple.[36] For Scarf, this basic model is, in one permutation or another, the root of most significant problems in relationships. Other writers don't make this conflict so central, but most acknowledge it as important. Napier, for example, asserts that "almost every couple experiences a version of this pursuit-distance agony."[37] Yet it is telling that "intimacy" names the reward this literature promises. Readers seeking autonomy, if any would actually formulate their desire in that way, are likely to be attracted to books offering assertiveness training and the like. Within the discourse of intimacy, autonomy is rendered part of the intimacy process. A completely intimate, or "integrated," relationship recognizes each individual's autonomy, his or her separateness and differences.

How couples are supposed to approach, much less reach, this nirvana is a question that advice books answer more or less in the same way: improved communication. So even if intimacy cannot be defined as a kind of talk, good talk is the primary path to achieving the goal. What this means, however, differs from writer to writer. Tannen, for example, assumes that simply understanding how men and women characteristically use language differently will help them communicate more effectively. But Tannen's book lies at what we might call the "intellectual" extreme of advice literature in that it is heavy on description and explanation but light on explicit solutions and lacking behavior-changing exercises entirely.

Most of these books actually try to teach partners how to talk differently to each other. At the other extreme, the "manual," we find books like De Angelis's, which spend most of their time giving instructions. Her book contains headings such as "How to Express the Complete Truth," the need for which is explained by the "secret" that "most communication problems stem from communicating only part of the truth, not the Complete Truth.[38] The "Complete Truth" for De Angelis consists of all of the feelings on your "emotional map": anger, hurt, fear, remorse, and love. She tells the reader to make sure to cover each emotion in discussing a conflict with a mate. In another section, De Angelis instructs the reader to write and exchange "Love Letters" with his or her intimate partner. These letters cover the regions of the emotional map and add a new area, "intentions and wishes."[39] What is being taught by these formulas is not simple self-expression but a method for channeling emotions. The reader learns not only to say what he or she feels but what feelings to have.

Some of the differences in advice about intimacy stem from the differing psychological theories that advisers invoke. While all intimacy writing has a historical connection to psychoanalysis, the connection is merely vestigial in much of this material. Indeed, because of cognitive therapy's claim to be able to change present behavior without reference to that behavior's historical causes, it is often the psychology of choice for advice book writers. While psychoanalytic and cognitive approaches both treat intimacy as fundamentally a matter of communication, they differ on the causes and treatments of miscommunication. Cognitivists locate miscommunication in specific patterns of misunderstanding—sometimes called "automatic thoughts"—bad habits of mind that can be replaced by better habits of mind. They usually see their job as simply to teach partners to talk and listen to each other more effectively. So Beck provides couples with lots of exercises designed to help individuals change their relationships by changing their automatic thoughts. The title of his book, *Love Is Never Enough*, accurately conveys its practical tone and the (relatively) modest claims it makes. Intimacy here is not the Holy Grail but one kind of communication. But the cognitive approach need not treat intimacy in this way. De Angelis's much-simplified cognitive model promises a great deal more—how to make love all the time. Those with an analytic approach, such as Scarf, regard miscommunication as a symptom of unconscious processes, memories, or patterns. The assumption of these books is that it is important to understand how patterns of miscommunication arose. Some of this may be attributable to a questionable article of psychoanalytic faith, that understanding a symptom's etiology is a necessary step to bringing about its cure. But it is also a function of the analysts' assumption that problems in relationships stem from complicated but hidden patterns, both intra- and interpersonal, patterns that are likely to reassert themselves unless they are exposed and explained.

Nevertheless, Scarf also provides "tasks" for her readers, albeit many fewer than Beck or De Angelis. If Tannen tells how to read your partner's talk, De Angelis what you should be telling him or her, and Beck how to change what you are thinking, Scarf provides exercises designed to change the unconscious projections that she sees at the root of most marital conflict. It is thus the pattern of talk within the couple that is her chief concern. One "task" she recommends involves having each partner, during a half-hour set aside for the purpose, talk only about him- or herself—and not say anything about the other partner—while the other partner must listen but not respond. The point of the task is that it "compels the members of the couple to face each other as separate, autonomous people."[40] This is an exercise, not of self-revelation, but of self-discrimination. It teaches each member of the couple to listen and to hear what the other is saying and to distinguish that from his or her own feelings, thoughts, and desires. According to Scarf, "What members of the couple often discover is that while the entire exercise is autonomy enhancing, the process of going through it makes them feel unaccountably *intimate*. Being separate persons, in each other's presence, promotes a sense of closeness."[41] This sort of thing seems to be a "talking cure" in a third sense, for it is not designed mainly to change the way the partners talk, nor is it confession to a psychotherapist. Here structured talk is designed to change behavior in a much more general sense.

It is perhaps curious, given the strong emphasis that intimacy advice books place on talk, that almost all of them include technical information as well as advice about sex. This feature connects contemporary advisors to Stopes, whose *Married Love: A New Contribution to the Solution of Sex Difficulties* focused on physical relations but saw them as fundamental to marriage as a whole. It is, of course, not surprising to find the sexologists Masters, Johnson, and Kolodny devoting most of their book to understanding and improving sexual performance, but Scarf's section on this subject seems a non sequitur. The general assumption of these texts seems to be that couples now are as much in need of information about how to physically please each other—and, often, how their own bodies work—as Stopes believed they were in the post-Victorian era. One wonders if these texts include material on sexual mechanics simply as a result of a publishing formula that demands that such material be there because either readers expect it or it enhances sales—or both. But it is also true that physical intimacy is historically what has distinguished the "intimate" relationships this discourse concerns. In others words, whatever else constitutes intimacy, sex remains a part of it. The general assumption is that the sexual aspect of a relationship is strongly determined by its general psychological or communicative state. That is to say, the more the partners succeed in the intimacy process, the more likely they are to have satisfactory sexual relations. Schwartz, however, has found something like the opposite to be true. She discovered "that sex can get *too* comfortable" in peer marriages resulting in a loss of passion and desire:

> Peer partners get so close that some complain that an "incest taboo" sets in. They are each other's best friends, and if they aren't careful, that is exactly what they will start acting like in bed. Many find ways to get around this overfamiliarization problem, but the fact is that their absolute integration in each other's lives has to be leavened with some artifice to put romance back into the relationship.[42]

Schwartz here suggests, albeit in a subsidiary way, more or less the same strategy that advocates of romantic marriage like Stopes and Glyn suggested in the 1920s. While Schwartz's grounds for this suggestion are unusual, most of the advice books counsel some recourse to romantic artifice. This is just one of the ways in which intimacy discourse has coopted the discourse of romance for its own ends. Intimacy writers are much more likely to claim to incorporate romantic love as an element of their model than to argue against it. According to Francine Klagsbrun, for example, "Blaming romantic love when marriage turns difficult is like blaming a child for being too bright when she doesn't live up to expectations. . . . All marriages, not only those that fail, begin with unreal expectations that color much of what happens between partners."[43] As is typical, Klagsbrun makes romantic love a stage in the normal course of marriage. Scarf calls this stage "idealization," and, though she doesn't explicitly link it to romance, the name suggests the same "unreal expectations" usually attributed to romance.[44] Intimacy typically naturalizes romance and fails to take account of its cultural and historical development, to say nothing of its own.

Case History as Genre

Romance is characteristically expressed in narrative form, and its most important expressions have always been fictional. Intimacy, on the contrary, is most typically manifested in the rhetorical modes of exposition, analysis, and instruction—all of which claim nonfictional status. Narrative does play an important, if subsidiary, role in these texts, however, most of which prominently feature case histories. One might classify the rhetoric of intimacy as having a scale with the case history at one end and instruction on the other. Books in the analytic mode, like Scarf's *Intimate Partners,* are arguments built on the interpretation of case histories. The more cognitivist books, such as Beck's *Love Is Never Enough* and De Angelis's *How to Make Love All the Time,* give brief case histories, but they are offered as examples to explain or justify the concepts and instructions being taught. For those working analytically, case histories are necessary because only this mode is able to illustrate the patterns in the requisite complexity. While in the most instructional texts, case histories that are included seem to function as little more than the examples or illustrations they claim to be, in the most case-historical texts, the case histories take on a life of their own, their specifics exceeding the generalizations that the analyst makes on the basis of them.

The specificity of the case history illustrates that the differences between romance and intimacy are rooted in fundamentally differing modes and forms rather than merely in differing ideas about love. We don't normally think of the case history as an independent genre. On the contrary, under the influence of rhetoricians such as Hayden White, many would be inclined to assume that the case history, like any other history, must be emplotted in the form of tragedy, comedy, romance, satire, or perhaps some other literary genre.[45] Without denying that case histories do indeed impose form on their factual content, or that their form is sometimes a familiar, literary one, I want to argue that the case history itself has become a genre with its own rules and expectations. This genre does have a literary antecedent, realism, but it is one that is typically denied generic specificity. Northrop Frye, for example, names four archetypal narratives, tragic, comic, romantic, and ironic, three of which also name genres. Realism, Frye says, can appear in either the low mimetic or ironic mode, but it is not itself a mode.[46] Frye takes realism at its word by defining it as closeness to life. What he is missing by this definition is the distinctive attitude or stance that realism assumes toward its material. The issue here is not the hierarchical relationship of the narrative to its subject but the epistemological one. The realist writer presents his or her material by means of the fiction of the nonfictional report. The narrator is an observer, and the story is what happened. The point here is that realism resists the traditional generic forms because they betray an authorial interest or politics. The case history, we might say, is the extreme form of realism. It is only minimally emplotted. Within the narrative, there are no heroes, no quests, no romance, no adventure, and no triumph over obstacles, even if a cure is accomplished. While the doctor is sometimes the explicit or implicit hero of a case history, this is seldom the pattern in intimacy discourse. There the focus is on the couples' stories and not on the therapist's brilliance. Like realism in William Dean Howells's conception, the stories told by the advice books' case histories are ordinary. They are offered because they are common, in contrast to Freud's "Wolfman" and "Ratman," which are of interest for their extreme abnormality.[47]

Perhaps the most salient aspect of the case history's minimalism is its lack of an ending. Especially as these histories are used in intimacy writing, we seldom know what happens to the couples after the moment of their story that is relevant to the author's discussion. Even if we are given a brief sentence or two telling us, for example, whether the couple stayed together or got divorced, such statements function not as endings but as epilogues. The point here is not that the stories lack "closure." For one thing, the use of the histories as examples provides an argumentative closure even if a narrative one is missing. Second, there is little in the way the stories are told that would encourage the reader to keep wondering about the couples discussed—unlike, say, in a soap opera, where the narrative structure is designed to keep such wonder going. Rather, the case histories lack the dramatic structure we expect of most narrative, a structure that requires—even if one is not always provided—a formal resolution of the problem or problems the narrative describes. Case histories in intimacy writing are never tragic, comic, or romantic.

Such histories are not ironic either, but for a different reason. Like *New Yorker* stories or independent films, they are slices of life and never the whole of it. And like these genres, the case histories are distanced from the reader. The character of the distancing differs, however. The fictional genres mentioned usually depend heavily on irony or, sometimes, exoticism. Framing the slice of life as art removes it from the ordinary, no matter how common the events narrated. The effect of the case history is just the opposite: it is told in order to seem mundane even while it is also meant to reveal truths about relationships that the reader has heretofore not recognized. The narrator of a case history must avoid seeming to look down on his or her subjects while at the same time maintaining the ethos of expertise. The narrator knows things about relationships that you and I and the subjects do not, but it is vital that he or she not seem to condescend to us. Perhaps in response to this dilemma, intimacy writers almost always draw on their own relationships for material, rendering themselves, at least in those passages, equals of the others whose histories they tell. Napier's *The Fragile Bond,* while it includes many shorter case histories, is as a whole a case history of the author's own marriage.

The structure of romantic narratives encourages the reader to identify strongly with one or more of the characters. I have argued that it is the triangular structure of intersubjective relations that makes romance so compelling of the reader's emotional involvement. Case histories lack this structure, even if they tell the story of a love triangle. They do engage the reader emotionally, however, and if this engagement is probably at a lower level of intensity, this doesn't stop reviewers and publishers from using adjectives such as "riveting" and "compelling" to describe them.[48] The best of the advice book writers do manage to make their case histories page-turners. While they rely on many of the same techniques as fiction writers, they also appeal to a different kind of reception. Rather than instructing the reader to identify with particular subjects, intimacy writing poses the question of such identification: Do I see myself as behaving like that man or woman? Is my relationship similar to the one described? Admittedly, the question of identification, once posed, is an invitation that may be hard to resist. The point is that not identifying is an option that will not destroy either the message or the pleasure of the text.

The question of the pleasure such texts bring seems to me to be central to any attempt to understand them. At least one author of these books notes a phenomenon that might be called hyperbolically self-help book addiction.[49] While one can assume that self-help reading usually begins out of a desire to solve or understand personal problems, its continuation seems to depend much more strongly on the feelings the reader gets from reading than on the success or failure of the solutions presented. On the one hand, if a solution were discovered, there would be no need to continue to consult additional texts. On the other, if solutions repeatedly failed, one would assume that the reader would conclude that reading such books was not a good means of solving the problem. It is likely that many readers find that these books are pleasurable in themselves because they offer a discourse very like the one that many of them claim women use with close female friends. This is the sort of talk that Tannen describes women using to establish and maintain connection and intimacy and that she labels "troubles talk." The point of such talk is not to arrive at solutions to problems but to share emotions. Men typically misunderstand this sort of talk and respond, not with troubles of their own, but with solutions for which they mistakenly believe that women are asking.[50] Obviously, self-help books must offer solutions, but the case histories themselves may for many women be the principal attraction of these books. Such attraction would involve identification, but of a different kind than is typically produced by a fictional romance. The reader here does not lose herself in an extended flight from her own more or less mundane existence. Rather, I am guessing that she responds as she would to a live interlocutor, sharing the emotions of the case subjects and silently offering troubles of her own.[51] One bit of evidence that case histories are appealing as emotional experiences comes from John Gray's *Mars and Venus in Love,* a sequel to his mega-seller *Men Are from Mars, Women Are from Venus.* Subtitled *Inspiring and Heartfelt Stories of Relationships That Work,* the sequel adds little to the original except case histories.[52] Since the case histories mainly involve people who found the earlier book helpful, this more emotionally engaging sequel also serves as an advertisement for the original.

If entertainment is one of the uses of advice books, one is led to speculate further about other uses. The address of such books is often curiously divided, sometimes directed to an individual, sometimes to a couple. And even in books like *Intimate Partners,* in which the focus is explicitly on the partners' interactions, intimacy is still sometimes treated as a capacity of the individual. Most intimacy writing makes it clear that intimacy is not something that depends on the relationship alone. Rather an individual may be more or less capable of intimacy depending on his or her gender, childhood, family history, and experiences in other relationships. An emphasis on one among these factors distinguishes many of the different approaches within the discourse. Scarf focuses on family history, Tannen emphasizes gender, and so on. The focus on the individual enables the writer to offer help to the individual reader. While having a couple together at a therapy session allows the therapist to observe and intervene in their interaction, books by convention presume a solitary reader, even if they encourage both partners to read and to do the suggested exercises or homework. And while some couples doubtless do make such use of self-help books, my guess is that they are much more frequently read by only one member of a couple or by singles. If I am right, I think it can be concluded that the advice books probably do more to change consciousness than to change behavior. In other words, like the fictional narratives of the discourse of romance, these books work primarily by providing terms, images, and stories by which love is understood, relationships are constituted, and lives are forecast.

Greater Expectations and Other Problems

Giddens concludes *The Transformation of Intimacy* with a chapter entitled "Intimacy as Democracy." By this point in the book, it has already become clear that it is more than a mere discussion of an historical transformation. It is in fact a theoretical argument written in the discourse of intimacy. As I have suggested above, I believe that the discourse of intimacy does embody important democratizing impulses. It has, I agree, contributed to what Giddens calls "the democratization of personal life."[53] The new sense of "intimacy" means something substantially more than "companionship," in both senses in which that term has been used. Intimacy assumes companionship as a condition but does not regard it as sufficient. In its most complete manifestations, intimacy demands emotional, economic, and political equality of domestic partners. That this demand is emancipatory there can be no doubt.

Built into the discourse of intimacy, however, is a limitation on its transformative capabilities. Recall how Scarf treats the basic conflict between intimacy and autonomy as typically manifesting itself in a man who cannot accept his own need for intimacy and a woman who cannot accept her need for autonomy. Scarf allows that this typical pattern is sometimes reversed, and she thus avoids treating gender roles as if they were natural conditions. But not all, and perhaps not many, writers of self-help books treat gender in this way, a problem that is at least partly structural to the genre. Current gender roles are part of the context of the problems that these books are meant to solve. While a change in such roles might also be a solution, intimacy advice does not take that route. Such writers assume, probably accurately enough, that gender roles are difficult to change and that individuals seeking better relationships are looking for ways that will work under present conventions. Thus, they accept the status quo.

This limitation on the transformative potential of advice books obtains even for writers like Scarf who do not naturalize gender roles, since they do not make challenging these roles central to their projects. However, if Scarf's understanding of relationships were internalized by both parties, it could be argued that the result would be a change in gender roles. The same cannot be said for many other writers in this genre. Tannen, who as an academic is doubtless more often exposed to feminist critique, concludes her book with a chapter entitled "Living with Asymmetry," an explicit defense of her naturalization of gender. "Not only do we not escape . . . discrimination in our most intimate relationships, but we can hardly conceive of them apart from gender-based alignments that are inherently asymmetrical—implying differences in status."[54] She makes clear that she believes this condition is not a cultural convention but a result of "physical constellations" rooted in nature. In explicit opposition to many feminist and queer theorists, Tannen asserts that "gender is a category that will not go away."[55] Even if that claim is persuasive, however, it does not follow that genders will always be categorized as they are now, but Tannen writes as if the current gender arrangements were inevitable.

More troubling than Tannen are those writers who not only take for granted current gender roles but also actively endorse them. The most extreme example of this kind is Gray, whose title *Men Are from Mars, Women Are from Venus* makes the problem plain. Gray treats men and women as if they were different species with utterly contrasting natures. Men and women are "supposed to be different," Gray claims, and, though he doesn't reveal whose supposition is being invoked here, that sounds very much like a theological statement.[56] Every section of his book emphasizes some way in which men and women are completely different. Indeed, the entire premise of the book is that these two species "speak different languages" and thus need to be taught to interpret each other if communication is to succeed. The book reads like a series of exercises in decoding, the assumption being that the surface text of the partner's speech is never to be trusted. So invested in the essential opposition of male and female is Gray that he resorts to binaries that collapse without the need of explicit deconstruction. Thus, women need "validation," but men need "approval"; women need "reassurance," while men need "encouragement."[57] These are distinctions without differences, but Gray needs them in order to reinforce the gender roles on which his advice depends. Clearly, books like *Men Are from Mars* perpetuate, rather than transform, the current state of gender relations structured by male domination. Moreover, I don't think it is a coincidence that *Men Are from Mars* is by far the largest seller of the books discussed here. By endorsing gender essentialism, Gray was able to simplify his advice and also could tap into a more conservative readership than could, say, Scarf.

This tendency to accept and even endorse the status quo in gender roles is only one reason why I am skeptical of the larger utopianism of Giddens's conclusion. Leaving aside the highly questionable notion that intimacy will bring about large-scale social change "from the bottom up," there are much more immediate, internal problems to be mentioned.[58] The most obvious concerns the scale of the transformation, the degree to which the "pure relationship" has actually made, as Giddens claims, heterosexual marriage "just one life-style among others."[59] The recent "Defense of Marriage Act," which exempted states from recognizing homosexual marriages that might become official in other states, would seem to indicate that it is a rather small degree. That is especially true since no state actually does recognize marriages other than heterosexual, and only Vermont has created any form of legal recognition for homosexual relationships. Moreover, as I have argued, intimacy advice books exhibit a bias in favor of heterosexual marriage even when the legitimacy of other relationships is recognized.

Of course, it could be argued that the "Defense of Marriage Act" demonstrates the weakness rather than the strength of the traditional role of marriage, since it would not need to be defended were it not under some form of "attack." So Giddens may be right about the replacement of marriage by the pure relationship as a trend, but there remains a more insidious problem with his evaluation of the new intimacy. Some of the advice books written in this discourse may offer a genuine vision of liberation, but they also entail a kind of coercion. The "mechanisms" of intimacy, as Giddens rightly calls them, are not neutral, whatever their usefulness.[60] The premium that the intimacy model places on communication and self-revelation makes it much like the "discipline" that Michel Foucault has shown to define modern institutions, including the factory, the school, and the prison.[61] The therapies and exercises prescribed in intimacy advice literature are extensions of the technologies of the soul Foucault describes, for example, the confession of the Church and of the psychoanalytic couch.[62] While they offer a certain kind of self-control, a form of freedom, they also may, like a virus in a cell, represent an alien power that takes over from the inside. The intimacy model threatens to bring the confession out of the consulting room and into the bedroom.

Foucault's own constant reminder that power is productive should caution us against assuming that intimacy therapies are necessarily repressive. They can be productive of liberatory change. But several conditions are cause for concern. For one thing, all of this psychic technology is being used in the service of attaining a state that cannot be defined with any clarity. Freud said that a healthy individual was one who could love and work. While this is doubtless more difficult than it sounds, it is baby stuff compared to the task of trying to decide if you have reached intimacy. More troubling still is the fact that the therapies that advice books recommend often involve the internalization of oppressive social conditions. To perform Gray's readings and his exercises is to accept—without being explicitly asked to assent to—gender roles defined by male dominance.

Even if we discount concerns about internalizing oppressive technologies or oppressive social hierarchies, however, it is still not entirely clear that intimacy represents an unambiguous improvement over romance. One of the chief complaints about the vision of romantic marriage articulated in the 1920s was that it raised expectations of matrimony far beyond what that relationship could actually yield. While the discourse of intimacy may at first seem to offer more modest expectations than did romance, this is not always, and perhaps not even often, the case. If the discourse of romance promised enduring passion and spiritual transcendence, the discourse of intimacy promises "love that will last a lifetime" and psychological transcendence. It says that you can have autonomy and intimacy at the same time without conflict, in you or in the relationship. Moreover, the degree of promised closeness may be as extreme as the degree of rapture promised by romance. The intimate partner is not merely a companion but a soul mate. Anything less seems to be grounds for therapy or for searching elsewhere. In this way, intimacy may become just as productive of dissatisfaction as romance has been. The discourse of intimacy doubtless entails its own illusions, but they may be much harder to recognize in their masquerade as truth.

6

Relationship Stories

In a relationship you're just screwing the guy. In a meaningful relationship you're screwing him and also he's your best friend.
—Alison Lurie, *The War between the Tates*

The love story is so familiar in our culture that we rarely give it a second thought. "Boy gets girl, boy loses girl, boy gets girl back" is exhibit A of standard plots in all fictional media. As we have seen, print fiction and movies of the first half of the century were typically told in the discourse of romance, focusing on courtship leading to marriage. So it is significant that beginning in the 1970s a new film genre emerged dealing with relationships rather than the inevitable pairing of love and marriage.[1] These "relationship stories" are perhaps the strongest evidence we have that the discourse of intimacy has broad influence in our culture and is not restricted to popular psychology. By taking the relationship—rather than courtship, marriage, or adultery—as their primary subject, these films provide strong confirmation for the idea of a fundamental transformation in the way that intimate relations are understood and practiced.

Like the self-help books discussed in the previous chapter, relationship stories are also a response to the crisis in marriage, but, as we will see, they are a different sort of response. The advice books are aimed primarily at helping married people stay married or be more happily married, although they may be used by single people hoping to have more successful relationships. The relationship stories I'll be discussing here, with the exception of *Husbands and Wives,* are devoted mainly to the condition of being single. They are not about courtship in the way that traditional romantic comedies are. Marriage may have been part of the main characters' past and may be part of their future, but it typically is not their present state. Moreover, the basic condition of life that these films take for granted is serial-monogamous relationships that may or may not be marriages. If the ideal of nonfictional intimacy discourse remains "until death do us part," most of the films under discussion seem to assume that for most people that ideal is impossible. Like the advice books, relationship stories tell us about how relationships work, but their function is not to help us have better relationships. It is rather to help us cope with the reality that our relationships are likely not to work.

The genre of the relationship story is characterized by innovations in both form and content. Formally, these films often deviate from what has been called the "realism" of studio-era Hollywood. That is, they do not tell their stories in a way that seems to discourage the audience from thinking about the *telling* of the story and to encourage them to think only about what is being told. Relationship stories use various devices to frame the material, often with the effect of making the story seem like autobiography or confession. The devices could be called "reflexive" because they draw attention to the medium of cinema, and they render relationship stories a genre that has much in common with the nonfictional case history.

Relationship stories are also reflexive in their treatment of relationships. Instead of just depicting them, these films constantly offer comments on relationships, sometimes in dialogue, sometimes in asides or "interviews." This commentary renders relationships in general as a problem, rather than merely as the topic of the film. The content of the stories the relationship genre tells reflects the social reality that a majority no longer falls in love and marries only once in a lifetime. Thus, these films do not typically follow the old marriage or adultery plots. Rather, as the name suggests, their plots typically start from the premise of serial relationships that may or may not be marriages. A relationship, for purposes of these films, is any continuing sexual association between two people. As a result, sex is no longer the implicit payoff of these narratives but rather another aspect of the relationships they depict. Finally, since serial relationships are assumed to be the norm, the ending of these films can't be read as fully comic or fully tragic in the manner of earlier romance genres. While relationship stories end both "happily" and "sadly," no ending can ever be assumed to be final. Another breakup or another relationship is always possible, if not likely.

Fictional Case Histories

It is a curious condition of the films I will focus on in this chapter that they do not typically tell a story simply and directly. Often relationship stories are told using flashbacks and other complex chronologies. Even more frequently, these films frame their stories using such devices as voice-over narration, "witness" or character interviews, and stand-up comedy. These devices exist entirely or partially outside the story, or diagesis. They typically distance the audience from the action, reminding us that what we are seeing is a film, a version, a construction, a work of art, but not the "reality" in the sense that studio-era films seem to offer. Yet the effect of this framing is not to render the film less real but to render it all the more real. The simple story of older Hollywood films is now understood by most viewers as a fantasy, the illusion of reality. What the films of Woody Allen, Albert Brooks, Paul Mazursky, Rob Reiner, and others give us is the reality of personal experience: a subjective reality that is the more real for being admittedly subjective.

This style of storytelling is the fiction-film equivalent of the case history. The opening of *Annie Hall* (1977) defines what follows as the confession of its protagonist, Alvy Singer. We see Woody Allen, the co-writer, director, and leading man of the film, addressing the camera. We will learn that he is playing Alvy in this scene, but that would not have been immediately obvious to most viewers in 1977, who would have known Woody Allen as a stand-up comedian. Moreover, *Annie Hall*, like many of Allen's films, depends on the conventions of autobiography. This is one reason why audiences typically assume that these films are literally autobiographical.[2] So even if the film is presented as Alvy Singer's story, that story is told as if Alvy Singer were a nonfictional person, a strategy that works because of the audience's conflation of Woody and Alvy. The initial address to the camera, for example, is part comic monologue, but it is also part personal confession. Woody Allen's stand-up routines also invoked confession, but the opening of *Annie Hall* goes beyond Allen's routines in the degree to which it asks the audience not just to laugh but also to empathize with the speaker. Alvy in this opening address is both performing and engaging in serious self-revelation and analysis, and the audience is thus invited to experience the story that follows as a continuation of the latter.

In his monologue, Alvy tells two jokes that he offers as keys to his own personality. The first joke tells us about his attitude toward life: "Two elderly women are at a Catskill mountain resort, and one of 'em says, 'Boy, the food at this place is really terrible.' The other one says, 'Yeah, I know, and such small portions.'" Alvy immediately glosses the joke: "That's essentially how I feel about life. Full of loneliness and misery and suffering and unhappiness, and it's all over much too quickly." Alvy will later tell Annie (Diane Keaton) what is in effect another version of this same joke, that all people may be divided into the horrible and the miserable: the former being those with unusually severe afflictions, the latter being everyone else. The cynicism of this joke is one aspect of Alvy's character, but besides its general pessimism, it may be read as a more particular statement of the film's main point about relationships. That won't become clear until the very end of the movie, however.

The second joke serves as an analysis of Alvy's problems in relationships. The joke, attributed by Alvy to both Groucho Marx and Freud, goes, "I would never want to belong to any club that would have someone like me as a member." Alvy tells us, "That's the key joke of my adult life in terms of my relationships with women," and then goes on to admit that he has been going through some sort of "life crisis" associated with turning forty. If the first joke expresses an attitude, this one clearly reveals a condition, emphasizing Alvy's presentation as a "case."

Alvy follows the jokes with another revelation, one that comes in the middle of the part of this opening address that is most like a stand-up routine. Alvy has been going on about what kind of old man he will become but interrupts himself with a sigh. It is as if the speaker, like a patient with his analyst, knows that he has been avoiding the very subject about which he most needs to talk. If the monologue up to this point could all have been a stand-up routine, Alvy's tone of voice and facial expression prohibit us from understanding the following as anything other than a confession: "Annie and I broke up, and I still can't get my mind around that. You know, I keep sifting the pieces of the relationship through my mind and examining my life and trying to figure out where did the screw-up come." On second viewing, we realize how unusual this statement is and how risky for Allen as a filmmaker, for it reveals the outcome of the narrative the film will tell. We know from the start that we are watching a movie about a failed relationship. At an earlier point in film history, this could only have been the beginning of a melodrama or a farce, but *Annie Hall* is neither of these.

Alvy's confession of the relationship's failure does more than give away the film's ending, however, for it also frames the story as Alvy's reflection on the relationship, as his sifting the pieces through his mind and examining his life. It will be the pieces that we will see. While the film does tell us the story of Alvy and Annie's relationship from beginning to end, it does not tell it in chronological order, and it is intercut with flashbacks to Alvy's life before this relationship and by other interruptions. Given all of this fragmentation, it is not surprising that *Annie Hall* doesn't present a continuous narrative in which events seem to follow from one another. Rather, we get vignettes that are meant to typify the relationship, giving us the feel of a life being examined. The first scenes we see after the opening monologue are of Alvy's childhood. Even the first scene in the film's present involves Alvy expressing his paranoia about anti-Semitism to Rob (Tony Roberts). These scenes don't bear any narrative connection to the story of Alvy and Annie. Rather, they tell us about Alvy's psyche, revealing his neuroses and, perhaps, some of their causes.

Overt confession is not the only way that relationship stories are structured as case histories. The beginning of *Manhattan* (Woody Allen, 1979) suggests a different kind of personal statement. Its story is framed by an opening visual and aural celebration of New York that is not narratively significant. We see incredibly beautiful images of New York while listening to Gershwin's *Rhapsody in Blue*. That this is a highly romantic treatment of the city, however, is acknowledged by the voice-over narration. Five times we hear Woody Allen's voice giving us a different beginning to a book he is writing, and in one of them he admits that he "romanticized [New York] all out of proportion." This opening warns us about the romantic cast of the film we are about to see, while it also alerts us to its ambition to be an "art" film. It tells us not only that *Manhattan* has pretensions to move beyond mere entertainment but also that it is presenting a self-consciously constructed world. The black and white photography is meant to remind us, not of documentary realism, but of the fantasy of classic-era Hollywood films. The opening sets the tone of the movie, while at the same time making us aware that someone is setting a tone, that a picture is being created out of a particular sensibility.

Husbands and Wives (Woody Allen, 1992) lacks the introduction we found in *Annie Hall* and *Manhattan*, but it uses many internal framing devices. *Husbands and Wives* works as hard at looking like a documentary as *Manhattan* works at looking like a collection of art photographs. The first thing we notice is the handheld camera, which gives a cinema vérité feel to much of the film, and especially to the first scene. The documentarylike photography is supplemented with interviews with the film's characters, in which they comment on their lives and each other, and with objective voice-over narration. The handheld camera and frequent instances of actors addressing the camera make the film harder to watch than the others I'm discussing here. Even though we are meant to identify more strongly with Gabe Roth (Woody Allen) than the other characters in this film, he is not its center in the way Alvy was in the earlier film. The interviews give voice to most of the major characters, and what they say in them often contradicts other characters' remarks and sometimes even their own earlier statements. We as spectators are asked to evaluate these differing interpretations and claims. This makes *Husbands and Wives* the most case-historical film among the relationship stories, and the one that has moved farthest from the conventions of romantic comedy. Indeed, perhaps the chief popular objection to the film on its release was that it wasn't funny but depressing.

Other directors of relationship stories have not so elaborately framed their films, but most instances do involve some framing. Paul Mazursky's *Blume in Love* (1973) makes use of flashbacks and subjective voice-over narration by the protagonist. Rob Reiner's *When Harry Met Sally* (1989) is less explicit in its framing, but it intercuts witness interviews with episodes of the narrative, which provide another level of reality to compare and contrast with the main story. Of the films I will discuss in this chapter, only Mazursky's *An Unmarried Woman* (1978) lacks explicit framing devices.

This style of storytelling distinguishes the relationship story from most romantic comedy. The screwball comedies I discussed in Chapter 3 do not make use of complex narration. They tell tight, straightforward narratives that begin at the beginning—often with a couple's first meeting—and end at the end—the couple's happy union or reunion. The events that are represented are related to each other by a relentless logic of cause and effect. For the most part, these narratives are unframed; they do not acknowledge a storyteller.

These stories and others typical of the discourse of romance work by engaging the viewer's (or reader's) identification with at least one member of the central couple. I have argued that a major innovation of romance narratives was according subjectivity to the major characters, thus making the love triangle an emotional investment for the audience. Relationship stories typically offer a different sort of subjectivity, one that makes identification more difficult because it is more pervasive. If all of *Annie Hall* is Alvy's confession, then it presents his view of things and not things as they are. We are asked to decide whether we want to identify with Alvy, to accept this point of view or to be skeptical of it. The framing devices and, to a lesser extent, the complex chronology of relationship stories distances their characters from us. Instead of making us want what the hero wants, these films ask us to stand back and analyze him just as he often analyzes himself. The films' humor usually derives from this stance and not from the characters' zany reactions to embarrassing, difficult, or improbable situations, as in screwball comedy. The distancing effects that relationship stories produce don't make it to the level of Brechtian alienation. We still are meant to care about the characters and to understand them realistically, but we are supposed to be aware that we choose to do so.

Relationship School

There are times when these movies seem not merely to share the same assumptions about relationships as contemporary self-help books but actually to be repeating the same advice. If the premise of the discourse of romance is that love is natural and historically unchanging, then romantic stories need not, and perhaps could not, spend their time analyzing or commenting on love. Love used to be something that happened to the characters, its power lying precisely in its not being entirely comprehended by the rational mind. In relationship stories, on the contrary, the characters are almost continually in the process of struggling to comprehend their own feelings and actions, those of their partners, and the patterns of relationships in general. We have already seen how *Annie Hall* begins with a commentary on Alvy's relationships with women, but this is, as I have been arguing, the frame, not the picture. There is also much commentary within the narrative itself, however, presented in dialogue, in asides, or by other more intrusive means. And *Annie Hall* is not at all atypical; the other films in the genre share its penchant for talking about love.

Relationship stories aren't content simply to show us an instance of love; like advice books, they want to get beneath the surface and show how love works. *Annie Hall* offers a particularly telling instance of this in a scene that uses subtitles to reveal what Alvy and Annie are thinking as they converse with each other. Revealed in this scene are the insecurities the two feel in first getting to know each other. While this is hardly a surprising revelation, the idea that we are able to see into the characters' minds is emblematic of what the film as a whole is doing. Later in the film, we hear Annie and Alvy's private thoughts as they both consider ending the relationship. These devices reveal conscious but unexpressed thoughts. Flashbacks to Alvy's childhood add another dimension, opening up his unconscious to scrutiny. Just as some of the advice books often claimed that a person's family history is a key to understanding current behavior in relationships, Allen suggests that Alvy's childhood can help us to understand his relationship with Annie.

Interestingly, *Annie Hall* is the only film I'm discussing in this chapter in which the lovers' families play any role at all. In the screwball comedies, fathers and mothers, aunts and uncles, or other relatives are almost always present. In relationship stories, friends replace relatives as the chief social grouping. This is doubtless an accurate reflection of the declining significance of blood relations in the social lives of urban Americans, but it also is another indication of the relative insignificance of marriage in these films. Friends provide emotional support in many of these films, and in several they serve up advice about relationships to the protagonists. *An Unmarried Woman,* for example, features a group of women who meet regularly and discuss their relationships. Their emotional bonds mirror the female friendships described in books like Deborah Tannen's, although here they seem to compensate for the absence of emotional closeness in these women's relationships with men. At the beginning of the film, only Erica has what she believes to be a satisfactory relationship. These friends provide a dark image of the state of modern love, illustrating the difficulties of being married or single.

Psychoanalysis was the first theory that claimed to be able to understand interior and unrevealed mental processes of others. One way that relationship stories are able to work commentary into their narratives is by referring to or depicting psychotherapy. Psychoanalysis figures in all three of the Woody Allen films I'm discussing here, and there are scenes of therapy in both of Mazursky's films. These explicit references make it clear that cinematic relationship stories are as much indebted to the talking cure as are the self-help books.

Annie Hall contains only a few scenes that actually take place in the consulting room. Rather, analysis is more often invoked in dialogue between the characters. One instance where we do see the protagonists in therapy is a scene late in the film in which both characters are shown in split screen in their psychiatrists' offices. Alvy has played the role of Annie's teacher throughout most of the movie, a fact underlined by repeated dialogue about him encouraging Annie to take adult education classes. But in this scene Annie explains to her analyst that she refused to have sex with Alvy the other night, something that she wouldn't have done before her therapy: "Since our discussions here, I feel I have a right to my own feelings. I think you woulda been happy because I really asserted myself." Alvy is paying for Annie's analysis, which he begins to resent when it leads her to feel less dependent upon him and threatens the relationship: "I'm paying for her analysis and she's making progress and I'm getting screwed. . . . She's making progress and I'm not making any progress. Her progress is defeating my progress."

Several issues are illustrated in this piece of dialogue. The first is that, in spite of its ubiquity, psychoanalysis is not treated as a panacea or miracle cure. Indeed, while all of the characters in Allen's relationship stories seem to have analysts, apparently such analysis is interminable. Moreover, several of these analysts are depicted as worse off than their patients. In *Manhattan,* one of them weeps to his patient over the phone and later is unavailable because of a bad acid trip. In *Husbands and Wives,* an analyst ends treatment so that he can sleep with his much younger patient. Alvy's lack of progress, then, seems to be par for the course of therapy. The fact that Annie is making progress illustrates another pattern typical of Allen's relationship stories. Alvy has been the teacher throughout most of the relationship, but here we see his pupil beginning to develop out of that role. She is learning to be her own person, someone who is more capable of having a successful relationship.

A similar pattern occurs in *Manhattan,* where the character played by Allen, Ike, is clearly presented as Tracy's (Mariel Hemingway) teacher in matters of history and art. Like Erica in *An Unmarried Woman,* Tracy will in the end refuse her lover's request that she abandon her work to stay with him. As in Alvy's relationship with Annie, there is an imbalance of power in this relationship. What is new in *Manhattan* is that this imbalance seems to trouble Ike. He is attracted to Mary (Diane Keaton) because she is willing to argue with him rather than accept his intellectual superiority. This pattern, which will be treated again in *Husbands and Wives,* presents a problem of conflicting desires. In retrospect, Ike describes his relationship with Tracy as "relaxed," but it is clear that there is an excitement in Mary's challenge to him that Tracy did not provide. Ike wants both comfort and excitement, but the two don't go together. *Manhattan* does not present Tracy merely as Ike's protégé. In matters of ethics, it is Tracy who is the teacher. It is she who utters the film's two

Manhattan: The "little girl," Tracy (Mariel Hemingway) is taller and wiser than Ike (Woody Allen).

most unambiguous messages. When Ike breaks up with Tracy, he questions what she means by saying that she loves him—in fact questions whether anyone knows what love is—and she responds: "We have laughs together. I care about you. Your concerns are my concerns. We have great sex." This clear definition, at once both simple and profound, suggests that she has thought about the matter more deeply and seriously than has Ike, and perhaps more deeply and seriously than Ike is capable of thinking. Later in the same scene, when Tracy objects to Ike's trying to make it seem as though his breaking up with her is to her advantage, Ike's response is to say, "Don't be so precocious." He will offer a similar response at the end of the film when Tracy tells him why she is going to England to study acting, repeating an argument that he has earlier offered her about the value of this experience. It is Ike at this point who clearly seems immature and unreasonable in his assertion that she shouldn't go. Tracy's response to him, "You need to have a little faith in people," is the film's closing line. Not only does it seem like the position the film is taking on the events it has depicted, but it is also a specific rebuke to Ike's behavior throughout.

Men in relationship stories usually discover that they needed a relationship more than they believed they did. Women, on the other hand, often develop a different sort of self-knowledge, a reflection of the new reality of women's increasing independence in the wake of second-wave feminism. Most of the relationship stories feature women who learn that they can trust themselves and survive on their own. This is another reversal of the screwball comedies, where women typically learn that they can't be happy on their own. Both Mazursky's films feature a woman's developing independence as their main course of action, though in *Blume in Love* we see it from the man's point of view, while in *An Unmarried Woman* we see it from hers. Independence in these films doesn't mean not being in a relationship. Rather it means being in one as an equal, not an inferior, not, to use a somewhat anachronistic term for these 1970s films, as a "codependent."

Blume in Love begins with Blume's wife Nina (Susan Anspach) coming home to find him in bed with his secretary. Blume (George Segal) is surprised when Nina throws him out, and he spends the rest of the movie trying to win her back. Pauline Kael called this movie "a hip updating of *The Awful Truth*," and it does begin and end in a similar way, with an infidelity and a reconciliation.[3] But *The Awful Truth* offers us no sense of the heroine's development, or the hero's, for that matter. In that movie, the estranged husband, Jerry (Cary Grant), was planning to marry someone else until his soon to be ex-wife, Lucy (Irene Dunne) dragged him away, the point being that their separation was a mistake. That's not the point of *Blume in Love* because Blume's transgression gives Nina the opportunity to discover herself. Her decision to take Blume back makes sense only because she has been away from him and can understand why she is doing it. This may be why Nina lacks any comic dimension. The humor is provided by Segal's Blume and Kris Kristofferson's Elmo, the man Nina takes up with after the separation.

In *An Unmarried Woman* we find Erica (Jill Clayburgh) being left by her husband Martin (Michael Murphy) for a younger woman. Erica believed herself to be happily married, and her husband's revelation is devastating. The movie's plot involves neither the remarriage to Martin that we would expect from a studio-era film nor even a marriage to someone new. Rather it is the story of a woman's development as an independent

An Unmarried Woman: Martin's (Michael Murphy's) confession that he is having an affair is as traumatic for him as for his wife, Erica (Jill Clayburgh).

person. As Erica explains late in the film, after having struggled to reach such understanding, "The problem was that I did everything as 'Martin and Erica' and not as me." Thus, although she finds a relationship with Saul (Alan Bates), who loves her and who is very clearly not a repetition of Martin, Erica nevertheless refuses to leave her job and go away with him. The film ends, not with a marriage, but with a relationship that may or may not weather this conflict. In this film's world, marriage is not the key to happiness.

If women often seem to make progress in relationship stories, the male characters, who are most often significantly flawed, usually do not. This is true especially of the characters Allen himself portrays, even though the association of these characters with the writer and director of the films may make this hard to perceive. If the women in Allen's films are often depicted as his students, the characters he plays are the ones most in need of relationship school. Yet these characters seem in some sense incorrigible. They are prone to repeat the same patterns. For example, although

Alvy is able to see that he seems to want only women who will reject him, that knowledge doesn't help him to change. Ike learns that he should have stuck with Tracy, but it is unclear whether he learns the larger lessons she articulates. It is pretty clear that Gabe learns nothing at all, except that he seems to make the same mistakes over and over again. Mazursky's men don't develop either. Blume exists in a romantic time warp, in love with the wife who left him and trying to relive their history together. It is the romantic aspect of this film that his persistence is finally rewarded. Martin, like the other men, also learns only that he made a mistake, but in this case not in time to win Erica back. The way these male characters are drawn seems to illustrate Giddens's point that men typically lag far behind women, "the emotional revolutionaries of modernity," in the ability to construct their own emotional narratives and thus continue to "have problems with intimacy."[4] Two other members of the genre, Albert Brooks's *Defending Your Life* (1991) and Stephen Frears's *High Fidelity* (1999), make this male inadequacy their premise and tell stories about men who finally can overcome it. Men in these films grow up by recognizing their need for intimacy, rather than by learning to deny it, as was the case in *Casablanca*.

There is another lesson common to relationship stories that *An Unmarried Woman* puts into the mouth of the psychiatrist, Tanya (Penelope Russianoff), whom Erica visits in an attempt to recover from the loss. If the shrinks in Allen's films are typically excuses for the characters to reveal themselves, Mazursky here gives us a much more interactive therapist in scenes that are at the same time funny, moving, and almost too real to be comfortably watched. The humor derives in part from Russianoff's Buster Keaton–like stone face and the New Age atmosphere of her office where the doctor and Erica face each other in the lotus position. Erica's confessions also have their humorous aspects—for example, her telling about getting her first period—but when she describes her loneliness in the wake of her divorce it is hard not to cry right along with her. What makes the sessions both convincingly real and difficult to watch is their slow pace and lack of clear direction. We are made to feel Erica's confusion and her fear. Tanya's lack of emotion contributes to our unease. We want her to comfort Erica, but what she does instead is ask difficult questions and give hard advice. Most important, she says that if she were in Erica's situation that she would "get back into the stream of life" and start seeing some new men. The answer to Erica's loneliness is to risk a new relationship. This is, in a nutshell, the basic lesson of the relationship stories. Though your relationships have all been bad, there is always hope that the next one will be better.

As usual, it is *Annie Hall* that articulates this last position most directly. At the end of the film, Alvy tells a joke in voice-over. "This guy goes to a psychiatrist and says, 'Doc, uh, my brother's crazy. He thinks he's a chicken.' And, uh, the doctor says, 'Well, why don't you turn him in?' And the guy says, "I would but I need the eggs."' Then Alvy glosses the joke: "Well, I guess that's pretty much how I feel about relationships. You know, they're totally irrational and crazy and absurd and . . . but, uh, I guess we keep going through it because most of us need the eggs." This is, of course, another version of the same paradox that was presented in the joke about the two women in the Catskills. Both jokes are about persisting in spite of a lack of a rational payoff for one's efforts. The second version is both softer and bleaker, for the payoff is not bad food but illusory food. Coming immediately after we have seen a reading of Alvy's first play, in which art improves on life by having the fictional Annie come back to Alvy, "I need the eggs" provides an oddly upbeat end to the film even though its message is cynical. It says, "I know very well that relationships do not give me what I need, but still, I will persist in behaving as if they did." But the shift in pronouns in the last sentence—"*we* keep going through it because most of *us* need the eggs"—renders Alvy no longer perverse but normal. Like Alvy, the film suggests, we all persist in trying to find the right relationship despite the pain and the odds.

Perhaps the explanation for this cynicism, which is an aspect of this group of films as a whole, is that although relationships are analyzed and patterns revealed, there is little hope offered for better relationships. Clearly, if only women are portrayed as making progress, heterosexual relationships are not likely to improve. But there is another limitation that seems built into the genre rather than an aspect of modern love itself: these films cannot show the way out of the patterns they depict. Consider once again Alvy's joke about not wanting to join a club that would accept him as a member. It could be read as a statement about desire in general, as in the psychoanalytic theory of Jacques Lacan: desire can exist as desire only so long as it remains unsatisfied. The Alvy of the joke has found the perfect object to sustain desire, the club that will not allow him to join. But in the advice books discussed in the last chapter, problems like Alvy's are not treated as fundamental to human subjectivity. Rather, they are described as potentially correctable patterns of learned behavior. Thus, Alvy's penchant for women who will reject him might be interpreted as his participation in the pursuit/distance model. He is the pursuer who depends on the distancer he is chasing not to allow herself to be caught. This is borne out by the events of the film. Alvy is clearly the pursuer in the beginning of the relationship, and he will end up in that role as well. But when Annie decides that they should live together, Alvy pulls back. He doesn't want Annie to give up her apartment, and is willing to pay the rent so she can hang onto it. But unlike the advice literature, *Annie Hall* offers us neither a name nor an explanation for Alvy's perversity, much less instructions on how he might break out of the pattern. As a result, the lessons this film and the others like it teach seem entirely academic.

The Problem of Sex

Viewers of screwball and other romantic comedies know that it is such a film's job to get the central couple married off. What make up the individual stories of these films are the obstacles to that end, an end that nevertheless must remain officially in doubt. Metaphorically, as I have suggested, these films can be read as extended episodes of foreplay in which consummation is deferred as long as possible. More literally, the films depict the sanctioned form of courtship of the period in which sex was postponed until after marriage. By the 1970s, sex had become a part of "courtship." A film in which a couple in love did not have sex would have seemed like a Doris Day movie—that is, hopelessly out of date. The structure of the relationship story had to evolve into a different form than that of the love story. Now sex marks the beginning of the relationship, but it also becomes a central problem for the couple as the relationship develops.

Sex is *the* problem in *Annie Hall*. It is the most significant issue between Alvy and Annie, and it is depicted as a difficulty in Alvy's previous relationships. In a scene with his first wife, Allison (Carol Kane), Alvy obsesses about the Kennedy assassination as a way to avoid having sex. At a party with his second wife, Robin (Janet Margolin), Alvy tries to get her to have sex with him in the bedroom to which he has retreated to watch basketball on television. She responds, "You're using sex to express hostility." In the next scene, Robin and Alvy's lovemaking is interrupted by a siren. The city makes her too tense, but he can't live in the country. The scene concludes with Alvy going off to "take another in a series of cold showers." But even before we have witnessed these flashbacks, we have already seen that sex is a source of conflict between Alvy and Annie. It is significant that in one of their first scenes together we see Annie tell Alvy that she doesn't want to have sex with him. We see this before we are shown an earlier time in their relationship when sex was good between them. The effect of this chronology is to render the good sex of the beginning of the relationship an exception. As a rule, sex is a problem.

In *Husbands and Wives* there are sexual difficulties for both of the original married couples, one pair fighting over whether to do it, the other not finding their sex satisfying. And it's not just Woody Allen who defines sex as a problem. In *When Harry Met Sally,* the first time the two protagonists have sex, it nearly ruins their relationship. Friendship is defined in this film in opposition to sex. Although one of the earliest scenes in *An Unmarried Woman* shows Erica dancing ecstatically around her apartment after she has just made love to her husband, we soon see the almost obligatory example of him wanting to when she does not. Sex is even more of a problem after Erica has become an unmarried woman. It's a problem for Blume also, who rapes his estranged wife when she refuses his advances. How did what used to be the unstated but obvious goal of romantic comedy come to be a constant source of strife in relationship stories?

The "sexual revolution" of the 1960s is the essential background to this change, for it entailed shifts both in sexual practices and in what could be represented on screen. Woody Allen's career as a stand-up comic and some of his earlier films—for example, *Everything You Always Wanted Know about Sex* (1972)—strongly reflect the moment of this change. As Adam Gopnik observes, the ideal to which Allen's early comedy aspired was the *Playboy* lifestyle.[5] The persona Allen created was a frustrated lecher, the nebbish who thought only about sex. This is a character who could have been brought to life only after the lifting of censorship in the 1960s, but he is a product of pre-1960s sexual restrictions. The sexual revolution, enabled by the new birth control pill, made premarital sex the norm, while at the same time it became possible for sex to be openly discussed and represented on the screen.

The rise of feminism also contributed to the new sexual attitudes and practices. We have already seen how the new assumption of women's independence is one of the realities that relationship stories represent, and feminism also made sex something that couldn't be presented as if the male point of view were the natural one. Gopnik thinks that feminism has made lechery unfunny because it is not politically correct, but the reality is much more complicated.[6] Feminism certainly helped make sex the problem that relationship stories take it to be. Feminist thought has sought to question the assumed naturalness of sex that made the *Playboy* lifestyle seem like an ideal. But as I have argued, feminism also made it possible for women to imagine their own ideals, which typically conflict with *Playboy*'s. Not all post-1960s films significantly reflect these changes, but the relationship stories do. This does not mean that these films are "feminist" in their politics. Rather, it means that they depict situations in which the effects of feminism are felt. For example, there are no women in the relationship stories who work only in the home. Woody Allen may be the misogynist he is sometimes made out to be, but the heroines of most of his films up through *Husbands and Wives* are successful career women.

That sex is at least as much a problem as a pleasure in relationship stories may be these films' acknowledgment of the same reality the advice books mark by their almost obligatory discussion of sexual mechanics and technique. In the discourse of romance, the sexual act, though never present explicitly, was always taken to be a pleasure. Marriage, at least in the post-nineteenth-century, fairy-tale formulation of romance, derived its value from the fact that in it the unfulfilled desires of courtship could be satisfied. In the older, tragic formula for romance, marriage was presented as devoid of sexual pleasure, but such pleasure could be reliably discovered in adultery. Now that we have liberated ourselves from sexual restrictions and ignorance, sexual pleasure ought to be available in the relationships we choose to make, yet the evidence of the discourse of intimacy suggests that it is not readily so.

If the advice literature suggests that the solution to this dilemma lies both in greater knowledge and in better communication, the films seem to offer no solutions at all. The implication is that sexual problems are actually a reflection of deeper difficulties in the relationship. Thus, Alvy's avoiding sex with his first wife and Annie's avoiding it with Alvy seem to have little to do with any inadequacy of technique. But while the other chapters of advice books might help these couples, the films show them as much more likely to end their relationships rather than to work on them. If the advice writing shows a bias toward marriage—that is, toward staying in one's present marriage—relationship stories seem to reflect a different bias. While they are not opposed to marriage, they assume that marriages and other relationships are likely to fail.

Images of Romance

In intimacy advice books, we saw the discourse of romance subsumed into a moment or element of the intimacy process. In most of the films that tell relationship stories, romance also figures in a subsidiary way. Typically, romance in these films is represented not in the plot but in images that depict couples behaving romantically. In treating romance in this way, these films repeat a conception that is familiar to many viewers. As Eva Illouz observes, romance today is often understood as a discrete moment defined by special objects, settings, and activities, most of which are available as commodities. Print advertising often conjures up romantic associations by presenting a happy couple consuming appropriately.[7] Most relationship stories include similar tableaux. Although these scenes do, of course, involve action, they are discrete moments that contrast with the film as a whole. They thus differ from the "green world" (or Connecticut) of the screwball comedies, in which romance had a distinct space where most of the film's events often took place. Moreover, in the relationship stories, the action that takes place in these romantic moments is almost never pivotal. Relationship stories typically turn on moments of strife rather than moments of bliss. Romance is reduced to an aspect of relationships, and often one that seems quite ephemeral. The way the memory of Venice is used in *Blume in Love* illustrates this point, contrasting as it does with the tawdry reality of the Los Angeles where most of the film takes place.

There is, however, a sense in which many of these films use the entire visual world they create as a romantic backdrop. This is perhaps most obvious in Woody Allen's use of the cityscape of Manhattan, but Mazursky in *An Unmarried Woman* and Reiner in *When Harry Met Sally* also use New York to the same effect. Indeed, it may be the look of many relationship stories that results in our perceiving them to be romantic. *Manhattan* may be the film where this use of romance is most apparent. Gordon Willis's beautiful black and white photography turns almost every scene into a romantic image, but many scenes are especially appropriate as romantic settings. Some locations—the museums, for example, or Central Park—are romantic spots by virtue of what they are. Others are transformed by the way they are shot. The famous long shot of Ike and Mary silhouetted against the dawn over the East River and the Fifty Ninth Street Bridge is merely the most powerful of *Manhattan*'s many romantic images.

Manhattan: A museum is a setting for romance between Mary (Diane Keaton) and Ike (Woody Allen).

It's not just the look but also the sound of relationship stories that often gives them a romantic cast. Adding to the romantic character of *Manhattan*'s locations and photography is the lush music of George Gershwin. Since this music is used throughout the film, it complements the gorgeous images in lending a sense of romance to the film as a whole, a sense that is at least sometimes at odds with the events of the story. While *Rhapsody in Blue* is romantic music, Gershwin's popular songs have romantic lyrics that are evoked by the music even when the words are not present on the sound track. Many relationship stories make use of Tin Pan Alley standards, songs from another era that continue to be familiar to today's audiences. Why are these songs especially appropriate? They are, of course, romantic, but in what sense? Is it more than the personal tastes of the filmmakers that exclude the work of contemporary singer-songwriters that would seem to have more in common with the stories these films tell?

The standards of the pre–World War II era typically do not celebrate the innocent, uncomplicated love associated with fairy-tale romance; rather, they deal with people for whom romance is a source of pain and disappointment. Yet these songs remain romantic in the sense that the love they depict is an eternal condition and not something the songs themselves analyze. Cole Porter's "What Is This Thing Called Love," which plays during the beginning and end credits of *Husbands and Wives,* reflects this film's sense of the intractability of the problems of marriage but in a softer, romantic light than the film itself throws. The popular standards used in these films deal directly with the problems of love the films explore, but they also romanticize these problems and lend that romance to our experience of the story. Songs by, say, Joni Mitchell, might be overkill when used in comedies that are already so serious and analytic.

Manhattan is probably Woody Allen's most romantic movie. Among his relationship stories, only *Hannah and Her Sisters* might be said to compete for this distinction, its unusual happy ending perhaps suggesting that we give it the nod. What interests me about *Manhattan* is that the film continues to feel like an affirmation of romance even without a happy ending. *Manhattan* was the first film Woody Allen made after *Annie Hall,* and when it appeared, it was generally treated as a repetition—perhaps superior to the original—of many of the same themes. While there are many similarities, the two films also differ significantly. For one thing, *Annie Hall* is a film in which marriage figures only slightly. Alvy's two marriages are shown in flashback, but they are merely other relationships, more like his relationship with Annie than not. In *Manhattan*, on the other hand, marriage becomes much more of an issue. Again, the protagonist, Ike Davis, has had two previous marriages, but this time we see him interact in the present with one of his ex-wives with whom he has had a child and who during the course of the film publishes a book about their breakup. More important, the film's plot revolves around an affair between Ike's friend Yale (Michael Murphy) and Mary.

Manhattan also differs from *Annie Hall* in the pieces of relationships it depicts. While there are some romantic images and moments in the earlier film—perhaps the most memorable being the scene with the lobsters at the house in the Hamptons—it dwells on difficulties and conflicts. *Manhattan* doesn't give us the analysis of relationships that *Annie Hall* did or *Husbands and Wives* will. These films look at relationships in progress, while *Manhattan*'s focus is on the moments in which relationships form and when they end. In *Manhattan* there is a much higher proportion of scenes in which the couples depicted seem to be enjoying each other. Ike and Tracy are always depicted as a happy couple except in the scene where Ike breaks up with her. The same is true of Ike and Mary, and, in so far as we see them, of Yale and Emily (Anne Byrne). These mostly happy couples fit well against the romantic backdrops I described earlier. We don't see any scenes in *Manhattan* featuring the sexual problems that plague Alvy. On the contrary, the difficulties in the relationships in *Manhattan* seem to be less relational than internal. Alvy, Mary, and Yale all have trouble figuring out whom it is that they want. If Alvy's story is about trying to figure out why his relationships fail, then Ike's story seems to suggest that desire cannot be understood.

Manhattan's use of romantic images and situations fits within the discourse of intimacy, but there is a sense in which *Manhattan* seems to fall back into the older discourse of romance. I have already pointed out that Tracy utters *Manhattan*'s emotional wisdom. Her youth allows her to believe in simple, emotional "truths" that the more sophisticated, older characters can't grasp and that, if uttered by them, would likely be understood by the audience as merely one more "move" in those characters' intellectual or romantic games. But it is hard not to read this view of Tracy as itself highly romantic. Ike decides that Tracy is the right person, and although we are entitled to take this decision with many grains of salt, he implicitly rejects his earlier concern about their differences in age. In the terms *Manhattan* gives us, we cannot but affirm the rightness of Ike and Tracy's relationship, even though the film gives us no grounds to assume that it has a future, much less a successful one. Or is it *because* the relationship has no definite future that it seems romantic and therefore right?

Characteristically, *Manhattan* comments on its own use of romance. In the scene in which Mary tells Ike that she is still in love with Yale, Ike comments that "this is shaping up like a Noël Coward play, you know. Somebody should go out and make some martinis." The line would seem to refer not just to Ike and Mary's relationship but also to the film as a whole. Love triangles, which are insignificant in *Annie Hall,* are foregrounded in *Manhattan*. And while the allusion to Noël Coward is meant to suggest the farcical character of the events, *Manhattan* treats them seriously. It is precisely the achievement of making a very funny movie that does not ultimately trivialize its characters' behavior that renders *Manhattan* Allen's most aesthetically successful work.

Manhattan's romance is tempered by its posing a series of moral or ethical questions. The film does not settle these questions, but it does ask us to consider them. Ike is presented as a moralist. He worries about his relationship with the much younger Tracy, and the audience is also asked to consider the ethics of this relationship. More important for our purposes, the film addresses the ethical implications of serial monogamy and of infidelity under such a system. Ike tells Tracy, "I'm old-fashioned. I don't believe in extramarital relationships. I think people should mate for life, like pigeons or Catholics." But of course, Ike later notes that he "never had a relationship with a woman that lasted longer than the one between Hitler and Eva Braun." He has been unable to live up to his ideal. Tracy poses an alternative vision more in keeping with the reality the film is exploring: "Maybe people weren't meant to have one deep relationship. Maybe they we're meant to have, you know, a series of relationships of different lengths." This debate captures the ambivalence at the heart of *Manhattan*. It wants to preserve the hope of old-fashioned (fairy-tale) romance and the attractive trappings associated with it, while at the same time showing us a world where no one can live such stories.

Perhaps *Manhattan*'s central moral debate occurs in the scene where Ike confronts Yale after Mary has started to see him again. Ike condemns Yale, claiming that "you're too easy on yourself. . . . You rationalized everything. You're not honest with yourself. . . . You cheat a little bit on Emily, and you play around the truth a bit with me, and the next thing you know, you're in front of a Senate committee and you're naming names." Yale responds, "You are so self-righteous, you know. I mean, we're just people, we're just human beings, you know. You think you are God." The fact that this conversation takes place in an anatomy classroom, Ike sharing the screen with a humanoid skeleton, renders it farcical. Both characters are, we clearly understand, defending their own selfish interests. It is easy, I think, to assume that we are supposed to take Ike's position to be Allen's, but this scene makes both characters look foolish while leaving the point they argue unresolved. Relationship stories do not advocate adultery, as older romance narratives did covertly. One of the least romantic scenes in *Manhattan* is the one in which Yale persuades Mary to go off with him for a quick tryst in a hotel room. Unfaithful spouses or lovers are typically held up for ridicule, as Yale is here. Adultery was a much more exciting transgression when marriage was a much more difficult bond to escape legally. Since the reality with which these films deal is one in which marriage is not the only sanctioned relationship, infidelity is both less sexy and less evil. *Manhattan,* like other relationship stories, is about people trying to make new rules as the old ones lose their hold.

Romance in *Manhattan* is pervasive, but it is also tenuous. *When Harry Met Sally* has no reservations about romance, which it affirms in the face of the conflicting evidence of its characters' lives. Nora Ephron's screenplay is full of dialogue reminiscent of Ben Hecht and others who wrote the screwball comedies. It is sharp, fast, stagy talk, unlike the more realist scripts of Allen and Mazursky. And, as in screwball comedy, the dialogue is often scolding or argumentative, suggesting a sort of competition between the lovers. But we don't need to rely on such similarities to demonstrate the film's genealogy. *When Harry Met Sally* makes its connection to studio-era romance explicit in several extended references to *Casablanca,* including the incorporation of clips from that film's ending. This foreshadows *When Harry Met Sally*'s own ending, not in outcome but in style. And like studio-era romantic comedies, this film never leaves any doubt about what the outcome will be. You immediately figure out that Harry and Sally will end up together.

But if this film can be read as an updated comedy of remarriage, it is updated precisely by taking for granted the discourse of intimacy. Indeed, this film may be the first relationship story in which that genre itself becomes the object of reflective reference. As if to make sure that the audience knows what films to compare this one to, *When Harry Met Sally* begins with opening credits in white titles on a black background accompanied by jazz piano—the way a Woody Allen film typically begins. The opening scenes set up a debate between Harry Burns (Billy Crystal) and Sally Albright (Meg Ryan), University of Chicago students sharing a ride to New York City. Harry argues that men and women can't be friends because "sex always gets in the way." Sally disagrees. Not only is the debate an instance of the discourse of intimacy, but it also makes the claims of that discourse an issue. If Harry is right, then the Grail of intimacy can never be reached. Intimacy, as we have seen, is a form of deep friendship. Though Harry clearly gets the best of the verbal exchanges on the subject, it is the film's project to prove Harry wrong.[8]

That project is actually revealed before the debate occurs. The first scene after the opening credits features, not Harry and Sally or any other "characters" who will figure in the story, but an elderly couple filmed in documentary style telling the story of their meeting and reporting the number of years they have been married. There will be such documentary moments inserted at various points in the film, serving to mark transitions in the narrative but also to reinforce the film's position on romance. Besides long-lived marriages, what all the "documentary" couples' stories have in common is love at first sight. Several of the couples tell of having married many years after they first met but claim to have in some way known all along that the other was the right person. These stories are the ones closest to the plot of the film, in which it will take Harry and Sally twelve years from their first meeting until they finally tie the knot. The stories reinforce the romantic mythology of the "one right person," while at the same time providing examples of marriages that work.

The action of the film until its conclusion mainly contrasts with the "documentary" stories. Not only do the central couple's first long-term relationships fail, but the other characters in the film also constantly lament their relationships or lack of them. There is the klatch of women, familiar from *An Unmarried Woman,* who meet to discuss relationships. Marie (Carrie Fisher) is involved with a married man and keeps telling her friends what they have figured out long ago: he is never going to leave his wife. One of these conversations takes place while Marie and Sally are standing around a table in a bookstore featuring a display of self-help books with titles like *I Love You, Let's Work It Out* and *Women Men Love, Women Men Leave.* Sally is looking through *Smart Women, Foolish Choices.* In the previous scene, Harry has just told his friend Jess (Bruno Kirby) that his wife has left him for another man, though she has not admitted that that was the reason. Jess's comment comes straight out of such advice books: "Marriages don't break up on account of infidelity. It's just a symptom that something else is wrong." Harry responds, "Well that symptom is fucking my wife." Harry thought his marriage was happy. *When Harry Met Sally* is ambivalent about the discourse it both assumes and mocks; the account of relationships it provides may be accurate enough, but it doesn't seem to change anything.

In the bookstore, Marie notices someone in the "personal growth" section staring at Sally. It is Harry, seeing Sally again for the first time in five years. The last time they met, their respective relationships were new. Now they tell each other of their newly single status. Cut to a restaurant where Sally explains: "When Joe and I started seeing each other we wanted exactly the same thing. We wanted to live together but not get married because every time someone we knew got married, it ruined their relationship. They practically never had sex again." The idea is that not getting married and having kids will keep the romance alive. What precipitated their breakup was Sally's decision that she wanted to have a family, but she also realizes that in spite of their freedom, they weren't flying off to Rome or having sex on the kitchen floor. This problem is one that could only occur in recent times, when living together has become an alternative. But marriage clearly remains the long-term expectation, as Sally's change of heart and Joe's later marriage demonstrate.

The ending of *When Harry Met Sally* might seem to disqualify this film as a relationship story. It's the sort of "wild finish" we find in *Casablanca* and that helps to define the screwball comedy. The key element of such an ending is reversal. After Harry and Sally sleep together, their friendship falls apart. She refuses his offer to take her to a New Year's Eve party and goes alone. We see him wandering around downtown Manhattan trying to convince himself that he is having a good time. His glimpse of a laughing, happy couple produces a brief series of flashbacks of Harry and Sally's relationship, beginning with Harry's assertion, "You know, we can never be friends." These scenes of Harry are intercut with scenes of Sally not having fun at the party. Just as she is deciding to leave, we see him running to get there, as in the end of *The Graduate,* and we hear Frank Sinatra singing "It Had to Be You." Harry gets there just in time and tells her that he loves her. She is at first not convinced, but he persuades her as the New Year arrives. They kiss to the strains of "Auld Lang Syne." The scene is followed by one of Harry and Sally as interviewees, telling the story of their courtship and wedding as the elderly couples have been doing. There is no doubt about happily ever after here.

Yet in spite of this ending's over-the-top romanticism, *When Harry Met Sally* remains a relationship story by virtue of the grounds that it offers for the rightness of its long delayed match. Unlike Nora Ephron's more recent romantic comedies, *Sleepless in Seattle* and *You've Got Mail,* which feature lovers who fall for each other at a distance, *When Harry Met Sally* shows us a couple getting to know each other. This is not an easy task for a film, and few others accomplish it. Indeed, of the other relationship stories, only *Blume in Love* presents us with a couple who might be "soul mates," and there it takes a divorce for the characters to realize it. *When Harry Met Sally* makes its couple, in a phrase frequent in contemporary personal ads, "friends first." We believe in this

When Harry Met Sally: Sally (Meg Ryan) and Harry (Billy Crystal) are friends who comfort each other about their failed relationships before they embark on one together.

relationship, not mainly because the film has insisted that some marriages work, but because we have seen this couple be intimate with each other. The film's great visual trope for intimacy is the split-screen depiction of Harry and Sally in bed in their respective apartments talking to each other on the telephone. That they are often talking about each other's feelings about their previous relationships makes these scenes more, not less, intimate. They are sharing feelings for no reason but the desire to share them. Even the ending, for all its romance, is not uninflected by intimacy. In his midnight speech, Harry tells Sally that he loves it that she is cold when it is 71 degrees and that it takes her an hour and half to order a sandwich. As the advice books note, what is often attractive about the mate is also irritating or difficult. Harry seems already to have figured this out, making it less likely that it will surprise him later. Indeed, considering how well these two people seem to know each other, one can believe that they just might end up telling their story together in old age.

Antiromance: How Relationships Fail

If *When Harry Met Sally* is the most romantic of the relationships stories, *Husbands and Wives*, the most recent of the six films discussed in this chapter, is by far the most critical of romance. Though suffused with the discourse of intimacy, this film is not necessarily more representative of it than *When Harry Met Sally* is. Rather, we should understand these two films as reflecting different aspects of the discourse, which can be both hopeful and cynical. If *Husbands and Wives* seems more typical of the discourse, it is because in its fictional form, intimacy tends toward irony. Moreover, while both films make use of documentary-style interviews, *Husbands and Wives* presents interviews with the characters. Indeed, while *When Harry Met Sally* strives to be like a studio-era screwball comedy, *Husbands and Wives* strives to look like a cinema vérité documentary. This fictional use of documentary style is something Allen has borrowed from John Cassavetes, though the film as a whole owes more to Ingmar Bergman's *Scenes from a Marriage* (1973). Bergman's film, which is a drama, begins with its couple being interviewed for a newspaper article. But where Bergman has integrated the interview into the narrative—and does not repeat the gesture—Allen presents his interviews as commentary, the characters talking to an unseen questioner about the events as they move along. These interviews are not the only framing device Allen uses. There is also objective voice-over narration. These devices are complemented by the use of a handheld camera that in some scenes darts around from character to character as if it were reacting to the strife it is filming. If *Annie Hall* is presented as a confession and *Manhattan* as a kind of romantic memoir, *Husbands and Wives* is much more overtly a case history, or, perhaps, a group of case histories. It seems as though nothing that happens in this film goes without being analyzed, often from more than one point of view.

That constant analysis allows *Husbands and Wives* to wear its antiromantic position on its sleeve. In *Annie Hall,* Alvy in the wake of his first breakup with Annie asks a stranger in the street, "Is it something that I did?" to which she replies, "Never something you do. That's how people are. Love fades." But *Annie Hall* seems to reject that position, as Alvy remarks on how depressing it is. *Husband and Wives* repeats various versions of it and seems to embrace it. Gabe asks Rain (Juliette Lewis) if she thinks passion can be sustained. She replies, "I don't know.

In *Time* magazine they said you lose your sexual attraction for the other person in four years." Sally (Judy Davis) also directly questions romance: "I've learned that love is not about passion and romance necessarily. It's also about companionship, and it's like a buffer against loneliness." Jack (Sydney Pollack) comments on Gabe in an interview that his propensity to get involved with crazy women results from having grown up on "movies and novels where doomed love was romantic." Michael (Liam Neeson) confesses his romantic tendencies to Judy (Mia Farrow) and describes himself as being from a different era. He plans to take Sally to an intimate little Italian restaurant, but we never see this scene. Not surprisingly, the film is largely devoid of the romantic moments and images that predominate in *Manhattan*. In fact, the only really romantic moment in the film is the one between Rain and Gabe at her birthday party—a moment that we know, even as it is happening, can lead nowhere—or at least nowhere good—and it does not.

The film's view of passionate love is perhaps summarized in the words of Gabe's novel: "The heart raged and demanded, grew melancholy and confused, and toward what end? To articulate what nitwit strategy? Procreation?" The heart, according to the novel, is driven by the biologically different predispositions of men and women. Like Rain, Gabe's novel casts doubt on the survival of passion:

> What happened after the honeymoon was over? Did desire really grow with the years, or did familiarity cause partners to long for other lovers? Was the notion of ever deepening romance a myth that we had grown up on like simultaneous orgasm? The only time Rifkin and his wife ever experienced a simultaneous orgasm was when the judge handed them their divorce. Maybe in the end, the idea was not to expect too much out of life.

In an interview, Jack says pretty much the same thing: "The thing that's so tough, that kills most people, is unreal expectations." Of his novel, Gabe says to Rain, "I'm trying to show how hard it is to be married," and this seems to be the point of the film as well.

Husbands and Wives tells more or less the same story as *Manhattan* but in different styles, tones, and outcomes. Or to put it more accurately perhaps, the films pose the same problems for a similar group of characters, but they are understood from a different perspective. The films both deal with the intimate struggles of upper-middle-class, more or less intellectual New Yorkers. Each movie features a writer (played by Allen himself) who becomes romantically involved with a "girl" less than half his age. In each, the writer is a friend of another couple whose marriage is in trouble. In each, a third party—Mary in *Manhattan*, Michael in *Husbands and Wives*—becomes involved with two of the protagonists. Each film features a woman who is "too cerebral"—Mary and Sally—and one who is more emotional—Tracy in *Manhattan*, Judy in *Husbands and Wives*.

Unlike the earlier film, *Husbands and Wives* is told from *inside* marital relations, where its most important struggles are located. As in the intimacy advice books, extramarital relations in this film are just that: they are defined by the marriages to which they are tangential. *Husbands and Wives* begins its narrative with two couples meeting for dinner, this time at Gabe and Judy 's apartment. When friends Jack and Sally arrive, they announce rather blithely that they have decided to separate. This has a powerful impact on Judy, who takes the news very badly and has to be cajoled into going ahead with the dinner plans. This scene sets in motion a series of events in which we find Jack and Sally experimenting with other partners and returning to each other, and Gabe and Judy breaking up.

The "little girl" in *Husbands and Wives* is Rain, one of Gabe's students. Unlike *Manhattan*'s Tracy, Rain is neither innocent nor inexperienced. Moreover, she is not overly awed by Gabe's reputation. She dares to criticize the manuscript he has given her, and he responds as if wounded. But, as Gabe tells the interviewer, her criticism of him makes her much more attractive. Thus, Rain combines traits that *Manhattan* had attributed to both Tracy and Mary. It would seem to make her the perfect object of desire, and all the more perfect because she is an impossible one. It is significant that Rain is the only major character who is not interviewed, while even her former analyst and lover, a very minor character, is. Rain can't be interviewed because she must remain mysterious, an obscure object of desire.

Where *Manhattan* had made student-professor relationships into a joke, the matter is addressed directly in *Husbands and Wives*. Gabe explains in an interview that he knows of professors who regularly seduce their students, but he has never been involved with a student or cheated in a relationship. This gives Gabe something of the same high moral ground that Ike had in *Manhattan*, especially compared to Jack, who we find out has been with prostitutes and had a mistress at the time he and

Sally separated. In *Manhattan,* however, Ike's moralizing is undermined by the humorous way it is presented, and it is opposed by Tracy's more humane wisdom. In *Husbands and Wives,* Gabe's moral judgments seem to be affirmed, yet they are not rewarded. His physical relationship with Rain consists of one long kiss; he knows literally the taste of this desire, but he will not act on it. The heart here is refused by the head.

The end of the film finds Gabe alone, divorced from Judy, who has since married Michael, Sally's former lover. Jack and Sally are back together again. It seems that they can't live without each other, but the problems in their relationship persist. The last scene is an interview with Gabe, who describes himself as out of the game for a while. He comments that "he blew it with Judy," a difficult remark to comprehend because we don't know what Gabe could have done better. Gabe describes a new novel that he is writing, having abandoned the one he showed to Rain. In a brilliant little moment, the interviewer asks Gabe on the heels of this, "Is it different?" Gabe's answer, "What, the novel?" makes it clear that the interviewer meant his life and that Gabe wants to dodge the question. He says that the new novel is "more political and less confessional," and then asks, "Is this over, can we stop now?" At that moment one has the sense that Gabe experienced the interview as torture and that he is fundamentally a victim, though perhaps only of his own repression. He wants to stop confessing and wishes to retreat into the more impersonal realm of politics.

Reversing the pattern of *Annie Hall, Husbands and Wives* ends with a confession, and its ending needs to be seen as the absolute antithesis of the Hollywood ending. There is no hope for romantic marriage at the end of *Husbands and Wives*; we have seen nothing to make us believe that the new couple, Michael and Judy—much less Jack and Sally—will escape the traps into which the others have fallen. Romance itself—outside of marriage—comes off no better. But if *Husbands and Wives* is a powerful critique of romance, it does not escape from confession into politics, for it offers nothing by way of an alternative. Unlike *Annie Hall,* it is not properly cynical but rather verges on despair. At best, it suggests that we can only hope to muddle through relationships that will inevitably be painful and unsatisfying. What *Annie Hall* had stated as a joke has become in *Husbands and Wives* the simple and unhappy truth.

It may be, then, that *Husbands and Wives* marks the end of the cycle of relationship stories that *Annie Hall* initiated, just as *Unfaithfully Yours* represents the last gasp of the first cycle of screwball comedies. In both films, the originally comic premises of the respective genres have become dark and troubling. While Allen and a few imitators have made films in the genre since then, they no longer are breaking new ground. More important, traditional romantic comedies have been far more popular. As I will argue in the conclusion, this trend is a response to conservative political forces, but it does not necessarily reflect the retreat of the discourse of intimacy. It rather suggests that the discourse can be articulated in both progressive and conservative versions and that the latter is now dominant in movies. In films such as *Runaway Bride*, intimacy often becomes subservient to romance.

7

Marriage Fiction

All happy families are alike but an unhappy family is unhappy after
its own fashion.

—Leo Tolstoy, *Anna Karenina*

When I first thought about writing about the novels and stories of John Updike and Alison Lurie, this work seemed to be distinguished by its frank and almost obsessive treatment of adultery. It *is,* of
course, but given the history of prose fiction, its serious treatment of marriage itself is even more distinctive. Hence, I have come to think of this
work as "marriage fiction" rather than as "adultery fiction." What this
body of work illustrates is the new meaning of marriage once it has become a "pure relationship." Marriage used to be considered both natural
and socially necessary. Now its naturalness is in question, and only right-
wing public moralists regard marriage as a social obligation. Legally and
ideologically, marriage is today the most private of practices and a matter of individual happiness and fulfillment.

The novels and stories I'll be discussing in this chapter are concerned
with marriages that fail to provide such happiness.[1] Like the intimacy advice books and the relationship films, they deal with how love works most
often by depicting instances when it does not work. Marriage here is no
longer an obstacle to true love, nor is it necessarily the fulfillment of such
love. Indeed, the whole idea of "true love" is called in question by this fiction, since the troubled marriages depicted are never loveless. As a result
of the different status of marriage, adultery takes on new meaning as well.
It is not depicted in these books as the place where love best flourishes, so
it can be used neither to diminish marriage nor to romantically mystify it.
As in contemporary advice books, adultery is seen as an aspect of marriage and as a path, perhaps misguided and always painful, to the happiness and fulfillment sought in marriage.

Tony Tanner has argued that "marriage is *the* central subject for the bourgeois novel."[2] My argument has been something like the reverse of this, that marriage has been mainly left out of the novel, bourgeois or otherwise. I think that Tanner's own title, *Adultery in the Novel*, supports my point. Of course, adultery exists only in the context of marriage, but the issue here is precisely what is text and what is context. In the novel, marriage itself has rarely been in the foreground. Even in novels where marriage seems to constitute a large part of the story, it rarely turns out to be these books' real focus. Henry James's *The Portrait of a Lady*, for example, gives us a marriage that is a sham from the start. That James's novels so often involve a clash between rich Americans in search of romance and impoverished European aristocrats seeking wealth reveals that he continues to deal with marriage as alliance. As scholar Alfred Habegger has observed, *The Portrait of a Lady* "tells a conventional story of courtship and marriage, yet, conspicuously, there is not a single example of reciprocal love, except near the end."[3] Of course, that love is not inside a marriage. Or consider *Middlemarch,* where "Eliot spares Dorothea Brooke a devastatingly sterile married life" by having her husband quickly die, "freeing Dorothea to pursue her maidenly ideal of marriage."[4] In other words, *Middlemarch* becomes, like most novels, focused on courtship once Casaubon dies. The marriages in these novels are marriages of convenience for at least one of the partners. In these novels, neither James nor Eliot has imagined a marriage based on mutual romantic love.

Tanner claims that marriage is so important in the bourgeois novel because "for bourgeois society marriage is the all-subsuming, all-organizing, all-containing contract. It is the structure that maintains the Structure, or System."[5] I'm not sure that this is an accurate account of what distinguished bourgeois society from earlier social systems. Marriage was far *more* significant when it was a means by which political alliances were created among families of hereditary rulers. In the late eighteenth and nineteenth centuries, such alliances among bourgeois families remained economically significant, but they had lost their political centrality. Tanner is right, however, to say that marriage continued to be understood during that period as "a means by which society attempts to bring into harmonious alignment patterns of passion and patterns of property."[6] As a result, the fact of marriage, together with its rules and obligations, continued to have social significance. It is this social function of marriage that prevented the marriages themselves from taking center stage in fiction.

Marriage fiction becomes possible only when marriage has become a personal choice rather than a social obligation.

It is because novelists of the earlier part of this century remained burdened by this social conception of marriage that it has taken so long for marriage fiction to emerge. Those few authors who tried to write novels focused on marriage continued to be diverted away from it. William Dean Howells's *A Modern Instance* (1882) is a book about marriage, adultery, and divorce that "expose[s] the dangers of . . . romantic marriage."[7] The failed marriage of Bartley and Marcia Hubbard, however, is presented to show us both "the shortcomings of the society from which [they] spring" and [the marriage's] "own damaging effects on the social fabric."[8] Howells's subject matter—the "average," the "middle"—is what writers like Updike, Lurie, Saul Bellow, Raymond Carver, John Cheever, Sue Miller, Anne Beatty, and numerous others have taken up since the mid-twentieth century. Yet the middling world of *A Modern Instance* seems either boring or tawdry, perhaps because Howells always stands outside of it observing from a distance. We don't experience it from the inside as we do in Updike or Lurie.

Several critics have praised Henry James's *Golden Bowl* for presenting an authentic picture of marriage.[9] Like Howells, James was critical of the romantic vision of marriage that ended so many novels, and his novels avoid that convention.[10] *The Golden Bowl,* however, is about not just one but two arranged marriages. It does present more interaction among its spouses than we found in *The Portrait of a Lady,* but on the whole the novel stays true to form. Passionate love is located in the adulterous affair between Charlotte and the Prince. Intimacy, to the extent it is present at all, exists mainly between Maggie and her father.

The fiction of high-modernist writers such as James Joyce, D. H. Lawrence, and Virginia Woolf provides evidence that in the twentieth century marriage was beginning to be less understood as a social obligation. Woolf's *Mrs. Dalloway* and *To the Lighthouse* are especially important because of their focus on marital relationships. Nevertheless, as Stephen Kern observes, they depict "strained but dignified and contemplative marital love."[11] Partly this is a matter of the stream-of-consciousness style in which these stories are told, which distances us from the couples' interaction. We find neither romance nor intimacy in these novels, though they suggest an awareness of the lack of the latter. *To the Lighthouse,* however, makes explicit the change that enables the emergence of marriage fiction when Lily Briscoe, an observer of the Ramsays' marriage, realizes that she "need never marry anybody."[12] This is something that Mrs. Ramsay could not have realized because of the role marriage played in the society in which she came of age.

Marriage Fiction

Adultery functioned in earlier literature as it did—as romantic adventure and serious social transgression—because of the presumed infrequency of infidelity in real life. While the incidence of male adultery was probably quite high and the practice silently tolerated, female adultery was not tolerated and probably occurred with much less frequency. For both sexes, adultery was assumed to be the exception rather than the norm, an assumption that allowed men's affairs to be ignored. While this denial is still in evidence, it is now widely believed that adultery in recent times has been very common. The status of adultery today is interesting because, unlike other previously illicit sexual practices, including premarital sex and homosexuality, the popular attitude towards adultery does not seem to have changed. This condemning attitude is best explained by the personal betrayal that adultery entails rather than by beliefs in the general sanctity or social significance of marriage. Those beliefs remain widespread, but evidence suggests that they are in decline. Today, fewer people marry, couples routinely live together before marrying, and roughly 50 percent of all marriages end in divorce. Under the impact of these conditions, the meaning of marital infidelity must change. If marriage matters less, so does adultery.[13] While the majority clearly believe it is wrong to be unfaithful, it is the apparent hypocrisy of the adulterer that is most troubling. Rather than cheating, popular sentiment seems to hold, the adulterer should leave the marriage.[14]

Adultery is depicted in many of the films I've been calling relationship stories, but it is not their focus. The relationship stories are about being single, but in the books I'm discussing in this chapter, no one is single for very long. Adultery, the basis of the discourse of romance, was fundamental to romantic novels and films earlier in this century. Adultery may seem to be even more significant to the work of Updike and Lurie, since it is much more explicitly described there. I will argue, however, that it is in some respects less significant for being the more explicit subject of these books. The novels and stories I'm concerned with here are explicitly about the very thing romance couldn't discuss at all, marriage itself. But in becoming visible, marriage also comes to be a problematic state.

Like the relationship stories, this marriage fiction is an expression of the discourse of intimacy. To some extent, these novels and short stories represent something like intimacy itself. But if one is looking for the talk that the intimacy advice books promise—and the satisfaction it is supposed to provide—one will be disappointed. The married couples in this fiction do talk to each other, sometimes with remarkable honesty, but just as often to deceive. Instead of giving us fictional realizations of the "integrated" marriage, what Scarf called "relational heaven itself," this fiction presents an intimacy that, while both imperfect and inconstant, is also in itself potentially threatening and often restrictive.[15] While these novels and stories do show us what happens between the couple, they also give us a much greater sense of the separate, interior worlds of married people. This fiction insists on our isolation from even our most intimate others.

When Tolstoy asserted that "all happy families are alike," he was suggesting that there is no story to tell about a happy family. John Updike made this point in a review of Rougemont: "The essence of story is conflict—obstruction, in his term. Happy love, unobstructed love, is the possibility that animates all romances; their plots turn on obstruction because they are plots."[16] This remains a reasonable explanation for the lack of happy marriages in fiction, but it does not explain the relative absence of marriage itself. The discourse of intimacy does not entail the romantic assumption that there is nothing interesting about ordinary, functioning marriages. As one of the self-help writers puts it, "Conflict is an integral part of married life."[17] Even though most such books are not so forthright and often offer visions of conflictless "relational heavens," the very character and market for the books themselves belie these visions. The writers I'm dealing with in this chapter challenge Tolstoy's claim, not by depicting happy families, but by calling into question the very idea of the happy family. Happy families are all alike because they don't exist in reality, only in the realm of Platonic ideas. The families that Updike and Lurie depict are happy and unhappy at the same time. Just as these marriages are not "relational heaven," neither are they abusive or utterly dysfunctional. Marriage fiction gives us more or less ordinary marriages, and, if it emphasizes their problems, it does not neglect their benefits.

The writers I'm concerned with here do not give us misery on the scale of *Anna Karenina*. If the marriages depicted are troubled, they do not lead to tragedy. Endings are less important in this fiction than *experiences,* which, however painful or ecstatic they might be, are rendered as part of a life cycle. This, it seems to me, is where marriage and adultery in the novel would inevitably arrive once they stopped serving as symbols of the social order and transgression against it. I argued in chapter 1 that marriage in modern fiction is a matter of individual good or evil, happiness or unhappiness. But at the turn of twentieth century, marriage remained the only socially sanctioned relationship, and individual marriages therefore had a lot riding on them. Failure in love or marriage was still a personal tragedy. The reality of serial monogamy has made such failures routine and hence less disturbing, at least to readers. The experiences described remain affecting, but they are now familiar.

The fiction I'm focusing on in this chapter first appeared before the nonfictional expression of intimacy discourse had become popularized. The earliest works of marriage fiction were perhaps the first popular documents in the discourse of intimacy to appear. As such, they represent a very early response to the renewed sense of a crisis in marriage of the 1960s. Some commentators saw books like Updike's *Couples* more as an illustration of the crisis than a response. Marriage fiction lacks some of the therapeutic vocabulary of relationships that is typical of the cinematic relationship stories and may, as a result, seem a less convincing instance of the discourse of intimacy. The discourse of intimacy is defined, however, not by the use of psychological language, but by the way in which relationships are conceived. Intimacy is the central issue in marriage fiction, even if it is not named as such. This fiction is better able to deal with this issue because it can depict long-term relationships in a depth that the films do not. Conversely, such fiction typically presents marriages—and affairs as well—from the perspectives of individuals rather than by depicting the interaction of couples. These differences are largely the result of differences in media. Films typically present relationships through dialogue, whereas novels can augment or replace that kind of presentation with the silent thoughts of the characters or the truth about them known to an omniscient narrator.

High-modernist fiction writers such as James Joyce and Virginia Woolf challenged bourgeois assumptions about marriage, but they have become known for challenging the conventions of prose fiction. The fiction I'm concerned with here fits within the broad conventions of realism, but it also reflects a break in the history of the novel. Adultery, while depicted more explicitly, is no longer structural. Love triangles abound in this fiction, but they do not structure narrative succession in the way that they did in, say, historical romances. There we saw the reader's identification centered on an excluded subject who typically would be included at the end of the novel. In marriage fiction, romantic structure is sometimes present but is subverted. Lurie's first novel, *Love and Friendship* (1962), does retain the shell of the romantic structure, but we are asked to identify with Emily, the adulterous wife who is always included. The romantic character of her affair is mocked by the lack of any internal strife in her decision to stay with her husband. Updike's *Marry Me: A Romance* also retains but subverts the romantic structure, in this case by providing multiple endings. In this novel, we are never sure who we should root for. In Lurie's later novels, the lovers her married characters take up with aren't treated romantically; they aren't involved in grand passion, and we can't imagine them as potential mates. What drives our interest in these novels, and in *Couples* and the Maples stories, is not the question of who will end up with whom, but rather of the consequences of the characters' philandering.

The triangle can't serve as a structure of narrative succession in Updike's narratives because triangles have become permanent fixtures of his characters' lives. When we first meet *Couples*'s protagonist Piet, we feel that his wife Angela and his current lover Georgene are both included in something. It's not as if Piet is at one moment in love with Georgene and the next with Angela; he loves both of them and each loves him. As their nickname suggests, the spouse-swapping Applesmiths form a kind of family. They make two triangles but also a rectangle, as the novel observes.[18] Adultery is a constant in Tarbox. Triangles may break up and reform with new members, but they do not in general resolve into dyads as in romance narratives, where they always do. Piet's affair with Foxy may be the exception. It does finally lead to the dissolution of their marriages and their marrying each other, but the novel's ending leaves their future ambiguous. If in their new town "they have been accepted, as another couple," we can imagine the whole cycle repeating itself.[19]

Updike has asserted that *Couples* "has a happy ending. It's about a guy meeting a girl and the guy getting the girl."[20] Yet the guy gets the girl at enormous emotional cost. It is hard not to feel that the ending is as much Piet's loss as it is his gain, and Updike said that he "wanted the loss of Angela to be felt as a real loss."[21] The loss looms larger perhaps because of

Piet's passivity. He would never have asked Angela for a divorce. Foxy's husband Ken, a kind of Roger Chillingworth figure, is responsible for ending Piet's stay in the post-Pill paradise. Ken's failure to forgive his wife's infidelity renders him worse than Freddy Thorne, the dentist who extorts sex from Angela in return for arranging Foxy an abortion. (This may be a post-Pill paradise, but it's a pre–Roe v. Wade hell.) It is Angela who has the strength to decide to end the marriage in the wake of these events. Romance assumes that its lovers know what they want, even if they may also feel guilt and fear as a result. From internal evidence alone, we cannot know what Piet wants or that he knows what he wants.

Piet is not the hero of a romance but the subject of a case history. I argued earlier that the form of the case history is realist, which is to say a narrative with minimal emplotment. Updike connects his own work to Howells and realism when he asserts that "today's fiction . . . has turned, with an informal—a minimalist—bluntness of style, and with a concern for immediate detail that has given regionalism new life, and to areas of domestic morality and sexual politics that interested Howells."[22] Like Howells, he prefers "the middling," and he has said, "The idea of the hero is aristocratic."[23]

The novels and stories I'm dealing with here are not mere case histories, of course, and to claim for all of them minimal emplotment may seem risky. *Couples,* after all, is a theological allegory, and it is structured by the cycle of seasonal death and rebirth. But these metastructures seem to be a mere frame for a detailed landscape of domestic morality. We are not meant to treat these matters of everyday life as ephemeral or as mere symbols of something more significant. Like the advice book case histories, the fiction I'm discussing here does not fit any of the typical plot structures of romance, comedy, or tragedy. Irony comes closer, but the examples I'm discussing are finally too engaged to be described as ironic. Certain patterns of behavior may be treated ironically, but the world that these characters inhabit is not. Updike has specifically rejected the idea that *Couples* is a satire, and he claims, "You can't be satirical at the expense of fictional characters, because they're your creatures."[24] Lurie's novels are closer to satire, but it is the milieu that is satirized much more than the main characters. To refer to Frye's modes, these novels are firmly low mimetic: they are about people like us, no better and no worse. Critics who have read them as satire have failed to accept this identification and assumed their own and the author's superiority to the characters. Such critics render a moralistic judgment whether they know it or not.

The case history is fundamentally an illustration, an example of something. By itself, it offers neither explanation nor analysis, and it cannot have a moral. The point of a case history is never "Go and do thou likewise," nor can it be "Thou shalt not." A case history may show us a pattern of behavior that we would like to avoid, but if it were merely a matter of the will to do so, the pattern would not be presented as a case history. A case history tells the story of something that befalls its characters. A romance like *Tristan* could be written as a case history because the love of Tristan and Isolde results from the potion and is thus beyond their control. But all of the medieval versions of the Tristan story are emplotted as tragedies. The discourse of romance cannot make use of the case history because romance has too much invested in the outcome of the narrative. Whether the lovers end up together is the whole point.

It is not the point, I am arguing, of the fiction of Updike and Lurie, which is more interested in what it is like for couples when they are married. Since marriage is now only one of the forms that love between a man and woman might take, whether a couple get or stay married no longer has its old tragic or comic implications. Marriage fiction is thus free to examine marriages as particular—perhaps peculiar is a better word—relationships between two people. We do, of course, identify with the characters in this fiction, but since they do not know what they want, our identification cannot be a matter of simply wanting that. Piet, for example, doesn't know whom among his various partners he most wants. Foxy may be a better mate for him, but *Couples* is not told in such a way that the reader is likely to root for them. There is passion and there is love between Piet and Foxy, but their relationship is not idealized as it would be in the discourse of romance. Foxy is not presented as someone who will save Piet from himself, for he is no more faithful to her than he is to Angela.

Romance, of course, does exist in this fiction, but it is contained within the discourse of intimacy. To some extent, romance figures here, as it does in the relationship films, in particular moments or tableaux. *Marry Me,* for example, opens with its adulterous lovers meeting for a tryst on a deserted beach with a blanket and a bottle of wine. There is certainly something romantic about the old summerhouse in which Piet and Foxy make love. Just as often, however, lovers in these novels find themselves in humorously unromantic settings. In Lurie's *The Nowhere City,* the husband makes love to his mistress, a waitress he has met in a diner, at her dilapidated apartment that lacks even a shower.

More important than romantic settings, however, is the sense of adultery as an adventure that continues to exist in these novels. Piet's business partner, Matt Gallagher, tells him, "You have a kind of freedom I don't have. You can be an adventurer where I can't. I have to have my adventures here [at work]."[25] Piet's relationship with Georgene Thorne, in progress when the novel opens, may at first seem like anything but an adventure. It is so controlled, so carefully planned, so lacking in passion. Yet it is secretive, and there is throughout the novel the fear that her husband Freddy knows or will find out. Piet's affair with Foxy also begins without much sense of danger or risk, but once Foxy becomes pregnant by Piet, the affair has become all too risky. That episode concludes with Piet safely making love to Georgene, feeling that he has escaped: "He knew that he had exaggerated his trouble, that fate could be appeased."[26]

The most romantic of the texts I'm concerned with in this chapter is *Marry Me,* which is subtitled *A Romance.* Its first two chapters each focus on a particular tryst. The first, the afternoon at the beach, is barely an adventure, though there are some inconvenient teenagers who must be avoided. The second, a trip to Washington, is much more of one. In the first place, Jerry specifically tells Sally she cannot come with him on his business trip, but Sally shows up there anyway. Next, their return flight is canceled, and they find themselves stuck at the airport worrying about being seen together and how to explain Sally's lateness to her husband. Clearly, these obstacles create narrative tension by introducing danger that the lovers must try to avoid. They define the episode as romantic in the most fundamental sense. The rest of the novel presents even greater obstacles to Jerry and Sally, the last chapter playing with the reader's desire for a resolution by offering several endings, one a dream, one reality, and one a vain hope for the future beyond the novel. Yet the bulk of the novel is taken up with the third and fourth chapters, entitled "The Reacting of Ruth" and "The Reacting of Richard." Thus, the novel contains Jerry and Sally's affair within the context of their respective marriages. Typical of this kind of fiction, *Marry Me* makes the spouses' reactions more important than the lovers' relationship itself.

Another way in which adultery is contained is by self-reflexive distancing. It might be more correct to say that in marriage fiction adultery is an "adventure" to indicate this sort of treatment. One strategy is a mock-heroic presentation of the events, as is the case with Piet. His passivity makes him appear not as a knight-errant but rather as a more or less lucky fool. Even by naming Piet an adventurer, Updike diminishes the adventurousness of the acts themselves and makes us aware that his, like Matt's business dealings, are trivial as adventures go. Earlier in the novel, one character's account of an Orwellian vision of the future, in which a television in every room will permit everyone to be watched and "nobody could commit adultery," prompts another to respond, "My God. . . . They'll undermine the institution of marriage."[27] *Couples* thus seems to embrace the idea of the marriage-adultery system. Such acceptance is antiromantic even if romance can be seen as the product of this system.

These books are all written with an awareness of the cultural constructedness of romance, so that they can't give us the sort of experience Newland Archer had in *The Age of Innocence*. There the mere pursuit of an adulterous relationship is rendered as a legitimate adventure. Marriage fiction is much more likely to demystify this sort of romance. Jerry theorizes in *Marry Me,* "What we have, sweet Sally, is an ideal love. It's ideal because it can't be realized."[28] Sally's husband, Richard, doesn't get it; he thinks that "any romance that does not end in marriage fails."[29] In *The War between the Tates,* Brian explains his lover Wendy's attraction to him by referring to Rougemont: "Romantic passion, as De Rougemont has pointed out, is a plant that thrives best in stony soil."[30] He explains the demise of the relationship by reference to the same theory: "The way to cure a passion was by satiating it. Mere consummation was not enough; as long as the affair remained secret, the necessary stimuli to desire were there: absence, anxiety, delay, solitary longing."[31]

The novels of Updike and Lurie are about romance rather than being romances. They demystify the discourse of romance, even as they also invoke it. They are, of course, not the first novels to take this position. In *Madame Bovary,* Flaubert depicted Emma as pursuing her affair under the influence of popular romances. What distinguishes marriage fiction, however, is that it has a new discourse at its disposal. Emma must choose between her duty to her marriage and her desire for romance. In marriage fiction, it is intimacy, not romance, that is the ideal state.

Brave New World

I have so far merely touched on the changing social conditions that lie behind the rise of the discourse of romance and the emergence of the discourse of intimacy. The literature and films that I am discussing are in general not much concerned with such conditions. I have argued that society itself is no longer the main issue in the romantic literature of the turn of the century, and it is in general even less the concern of later works. The fiction I am discussing here is not exactly an exception to this rule; it too is focused on individuals and their relationships and does not treat marriage as a social building block. But unlike the advice books and relationship films, marriage fiction gives us a fairly robust picture of the society that its characters inhabit. What this fiction suggests is that changes in the social role of the family are fundamental.

Couples in particular takes as part of its task the attempt to explain the transformations that made Tarbox possible. If class is not an issue to the characters of this novel, it is something the narrator discusses. The Applebys and little-Smiths are introduced to us specifically in terms of their class and its changing habits:

> They belonged to that segment of the upper middle class which mildly rebelled against the confinement and discipline whereby wealth maintained its manners during the upheavals of the depression and world war. . . . Fenced off from their own parents by nursemaids and tutors and "help," they would personally rear large intimate families. They changed diapers with their own hands, did their own housework and home repairs, gardened and shoveled snow with a sense of strengthened health. . . . Having suffered under their parents' rigid marriages and formalized evasions, they sought to substitute an essential fidelity set in a matrix of easy and open companionship among couples.[32]

In the generation of Harold little-Smith's and Frank Appleby's parents, the social life of their class continued to revolve around extended families. While I suspect that this was most typical of the bourgeoisie, extended families were more important for prewar people of all classes. The society Tarbox reflects is one in which these older bonds have begun to melt into air. The rapid development of suburbs and of highways after the war meant that families were more likely to be geographically dispersed. No member of the Tarbox couples was born in that community. These are families who don't have grandparents within easy access or adult siblings or cousins living on the next block. Childhood friendships are not the basis for those of the adults. These couples were thus isolated in ways that earlier generations would have been much less likely to be.

As a result, the couples make a society among themselves. Not surprisingly for a novel set mainly in 1963, this social world is not a feminist utopia. Most of the women do only volunteer work outside the home. But it is a world in which separate masculine and feminine spheres of the Victorian era are well on their way to disintegration. The "easy and open companionship" that the Applesmiths create brings a mixing of genders that would have been unusual in the previous generation. It is this relatively new condition that creates the circumstances by which adultery becomes both a much greater temptation and much easier to commit. Classes also mix more easily in this world of the uprooted. If Updike calls the Applebys and the little-Smiths "upper middle class," it is because this is their American cultural identity. Strictly speaking, they are bourgeois, while most of the other couples are best described as petty bourgeois or professional managerial. But they all see themselves as middle class, and their social interaction gives substance to this conception.

The result is an expanded intimacy that comes to exist among the couples even before they become physically intimate outside their marriages. According to Angela, the couples are likened by Freddy Thorne to a church: "He thinks we're a circle. A magic circle of heads to keep the night out. He told me he gets frightened if he doesn't see us over a weekend. He thinks we've made a church of each other."[33] Another way that society has changed is that the real church no longer provides fellowship as it did in the past. Of the couples, only Piet and "the Catholics" attend church. Foxy's mother, in town to witness the birth of her daughter's baby, remarks that "you're fortunate to have found friends you can have *fun* with. Your father and I had no such circle. We were alone; alone with you. It's good, to be able to let off steam."[34] Foxy's husband Ken thinks the couples know each other too well. The novel suggests that both points of view are valid. Of the Applesmiths, the novel tells us, "The autumn of 1962, the two couples were ecstatically, scandalously close."[35] Intimacy here is not just a synonym for heterosexual love or relations; it is the condition that these people have attained with each other as a group. The novel suggests that this is wonderful, perverse, desirable, and inherently unstable. As Updike has remarked, *Couples* is an "elegiac story. It's a loving portrait of life in America."[36]

That *Couples* has often been read as satire has something to do with readers' unwillingness to accept it as an accurate picture of American life. When *Couples* was published in 1968, it seemed to reviewers something like *Rosemary's Baby,* an account of actions implausible in the place within which they were set. People in the suburbs just didn't behave like this. From having taught *Couples* in several university courses,

I can tell you that college-age students still find it implausible. The characters are too much like their parents for them to accept so much illicit sex. Even the ones who have experienced divorce are unlikely to know this side of their parents' marriages. But according to various studies of sexual behavior, this side of marriage is prevalent. The Kinsey report of 1953, the various Hite reports, and the recent and much disputed *Sex in America* (1994) show that roughly half of married individuals have had extramarital relations.[37] Yet as polls taken in wake of President Clinton's affair with Monica Lewinsky show, the vast majority of Americans do not condone adultery. The clear implication is that many people practice what they would not preach and that the prevalence of adultery is routinely met with denial by adults as well as college students.

What makes marriage fiction more disturbing than the relationship films is that it defamiliarizes the suburbs while the films ultimately depend on the commonsense view of city life. Even adult audiences are likely to think of the suburbs as too ordinary, too natural to merit analysis. Fiction by Updike and Lurie shows us that suburbia is a distinct environment with its own social and emotional ecosystems.

The suburban and small town environments of Updike and Lurie are the expected setting for married couples, just as cities are where we expect to find singles and childless couples. But it is not just the setting that accounts for the larger significance that families play in marriage fiction. Couples in cities have children too, though you would barely know it from seeing the relationship films. Children, however, also play a fairly minor role in the intimacy advice books. Some authors deal with problems that children may cause in a couple's relationship, but few actually understand them as integral to the emotional world of a marriage. This is curious, not only because the vast majority of married couples do have children, but also because the one social function that marriage is still widely held to fill is child rearing. Romance, avoiding the depiction of marriage, necessarily cannot deal with children. The result is that the romantic conception of marriage is one that imagines the couple as radically separate in their love. Children are to be expected, but they have nothing to do with the parents' relationship with each other. The discourse of intimacy also tends to focus on the conjugal couple as an isolated entity. While allowing the importance of the couple's own family history, the advice literature has little to say about the larger realm of human contacts in which any relationship exists.

Marriage fiction, though it usually doesn't present social relations in enough detail to satisfy, say, a Marxist critic, does give us a sense of family life in late twentieth-century America, including not only the children but also the pets. The families are nuclear units, excluding almost entirely the adults' relatives, parents, and in-laws. For the couples in this fiction, a divorce means not merely the end of a marriage but the loss—although not necessarily absolute—of other members of the household. For men and women in this fiction, familial relationships have value, and they form a significant part of the context for the couple's relationship.

The recognition of familial bonds does not mean that these novels treat children sentimentally. Lurie's *The War between the Tates* depicts this couple's two adolescent children not as pathetic pawns in their parents' struggle but as combatants in their own right. Before we learn of Brian Tate's infidelity, we are told that Erica Tate has grown to dislike her children: "In her whole life she cannot remember disliking anyone as much as she now sometimes dislikes Jeffrey and Matilda."[38] Not only are the children rude and disobedient, but their very presence is responsible for a growing distance between Brian and Erica. The acoustical permeability of their house makes the couple feel that "they dare not laugh or cry." Both sex and talk are thus inhibited, leading Erica to complain that "we live in the same house and sleep in the same bed and we never see each other any more."[39] After they separate, Brian's decision to return home is reversed after a brief encounter with Jeffrey and Matilda.

Brian thinks of his kids as "revolting (in both senses)."[40] This pun reveals what is new about the way children in these narratives are represented. They are no longer mere chattels. Like adults, they have their own subjectivity and their own loves. Angela and Piet's two children already have different metaphysics. One is innocent and fearful of death, the other has a "brave corruption."[41] In "Eros Rampant," Updike describes the loves of each of the Maples' four children, in addition to those of their pets and the couple themselves. The children love such various beings as the dog, dinosaurs, the Boston Bruins, and a teacher, but the point is that, like their parents, they love, and that their loves are particular. Even the children are "incorrigibly themselves."[42]

The Maples family is founded on love rather than property. When son John questions his parents' love for their children—"What do you care about *us*? . . . We're just little things you *had*"—Richard responds, "You're not little things we had. . . . You're the whole point."[43] The notion of family as property is also questioned by the negative example of Richard Mathias in *Marry Me,* who threatens to sue his wife's lover Jerry for alienation of affection:

> You know and *I* know, Jerry, that Sally was just as aggressive as you were in this affair, and probably more so. But in the eyes of the law, she's not a free agent. She's a chattel. In the eyes of the law, by turning my wife against me, you've caused me a great deal of mental suffering, mental and some physical, for which I have a right to be reimbursed.[44]

Richard's attitude is patriarchal, and it contrasts with the position Jerry articulated earlier when Richard had convened the two couples: "'Don't hate,' he begged. 'We're all too close to hate. We must all love each other now.'"[45] As with the Applesmith "family" in *Couples,* we know that this is not a practical solution. If the four adults can't make one big, happy family, however, the point is that they are all free agents bound to each other only by conscious or unconscious choice.

In Updike, the world beyond intimate relationships seems to exist only to impinge or mirror them. Society in Updike consists of the actual interaction of people, such as the Tarbox couples, or it doesn't exist at all. The idea that marriage might be the foundation of the larger social order is absent. By contrast, Lurie raises the issue of marriage and society explicitly in *The War between the Tates.* Early in the novel we learn that the Tates stood for "Marriage" as against "Divorce" in conversations with their friends the Zimmerns before the latter separated. This position is ironized by the Tates' own separation and likely divorce, yet the Tates continue to represent Marriage. Brian offers to marry Wendy when she becomes pregnant (for the second time) to save her and the child from social stigma. Wendy's response is to ask, "Isn't that just going along with everything that's fucked up in society? If you just do it because you're afraid of prejudice, isn't that sort of helping to perpetuate it?"[46] Wendy tells Erica that she is leaving town with her new boyfriend, Ralph, to raise the child in northern California away from the evils of civilization and that she does not plan to get married. "Once you're married you can't ever tell if the guy comes home on account of he wants to, or on account of he has to. I mean, who wants to have somebody fuck you just because it's his job." To which Erica replies, "But marriage isn't only sex: it's a social contract. If everyone thought like your friend, families would break up; parents would desert their children—" "'That's different,' Wendy interrupted. 'I couldn't ever desert a kid.'"[47]

The novel clearly favors Brian and Erica's arguments, but it does not entirely reject Wendy's in spite of her being a caricature. Regardless of which position Lurie might support, however, the significant fact is that Wendy's position is available. At the start of the century, it would not have been, and no one would have felt the need to state the sort of argument Erica makes in such bald terms. If both fictional and nonfictional discourse constantly endorsed marriage as the foundation of society, they did so more or less implicitly. What *The War between the Tates* shows us is that this position has lost its ideological dominance, that it no longer seems entirely natural or obvious.

Intimacy

Kern has noted that even modernist writers, who often dealt explicitly with sex, "were reluctant to explore marital sex."[48] This is a continuation of the conventions that had long kept marriage itself protected from the reader's gaze. Courtship and adultery could be represented, but marriage itself could only be forecast. In the work of Lurie and especially Updike, marital relations, both sexual and otherwise, are explored in explicit detail.

Couples opens with Angela and Piet undressing in their bedroom after a party, the one at which they have met Foxy and Ken Whitman for the first time. The scene, which is interrupted by the provision of background information about the characters and their home, is one that doesn't quite fit the models we have from either the advice books or the relationship films. The advice books show us scenes of noncommunication or examples of successful talk. The films show us moments of bliss and moments of strife, but these are usually pretty clearly distinguished. At the beginning of *Couples,* we witness a fight, but it is an intimate fight. They are talking about the new couple, the Whitmans:

> He spoke as if in self-defense. "I was just wondering at what stage they are. He seemed rather brittle and detached."
> "You're hoping they're at our stage."
> Her cool thin tone, assumed at the moment when he had believed their intimacy, in this well-lit safe room encircled by the April dark, to

be gathering poignant force enough to vault them over their inhibitions, angered him. He felt like a fool. He said, "That's right. The seventh circle of bliss."

"Is that what we're in?" She sounded, remotely, ready to believe it.[49]

The text tells us, right from the start, that Angela and Piet have intimacy. I don't mean that Updike is using the term exactly as the more recent self-help books do. In the late 1960s, it had yet to become a buzzword. Moreover, as we discover later, Piet feels a lack of closeness with his wife, the sort of lack that would now be described as a failure of intimacy. But what this first scene shows us is two people who, despite their verbal jousting, know each other deeply and do communicate. Indeed, it is the character of their jousting that conveys this impression. The scene concludes, like so many scenes in Woody Allen's films, with Angela refusing Piet's desire for sex. This will turn out to be a real issue in their marriage, but unlike in Allen, it is not the main issue. Their sexual difficulties are not finally what will cause them to break up. Rather, his greater desire and her lesser are part of the texture of this relationship, a relationship that is nine years old as the novel opens. We learn that the problem is not recent in origin, and there is no indication that they have become bored with each other. They have always been different in this way.

Different sexual needs and desires are typical of the marriages in Lurie and Updike. In *The Nowhere City*, Katherine, unhappy to have been dragged out to Los Angeles by her husband, submits passive-aggressively to her husband's advances even though they have been apart for six weeks. *The War between the Tates* features a couple who in lovemaking had for fifteen years "made each other happy." After the discovery of Brian's affair, however, Erica also begins to passively resist his desires: "It takes her up to five minutes to find and insert her diaphragm . . . and longer to get out of her nightgown than it takes Wendy to undress completely."[50] Whereas in Updike, differing sexual appetites seem to be incorrigible sources of marital conflict, in Lurie's world, sexual problems are symptoms of a larger failure of intimacy, sometimes a temporary one.

But even when conflict over sex is endemic to a marriage, it does not preclude sexual pleasure from being shared. In the midst of his affair with Foxy, Piet is still thrilled when Angela wants him. Updike's account of their lovemaking is at least as explicit—perhaps more so—than any depiction of illicit sex in the novel:

The woman's beauty caressed the skin of his eyes; his shaggy head sank toward the ancient alleyway where, foul proud queen, she frothed most. His tongue searched her sour labia until it found them sweet. She pulled his hair, *Come up*. "Come inside me?" He realized, amazed, he who had entered Foxy Whitman the afternoon before, that there was no cunt like Angela's, none so liquid and replete. He lost himself to the hilt unresisted. The keenness of her chemistry made him whimper. Always the problem with their sex had been that he found her too rich to manipulate. She touched his matted chest, *wait,* and touched her own self, and mixed with her fluttering fingers, coming like a comet's dribble, he waited, until her hand flew to his buttocks and, urging him to kill her, she gasped and absolved herself from tension.

He said, "My dear wife. What a nice surprise."[51]

The passage demonstrates the couple's literal and figurative connection to each other. It makes it clear that, although their sexual difficulties contribute to Piet's dissatisfaction, they cannot serve as a simple explanation for his philandering. Neither can a simple psychological explanation be invoked. Piet is not a Don Juan figure, not a seducer who acts under the compulsion to find new conquests. His passivity makes it impossible for us to imagine him in that role. Foxy tells her mother that the affair "wasn't his idea it was *mine*" and that she is afraid of taking advantage of him.[52] The most one can say is that Piet makes it known that he is available. Unlike the womanizer, who loves women but cannot love an individual woman, Piet "loved any woman he lay with, that was his strength, his appeal."[53]

Piet and Angela can and do talk to each other. So can Updike's other married couples, Jerry and Ruth in *Marry Me* and, especially, Richard and Joan Maple. This suggests that the lack of intimacy that his characters feel is not mainly a function of their inability to communicate. Updike's male protagonists are not strong, silent types. They have complex emotions that often get in their way. Jerry for a time is paralyzed by a fear of death that gives him insomnia and interferes with his work. These men are, unlike the typical male that Deborah Tannen describes, quite garrulous and articulate about their emotions. Jerry and Ruth's conversations in the wake of her discovery of his affair with Sally are extraordinarily intimate; the emotional bond between this couple is so strong that Jerry is incapable of breaking it despite his desire to do so.

These intimate conversations are remarkably honest, revealing the ambivalence that these spouses feel about each other. Such honesty, however, is always presented against the background of deception, usually on the part of both partners. Deception is a necessary condition of marriage, Updike's work suggests. When Piet deceives Foxy about his having slept with Georgene, the narrator tells us that in being deceived "Foxy closer approached the condition of a wife" to her lover.[54] The paradox is that such deception seems to exist in conflict with these characters' deepest desires. Both Piet and Foxy express similar dissatisfaction with their marriages: they feel their spouses do not know them. Piet complains to Angela that she has "no idea what I'm like inside." Angela's response makes the connection to his deception: "You mean you're having an affair and you want me to guess the woman?"[55] Piet says he does not mean that, and he does mean more than just that. Even her question illustrates this. She can't understand his complaint except in terms of the secret that she has guessed but that she doesn't yet believe. The intimacy Piet has with Angela is not enough; he seeks an even deeper intimacy, which Foxy seems to provide. Foxy tells her mother that her husband is "everything I could want but we don't make *contact*. . . . He's so good, Mother, he's so goddam *good*. He doesn't *see* me, he doesn't *know* me."[56] This longing to be known is at the heart of the discourse of intimacy. Where the romantic lover sought mystery and to remain mysterious, the lover under intimacy wants to break through deception to a true meeting of minds.

Piet and Foxy are married to good people, but they are not married to their soul mates. Both lovers believe that they are known by each other in ways of which their spouses are incapable. Foxy's letters to Piet give some substance to this belief, for there she reveals herself in ways that neither character does to a spouse. Yet the intimacy that is suggested between the lovers remains a promise rather than something the novel can actually depict. The novelist is no more able to represent the merging of souls than is the advice writer. As a result, the lovers' intimacy could be a romantic illusion, an appearance reinforced by Updike's romantic explanation that "it is Foxy who in some obscure way was turned on the lathe for [Piet]."[57]

Like the advice books, marriage fiction is much better at depicting failed intimacy than at representing the achievement of that state. Lurie's books characteristically follow a pattern established in her first novel, *Love and Friendship,* which begins with the memorable line "The day on which Emily Stockwell Turner fell out of love with her husband began much like other days."[58] The pattern is of marital breakdown, of a disintegration of intimacy. On the day that Emily falls out of love with her husband, the chief event is her husband's refusal to talk to her about his day. It is a scene that could have come straight out of one of Tannen's interviews. Unlike Updike's married couples, Lurie's do not seem to talk easily to each other. Given Tannen's work, one suspects that this difference reflects the authors' genders. Updike gives us the unusual moments when couples reveal and discover things about each other. Lurie presents a picture of the failure of communication under normal circumstances.

In *The War between the Tates,* this state of affairs is reflected in the way the novel is constructed. There is very little dialogue between the couple, and the story is told in alternating episodes from each spouse's respective point of view. The result is a very strong sense of the Tates' isolation from each other even when they are together. The novel opens from Erica's perspective, where we find her thinking about "her friend and husband, Brian Tate, [who] is away lecturing on foreign policy at Dartmouth. If he were there, she thinks, he would understand why she had screamed at the children. . . . He would listen to her, share her feelings, and console her afterward—possibly in bed."[59] But Brian is barely there for the rest of the novel. We don't get to see the Brian who listens to his wife and shares her feelings, nor do we find Erica thinking such nice thoughts about her husband. Their intimacy is a memory.

Where *Couples* is a novel that precedes the rise of second-wave feminism, *The War between the Tates* rides that wave. There is little sense in Updike's work of the battle of the sexes. His betrayed spouses often continue to care for their mates, and if they seek revenge, it is against the third party. Erica Tate, on the contrary, tries to build an alliance with her husband's young lover, Wendy. I don't think that the presence or absence of feminism explains this difference entirely. Gender also contributes. From the position of dominance that men hold, women do not appear as the enemy. From the position of female subservience, men are the enemy, since they are responsible for and benefit from women's oppression. It is a different kind of freedom that women seek, a freedom from men rather than from one man. In Lurie, it is men who typically first stray and who will leave a marriage to seek a better mate. Female characters often follow their husbands into adultery, but they are less likely to want to leave a marriage. When they do, it is not because they have fallen in love but because they no longer find their marriages satisfactory.

Erica Tate has something in common with Mazursky's Erica in *An Unmarried Woman.* Like Mazursky's heroine, Erica finds in her husband's absence that she can rely on herself. Brian prevented Erica from taking a job; after he moves out, she has no choice but to find one. That opportunity and Erica's self-discovery will change the character of their relationship. As in *Blume in Love,* the fact that Erica and Brian reunite at the end does not mean that nothing has changed, that the status quo has been reestablished. Conversely, the way in which Brian imagines their reunion suggests that they will reestablish their intimacy:

> They will talk for a long while after lunch, Brian imagines. Moving into the sitting room—Erica curled on the blue sofa as usual, and he in his wing chair—they will relate and explain all that has passed. They will laugh, and possibly at some moments cry. They will encourage each other, console each other, and forgive each other.[60]

Even if this novel has not presented much of this kind of talk, we have no reason to doubt Brian's vision, a vision that could serve as an advice book illustration of a successful marriage. Moreover, the passage, contrasted against the events of the novel, explains the value of such a relationship as a haven in a heartless world.

The Limits of Intimacy

Updike's collection of his short stories about the Maples, *Too Far to Go,* was published in 1979 when a made-for-TV movie was produced based on the stories. The individual stories were first published in magazines between 1956 and 1979. As the author describes the stories in his foreword, they "trace the decline and fall of a marriage."[61] The stories begin with Richard and Joan Maple recently married and end with their divorce twenty years later. The marriage thus "declines" for nearly the entire period of its existence. This long history gives us an unusual portrait of a marriage. The novels I'm discussing here give us at most a few years. As a result, the Maples stories depict more of the inner workings of a marriage than the other fiction I've been discussing.

The first story tells of Richard's attraction to a woman who visits them at their new apartment in Greenwich Village, but it is an affair that does not happen. The third story in the chronology, "Giving Blood," begins, "The Maples had been married now nine years, which is almost too long."[62] It was perhaps a shocking sentence when the story was published in 1963, and it retains an edge. Even in an age of divorce, we don't normally think of a marriage lasting too long. The sentence suggests that nine years would be "almost too long" for any marriage; the stories don't necessarily support that interpretation, but they do make it clear that the Maples' marriage ends up lasting longer than it should have. In every story from "Giving Blood" on, the marriage seems to be increasingly beyond repair. In the very next story, "Twin Beds in Rome," for example, Updike tells us, "Their marriage let go like an overgrown vine whose half-hidden stem had been slashed in the dawn by an ancient gardener." Yet a few sentences later, the story concludes, "She was happy, and, jealous of her happiness, he again grew reluctant to leave her."[63] This pattern of ambivalence runs throughout the collection. The marriage lasts too long because, in spite of the pain they inflict on each other and the unhappiness that they often feel, it is apparently too difficult to extricate themselves from each other. They have achieved an intimacy that they know it will be painful to lose.

Updike says of the Maples, "They like one another, and are mysteries to one another. . . . Yet they talk, more easily than any other characters the author has acted as agent for."[64] It is this disjunction that renders these stories so powerful. These people talk to each other almost too well. The honesty of their conversations is at times hard to believe, yet in spite of this openness, this apparently deep and intimate conversation, the marriage oppresses them. One answer to this conundrum is that their conversation is only apparently intimate, and that is to some extent true. Their honesty occurs only on the flip side of their repeated lies and deceptions, which are so much the norm in their marriage that only the last story, in which the Maples are divorced, is free of them. Moreover, their honesty, when it does appear, is often nasty and cutting. In "Giving Blood" they have a fight about what they were doing with other people at the party they had been to the night before. Joan tells Richard, "Let's not talk." But he cannot shut up. "It's your smugness that is really intolerable. Your stupidity I don't mind. Your sexlessness I've learned to live with." When this aggression produces the desired result, hurting Joan, it no longer seems desirable: "Plunged fathoms deep into the wrong, his face suffocated with warmth, he concentrated on the highway and sullenly steered."[65] Here as in almost everything with the Maples, ambivalence rules.

Another way to understand the Maples' talk is that intimacy here is not understood as the Grail that the advice books make it out to be. "Twin Beds in Rome" begins:

The Maples had talked and thought about separation so long it seemed it would never come. For their conversations, increasingly ambivalent and ruthless as accusation, retraction, blow, and caress alternated and cancelled, had the final effect of knitting them ever tighter together in a painful, helpless, degrading intimacy. And their lovemaking, like a perversely healthy child whose growth defies every deficiency of nutrition, continued.[66]

It is hard to imagine the phrase "a painful, helpless, degrading intimacy" occurring in the advice literature. There, intimate talk always seems to be depicted as warm and caring. As we have seen, the most common problem that these books discuss is a lack of talk. The Maples stories suggest that intimacy may be destructive to the individuals who practice it even as it sustains their relationship.

The Maples might seem to be "codependent" or "in collusion," but Updike has drawn characters who are too aware of themselves, whose boundaries are too well defined to fit these terms. Because these are fictional characters, we lack the evidence for such diagnoses. Moreover, it would be a mistake to take them to be typical or representative of the actual working of modern marriages. The Maples are exaggerated in the way fictional characters typically are, so that both the degree of their reflexivity and the number of their extramarital affairs are "unrealistic." The Maples stories don't disprove the advice literature, since they cannot provide evidence of behavior. Rather, these stories represent another permutation of the discourse of intimacy, marking one of its limits. If a relationship features deep, genuine communication, as the Maples' marriage does, then intimacy has been achieved, and the discourse has nothing more it can offer them. This couple, it must be concluded, knew each other well but could not finally find enough happiness in that knowledge to choose to stay married.

I need to emphasize that the destructive intimacy that characterizes the Maples is not outside the discourse I've been discussing in this section of the book. Updike is not offering a critique of intimacy, even though his view of marriage is not the same as that of the advice books. The discourse of intimacy, like the discourse of romance, offers a number of different and sometimes conflicting positions to those who speak it. The Maples stories certainly don't return to romance, and they don't offer a new way of conceiving of love either. What they suggest is that intimacy will not save every relationship, that partners may want things

beside intimacy. This is not, as Updike's foreword makes clear, meant to
be tragic, much less cynical. "That a marriage ends is less than ideal; but
all things end under heaven, and if temporality is held to be invalidating,
then nothing real succeeds." Updike here is articulating another version
of the pure relationship, and it is perhaps the purest. Unlike the advice
writers, Updike does not show a bias toward marriage, and, unlike the relationship films, he does not express a bias against it. The Maples' marriage was not a failure, despite its end and also despite its conflicts, since,
as he continues, "The moral of these stories is that all blessings are
mixed." For him the stories "illumine a history in many ways happy, of
growing children and a million mundane moments shared."[67] We glimpse
these moments through Richard's memories and meditations more than
through the actual interaction of the couple, yet even the conflicts we do
see lead us to imagine a couple at other times happy with each other.

If marriage fiction is part of the discourse of intimacy, it is also, like the
films discussed in the last chapter, at odds with the advice literature. The
intimacy advice books promise to make of their reader, to a greater or
lesser extent, someone new. But according to Updike, a second moral of
the Maples stories is "that people are incorrigibly themselves."[68] While it
is a lesson of the advice books that in a relationship each partner must understand the other as a separate self, that self cannot be incorrigible. The
advice books are committed to the possibility of utopian transformation.
For Updike, on the contrary, therapy may help people accept who they
are, but it cannot change them. As Joan puts it, "You're never cured. You
just stop going."[69] Psychiatrists play a role in each of the fictions, but that
role is neither transformative nor, as in the relationship films, revelatory.
The latter is true in part because it is only women who see the doctors,
but we experience the stories through the consciousnesses of male characters. Unlike Woody Allen's characters, Updike's men do not think of
themselves or their relationships in psychoanalytic categories. Instead,
they invent, with their wives and lovers, languages of their own. Of the
Maples stories Updike says, "A tribe segregated in a valley develops an
accent, then a dialect, and then a language all its own; so does a couple.
Let this collection preserve one particular dead tongue, no easier to parse
than Latin."[70] Like the proponents of talking cures, then, Updike also
seems to believe that relationships are defined by talk.

Perhaps the most moving story in the Maples sequence is "Separat-
ing," which is devoted to the problem of telling the children of the parents' decision. The children take the news pretty well, but Richard Maple

breaks down into tears. It is Richard who is moving out, who feels the most guilt, and who will lose the most. Richard, of course, is also the one who initiated the separation, so it might seem odd that he would cry. One critic observes of the husband's tears in *An Unmarried Woman* that they seem like a sham.[71] We don't know enough about him to feel otherwise. Richard's tears, on the contrary, seem real to us and even to his wife, though she recognizes that they have also served a rhetorical purpose: "In bed she explained, 'I couldn't cry I guess because I cried so much all spring. It really wasn't fair. It's your idea, and you made it look as though I was kicking you out.'"[72]

The point of the story, of course, is to dramatize Richard's ambivalence about leaving the marriage. The story concludes with him realizing, in the face of his older son's painful question, that he "had forgotten why."[73] Yet the story also explains the decision by an implicit analogy to the younger son's hating his school. Richard tells him, "We'll think about getting you transferred. Life's too short to be miserable."[74] Where previous conceptions of marriage and the family would have regarded the misery of father and son as the sacrifices they were expected to make, in the Maples' world, it is each individual's right to try to avoid misery. Yet the story also shows that even getting what you want is likely to be painful.

The Maples stories explore "loving detachment," the contradiction at the heart of intimacy discourse. As we saw in the advice books' preoccupation with the pursuer-distancer roles, this discourse makes the conflict between the desire for closeness and the need to be an independent self central to its vision of marriage. The advice books promise that these conflicting desires can be successfully managed or reconciled. Marriage fiction suggests that they often cannot be. Richard Maple feels his marriage to be a cage, a clinging vine that he must escape. It is hard to imagine that if he were only to practice the advice books' "homework" he would feel differently. The Maples stories show us a couple who, despite their genuine intimacy, simply want different things. It is to the point that Updike's work often presents this situation, while Lurie's does less often. In our culture, men remain more likely to choose independence at the cost of closeness, while women more often choose the opposite. *Couples, Marry Me,* and the Maples stories all depict husbands who to one degree or another want to escape their marriages. Despite the ambivalence each of them feels, the goal of escape is presented as a valid one. Lurie's fiction, on the other hand, seems to question that goal by making the alternatives to her characters' marriages unappealing. If these two writers' own perspectives are as reflective of current gender construction as they seem, then men and women appear destined to continue to have conflicts over closeness and independence.

It is important, however, to consider the kind of independence that men in marriage fiction seek. None of them follows Huckleberry Finn in "lighting out for the territories." They seek to leave one relationship only to form another. In this fiction, domesticity itself is not the problem, for the men in it crave the home as much as they crave other women. It should be obvious that these men are not seeking freedom "from women and their entanglements." They seem rather to be pursuing the ideal relationship. The fiction itself suggests the impossibility of that quest, but it does not therefore condemn the quest itself. This fiction stands as testament to the value of intimacy to men and women at the end of the twentieth century. If it does not depict gender relations as having reached a state of harmony, it also shows us a side of those relations not apparent in documents often held up as "most American" or reflecting the "dominant ideology." Thus, despite its frequent focus on failed marriages, marriage fiction remains a hopeful sign for the future of our relationships.

Conclusion

Other Media, Other Discourses: The Crisis Continues

> The social redemption of marriage in our time is precisely in intimacy as a countervailing force against the chaotic isolation promoted by free-market capitalism.
>
> —Jane Smiley

Other Media

Modern Love has traced two discourses, romance and intimacy, through their appearance in several genres of print and film. I argued at the beginning of the book that novels, movies, and advice books are important ways in which people learn about love, about how to love and be loved. Books and movies are not the only way these discourses are spread. I've already mentioned popular songs as an important vehicle, especially for romance, and women's magazines have long been a significant medium for the discourse of intimacy. Television talk shows are also full of intimacy discourse. They both use the language of therapy and make relationships the object of analysis. It is, however, beyond the scope of this project to say how the discourse is altered when it is used in this context. Fictional television programs convey both discourses, though they are filtered through the particular demands of its genres. Television, because it remains, in spite of cable, the closest thing to a genuine mass medium, is the most conservative in its representations of love and marriage. This means, not that what TV represents is what conservative moralists would approve, but that its conventions have been more limited and more stable over the relatively short course of its existence. Consider the soap opera, a genre that early television adopted from radio and that has changed very little since. "The American soap opera can be described as

215

a never-ending game of romantic musical chairs in which characters within a more or less closed circle keep exchanging partners until they (or the program) are taken off the screen."[1] The discourse of romance is the source of this formula, but it is transformed by the repeated failure of relationships. Soap operas are television's version of the women's picture, counseling courage in the face of loss rather than the hope that Hollywood romance typically encouraged. While prime time shows presented the extremes of safe, middle-class family life (situation comedy) and male loners (westerns and cop shows), the soaps gave us a steady stream of courtship, marriage, adultery, and breakup. It has been argued that melodramas such as these are "overblown . . . precisely because tellers and listeners feel that the emotion and meaning of events like heartbreak are not likely to be taken seriously."[2] Still, one might speculate that these stories helped to condition their predominantly female audience to the emerging reality of serial monogamy. And, like other romantic forms, the soaps lacked a picture of normally functioning marriage. Such a picture was to some extent present in the situation comedies of the 1950s and early 1960s, though it became less common after that.

Situation comedies have been television's other long-standing genre representing love and marriage. Unlike the soaps, romance has typically been a subsidiary discourse in situation comedies, which are built around some form of stable family, be it *The Adventures of Ozzie and Harriet*'s nuclear family, *Mary Tyler Moore*'s workplace family, or the apartment-building family of *Friends*. For the stability to be maintained and to prevent the comedy from becoming melodrama, romance cannot become a major plot line. The problem of romance on television is illustrated by the meltdown of the comedy-drama *Moonlighting* when its central couple moved from flirtation to serious involvement, a condition that destroyed the show's premise. Still, the detective genre makes romance possible by providing the constant adventure that situation comedies do not. Situation comedies are not celebrations of communal or individual renewal, not versions of New Comedy. They are rather affirmations of mundane existence, dwelling exactly on those aspects of life that romance excludes. This should make this genre the perfect vehicle for intimacy, but that discourse is present mainly in dialogue. When situation comedy tends toward case history, it risks instability. As one situation comedy writer and producer has noted, you can't "do a divorce" between a central couple and stay within the genre.[3]

The HBO series *Sex and the City* represents an interesting case in point. The show focuses on Carrie Bradshaw (Sarah Jessica Parker), the writer of a column about sex and the single girl in turn-of-the-millennium Manhattan. Carrie's columns, which provide a theme for each episode, are full of the rhetoric of intimacy. Because the show is not bound by broadcast censorship rules, it can treat in detail sexual issues that most situation comedies cannot. We thus get more of the texture of intimate relationships, and there is a sense in which this show is the television version of a Woody Allen film. Each episode gives us several relationship stories, some continuing, some not. But its form as a series means that these relationships must end. It is not surprising, therefore, that one episode directly lampoons intimacy advice. A couple experiencing difficulty in their relationship go to see a therapist, the author of a book with the punning title *Into Me See*. She turns out to be full of platitudes and silliness, and the therapy does nothing for the couple, who break up. The point is that they must break up if the series is to continue to feature its repertoire of situations. A continuing, successful marriage on this show would be just as impossible as a divorce between Ozzie and Harriet. Thus, the one marriage the show has featured was troubled from the start by the husband's lack of interest in having sex with his wife, putting her back into the same emotional situation as her single friends.

Popular songs have been devoted to romance at least since the beginning of sound recording, and those of the Tin Pan Alley era were overwhelmingly so. It has often been claimed that these songs, the most memorable of which became known as "standards," represent a sophisticated "adult" view of love, in contrast to the teenage sensibility of the love songs of the rock era. And, if one compares Cole Porter to the early Beatles, the case seems beyond argument. But Cole Porter is surely the most "adult" of the Tin Pan Alley songsmiths and one of the two or three best. There were lots of utterly uncomplicated celebrations of love in that era also, while the Beatles went on to write songs more complex than Porter ever dreamed of writing. Moreover, what the best Porter and the earliest Beatles have in common is the discourse of romance.

The difference between teen longing and adult longing is only the adult experience of getting what you want—and finding it or yourself still wanting. Neither genre focuses on living with the lover any more than romance narratives do. Moreover, both kinds of popular music treat love conventionally rather than as the expression of the songwriter's particular experiences. We can, for example, speculate that Cole Porter's life as a gay man entailed experiences that made him able to give such powerful expression to unrequited love and longing. But that expression did not lead listeners to conclude that he was writing autobiographically. These songs were understood as expressing universal rather than particular experiences.

As long as songwriters were writing for other singers, conventionality was the rule. The emergence of songwriters who performed their own material in rock and roll enabled a new stance toward the material. Starting around 1970, we begin to get a new genre of popular song and a new sort of artist that reflect the discourse of intimacy. The artist is the singer-songwriter, and the genre is the confession. The first big hit in this genre was James Taylor's "Fire and Rain." A song about loss rather than longing, it is also a work of self-analysis that was widely interpreted as autobiographical. It is a song about love that we probably would not call a love song because it seems to be about the singer more than about love in the abstract.

"Fire and Rain" was just the beginning. Joni Mitchell's album *Blue* (1972) made the singer's past relationships the object of intense and painful reflection. It is impossible to imagine Porter writing what Mitchell did in "River," "I'm so hard to handle. / I'm selfish and I'm sad." In "Every Time We Say Goodbye," perhaps Porter's most affecting love song, the singer blames "the gods above me" for the lover's leaving. Mitchell blames herself. The bluntness of this self-analysis makes this a personal, not a standard, statement. Another song on the album illustrates the particularity of the singer-songwriter's work. "A Case of You" describes peculiar incidents in a relationship that is finished but about which the singer feels ambivalence. There is longing here, but it is a longing for a specific person caused by the specific interaction of the two persons involved. While none of Mitchell's later records are as confessional as *Blue*, the project of self-analysis continues to run through many of her songs. In 1974, Bob Dylan issued his own confessional album, *Blood on the Tracks*, to which I referred in the introduction. This album made the case-historical aspects of singer-songwriting much more evident. The songs on *Blood on the Tracks* are often narrative, and several tell extended stories. While Dylan's persona on this record is less vulnerable than Mitchell's on *Blue*, these songs are also particular to the singer, distinguishing them from his early, folklike songs that were more popular when performed by other artists. The songs on albums like *Blue* and *Blood on the Tracks* are "relationship songs" rather than love songs, and this genre has since become a standard one for singer-songwriters, including such recent popular performers as Tori Amos and Alanis Morrisette.

Other Discourses

By mentioning television and popular songs, I hope to have shown the range of exposure that the discourses of romance and intimacy currently have in the media. But even if we imagine people not exposed to any of these media—a stretch, these days—this does not mean that they are likely to be unaffected by either discourse. Many absorb these discourses secondhand, from parents and friends, lovers and spouses. Where, for example, did the young teenagers in Sharon Thompson's study learn the discourse of intimacy? One guesses not directly from the books or films on which *Modern Love* has focused, though talk shows and magazines are likely sources. This does not mean that all of our ideas about love or all of our practice of relationships is determined by romance or intimacy. What these discourses teach directly or indirectly is not a simple script or set of rules. And what people take from them varies, not only with degree of exposure, but also with differing circumstances and temperaments. Moreover, while the discourses of romance and intimacy are both broadly influential, they are by no means the only social and cultural conventions that govern relationships. There remain the competing discourses of various religions, in addition to others deriving from marriage as alliance, and from various theories of sex and sexuality. But to these more or less coherent conceptions or ideologies, we need to add the ways in which marriage still figures in the social structure, however reduced that role may be.

While religion is a less powerful influence on such matters today than it was in 1900, it remains significant. Religion and romance were then likely to be opposed, but now they are usually combined. Formula romances are used by Christians to teach their conception of marriage and to try to encourage chastity outside it. More couples than not are married in religious ceremonies, and they often are required to take instruction by the clergy prior to receiving the religion's blessing of their union. This instruction will certainly include religious doctrine, but it may also rely on the discourse of intimacy.[4] And if the religion using this discourse continues to hold the patriarchal assumptions of Jewish and Christian scripture, then its politically progressive elements are likely to be vitiated even more severely than they are when presented in secular renderings such as *Men Are from Mars, Women Are from Venus.*

The rise of the Christian right, beginning in the 1970s in the wake of the "sexual revolution," second-wave feminism, and the gay rights movement, should be understood as a reaction against the very "transformation of intimacy" that Anthony Giddens describes. While fundamentalist religions have a direct and powerful influence over their members and their children, they have had less direct impact on the stories told in novels, films, and other media. But reactions against both romance and intimacy can be traced to the indirect influence of these forces and the fears that they exploit. Evidence of this counter-revolution is most obvious in film. Consider, for example, *Fatal Attraction* (Adrian Lyne, 1987), the third-leading moneymaker of its year and a film that makes infidelity into a crime worthy of death and the other woman into a monster. This "family values" movie is fundamentally and overtly antiromantic, turning the adventure of adultery into something terrifying. The strains of Puccini's quintessentially romantic opera *Madame Butterfly* serve as the background music for the film's adulterous affair, and they were originally used (in a rejected ending) to accompany the other woman's suicide. In pitting a stay-at-home wife against a single career woman, the film also opposed the equality that feminism sought to bring to society and to relationships. The film's association of sexual transgression and violence seems to be, as Linda Singer has argued, a reaction to the then recently recognized AIDS epidemic. According to Singer, the film "develops a narrative of sexual panic" that produces pleasure by making "anxieties more manageable" through the mechanism of displacement.[5] This film was designed to exploit people's fears about "everyday social experiments."

Not all of the conservative treatments of love and marriage have been antiromantic. In opposition to the relationship story, there has been a revival of more traditional romantic comedy. Perhaps the beginning of this trend was the extraordinary success of *Pretty Woman* (Garry Marshall, 1990). A version of the Cinderella story, this film updates the fairy tale by making her a hooker and him a corporate raider. Whereas in the original, all Cinderella needed (and wanted) was for the prince to marry her, in *Pretty Woman,* she wants not only that but also true love as defined by the discourse of intimacy. Yet the basic premise of the film—that a billionaire and a streetwalker could actually have such a relationship—remains embedded in the discourse of romance. By making their class differences so extreme, this film seemed almost a parody of Hollywood's history of cross-class romance—as its framing device, an apparently slightly crazed homeless man reminding us that the film is set in Hollywood, home of the dream factories, may be taken to show.

Pretty Woman initiated a series of films in which it was strongly suggested that there is one (and only one) right person for each of us. Nora Ephron's films from the 1990s are good examples of this trend. *Sleepless in Seattle* (1993) might seem to be a screwball comedy, since it contains the requisite triangle, but in this case it is a mere formality. The real obstacle in this film is geographical, as the lovers fall for each other on different sides of the continent. Moreover, the film's repeated references to *An Affair to Remember* (Leo McCarey, 1957) suggest that it is best described as a comic tearjerker. Ephron seems to be the contemporary master of "the delayed fuck," able to find plot devices that will allow her to keep her lovers apart (or, at least, out of bed) for most the movie.[6] The lovers in *Sleepless in Seattle* don't even meet until the film's closing moments. In Ephron's *You've Got Mail* (1998), a remake of Ernst Lubitsch's *Shop around the Corner* (1940), the lovers are brought together and kept apart by e-mail. *You've Got Mail,* like *Sleepless,* borrows from the screwball formula without actually becoming part of the genre. The source for this film was decidedly not a screwball comedy, as it lacks double entendres, fast talk, and the mock adultery. We are asked to believe that Ephron's couples are destined to be together, much as Churchill's Stephen and Virginia in *The Crisis* believed themselves to be. These films are truly fairy-tale romances.

We might describe Ephron's two 1990s films as devolved screwball comedies, films that return to earlier conventions of romance narratives. But they are not the most conservative of recent romantic comedies. That honor goes to two films that reverse screwball conventions to endorse marriage at the expense of friendship, intimacy, and romance itself. The more successful and interesting of these films is *My Best Friend's Wedding* (P. J. Hogan, 1997), but I will begin with *Forces of Nature* (Bronwen Hughes, 1999), where the mutation is much simpler and the derivation more obvious. Like the contemporary *Runaway Bride, Forces of Nature* is a descendant of *It Happened One Night,* but even though it borrows far more from the plot of that film, it shares much less of its spirit. Like Gable and Colbert, Ben Affleck and Sandra Bullock find themselves as strangers on the road together. In this case it is Ben (as his character is also named) who is trying to get to his wedding, and Sara

(Bullock) who is trying to persuade him that he doesn't really want to get there. As in Capra's film, we are invited to experience the growth of an erotic attraction and a friendship between two people who seem to have nothing in common. When the journey ends, we still don't know if Ben will go through with his wedding or elect to run off with Sara. The formula makes us expect the latter, but the film reverses the convention. Realistically, people don't often decide on a whim to throw over an intended mate for someone met yesterday. But no one expects realism from a romantic comedy, and when it comes in this package it feels more like cynicism than realism. Maybe Ben's fiancée is a better match, but we have no way of knowing this since we don't know her. The film builds our desire around Ben and Sara's relationship, and Ben's decision to go through with his original wedding is something akin to Tracy Lord deciding to go through with her plans to marry George Kittredge in *The Philadelphia Story.* We are left to assume that this movie endorses the social conventions of marriage over those of romantic love, in effect repudiating the film's own narrative.

My Best Friend's Wedding is if anything more cynical than *Forces of Nature,* but its reversal is less pure because our locus of identification is restricted to the heroine, Julianne Potter (Julia Roberts). Under such circumstances, we cannot be sure that she and her best friend, Michael O'Neal (Dermot Mulroney) are mutually in love. To make things more complicated, besides the best friend she has long been in love with, there is George Downes (Rupert Everett), her editor, who plays the role of her new best friend. George is rendered a safe best friend in a way not possible in earlier screwball comedies: he is gay. Finally, the woman Michael is engaged to, Kimmy Wallace (Cameron Diaz), does not fit the usual profile of the loser in a love triangle. She is too beautiful and has the strength of character to persist in spite of Julianne's efforts to sabotage her wedding. From a casting perspective, it is Dermot Mulroney who doesn't really fit the role, since he is nothing close to Roberts's equal as a star, and he lacks any other quality to reduce the gap. The result of this mismatch is that, as any number of reviewers observed, the real fireworks are between Roberts and Everett.

All of these complications serve to limit to some extent the audience's investment in Julianne's desire to displace Kimmy and marry Michael. The key question, however, is, To what extent? Does the film convince us that Kimmy and Michael belong together? Does it make Julianne sympathetic only at first, later painting her as cruel because of what she is willing to do to prevent Michael from marrying her rival? In my view, it does neither, and as a result, the ending, which in traditional comic form is a wedding, is not in fact convincingly comic. Kimmy, as her name suggests, is first portrayed as shallow and too immature for marriage. We are, I think, supposed to change our minds about this as we witness her persistence, but I did not. How can one help thinking that Kimmy's absurdly wealthy family is the real reason for Michael's interest? The message here seems to be the opposite of comedies like *It Happened One Night,* which at least overtly opposed marriages of alliance or economic interest. Thus, this film, like *Forces of Nature,* also seems to treat love cynically. Its fundamental situation is that Michael's deep friendship with Julianne is not accompanied by physical attraction, while his attraction to Kimmy lacks emotional depth. If the film were structured as a relationship story, it might have treated this disjunction as an interesting problem. As it is, *My Best Friend's Wedding* simply observes the disjunction and finally endorses the convenience (in all senses of the term) of the original plan. We are perhaps supposed to be comforted by Julianne's still "having" George, but the slightest reflection will show exactly how cold that comfort must be.

The cynicism of *Forces of Nature* and *My Best Friend's Wedding* differs from that which we found in *The Lady Eve* or *Unfaithfully Yours.* Preston Sturges seems to be suggesting that we know all very well that romance is an illusion, but still we believe in romance. If Sturges's cynicism were taken seriously—and I have argued that his films finally don't themselves take it seriously—then we would be led to question not merely romance but marriage as well. The contemporary cynicism holds that we know all very well that marriages are matters of property and law but that nevertheless we will pretend that they are about love. If the contemporary cynicism were taken seriously, we would not question marriage as an institution, but we would question the vision of marriage that has developed out of the discourses of romance and intimacy during the twentieth century. In this light, we have to read these most recent reversals of the screwball formula as part of the conservative reaction against the changes in intimate practices that have occurred since the 1960s. These films are, paradoxically, the same sort of response that produced the original cycle of the screwball comedies. Then, romance seemed to be a solution to the crisis of marriage, a way to make marriage seem more appealing. Now, romance is depicted as a threat to marriage, an incitement to divorce.

Divorce has become a frequent object of attack in recent political debate. While divorce laws were made more lenient in most states by the 1960s, there has been some attempt to reverse this trend. Louisiana, for example, created a special category of marriage, "covenant marriage," under which divorce is more difficult. Apparently, however, few Louisianians have availed themselves of the opportunity to make divorce more difficult. In the first year of its existence, only 1 percent of marriage licenses issued in the state were for covenant marriage. This instance strongly suggests that, regardless of the rhetoric, relatively easy divorce is now an accepted part of American life.

This has not stopped critics from arguing that divorce is a social evil. Judith Wallerstein's book *The Unexpected Legacy of Divorce* argues that children often suffer permanent damage as a result of their parents' divorce. Wallerstein says that parents should stay together for the sake of the kids and that the quality of the parents' relationship with each other—short of abuse—is not a significant factor in the children's well-being. Thus, she apparently would be happy with the pattern of marriage, sometimes called "bourgeois," in which it is expected that the husband will take a mistress and the wife may discreetly have lovers. Marriage in Wallerstein's conception is understood as being not primarily for the couple but for the children. This is a view at odds with both romantic and intimate conceptions of marriage.[7]

Curiously, Wallerstein's own reliance on psychoanalysis makes her accounts of the troubled lives of her subjects sound as though they were written in the discourse of intimacy. These subjects experience difficulty in forming intimate relationships, which they fear as inherently unstable. The trauma of divorce is for them a permanent scar. Wallerstein's research has been criticized for the small size of the sample, for bias in selection of the sample, for the lack of a genuine control group, and for making up composite characters who stand in for individual subjects. As a result of some of these flaws, "she greatly overstates the percentage of people who will experience serious problems because their parents got divorced," according to Andrew J. Cherlin, a social scientist who has also studied this issue.[8] But even if Wallerstein's research is accepted, it is not clear why parents who can't achieve intimacy with each other should give up that goal so that their children might achieve it. Moreover, one has to wonder whether it was the parents' lack of intimacy, rather than their divorce, that caused the child's problems in that area.

Wallerstein told Bumiller that she is "not against divorce," and her view of marriage as something that should be arranged for the children at least avoids the sanctimony of the religious right's view of marriage and the family. Her book, however, has been taken up by the antidivorce movement as evidence for scrapping no-fault divorce laws and imposing covenant marriage and other legal impediments. The antidivorce movement has been led by the Institute for American Values (IAV), whose president, David Blankenhorn, has interpreted Wallerstein's work as antidivorce. Wallerstein herself is a member of IAV, as are people such as Francis Fukuyama, who, besides arguing that history has ended, holds that gender equality has caused social breakdown.[9] (It's not clear how such breakdown can occur after history has ended, but that's another discussion.) What IAV and its supporters want is to return to a world where social pressure and legal regulation kept marriages together. They continue to see marriage mainly as a fundamental social building block and reject the dominant view that it should be a source of personal happiness.

While divorce remains the focal point of contemporary marriage crisis rhetoric, it is not the only complaint. The National Marriage Project, an academic research group based at Rutgers University and headed by two leading opponents of divorce, Barbara Dafoe Whitehead ("Dan Quayle Was Right") and David Popenoe (*Disturbing the Nest, Life without Father*), has been lamenting a general decline of marriage in America. The project reports that marriage trends in the United States over the past four decades indicate that Americans have become less likely to marry, and that fewer of those who do marry have marriages they consider to be "very happy."[10] What this group doesn't do is connect those two figures, which would seem strongly to suggest a correlation. Marriage, according to these people, is good for everyone, and they blame, among other things, current courtship practices, cohabitation, and a "loss of child centeredness." These moralists still believe that marriage is "a fundamental social institution" and "social glue."[11]

The discourse of intimacy rests in part on a demystification of romance. This might lead one to believe that we are returning to a less inflated view of marriage and its rewards. In fact, as I have been arguing, the opposite seems to be the case. We may no longer expect marriage to be one long romantic adventure, but we now demand of our partners a closeness that is equally unrealistic. The discourse of intimacy renders marriage in some respects more desirable but also more fragile, making it unlikely to reverse the current divorce rate. And even though the discourse is biased toward marriage, its conception of the pure relationship means that it is unlikely to reverse the trend in which fewer people are marrying at all. Should we continue to regard this state of affairs as a crisis?

One of the effects of the discourse of intimacy is to deny the culture the grounds for making marriage a moral compulsion. In this regard, the discourse reflects the social and economic conditions of modern love. What the contemporary crisis mongers fail to recognize is that the rise in divorce rates cannot be blamed on a decline in morality. Individuals don't divorce because they are more promiscuous or irresponsible than their forebears were; they divorce because the social role of marriage has changed, as have expectations of personal happiness and development. I have argued that the reduced significance of marriage as an economic unit and as a social building block is a condition that enabled the discourses of romance and intimacy to prevail. This reduced role has as its complement the increased autonomy of individuals, especially women. According to the anthropologist Helen Fisher, "Divorce is common in societies where women and men *both* own land, animals, currency, information, and/or other valued goods or resources and where *both* have the right to distribute and exchange their personal riches beyond the immediate family circle."[12] In earlier eras of Western culture, when women were property and were not permitted to own it, divorce was much less common. And, as Fisher also notes, "Divorce rates are much lower where spouses are dependent on each other to make ends meet. . . . [T]he low divorce rates seen in preindustrial European societies were . . . due to an inescapable ecological reality: farming couples need each other to survive."[13] One could add that farming people found the offspring that marriages produced an economic advantage, whereas those in industrial and postindustrial societies often find children to be an economic burden. As the discourse of intimacy would suggest, children are no longer the point of marriage. "Nearly 70 percent of Americans believe the main purpose of marriage is something else" than having children.[14] Within certain strata of American society today, children have become a luxury, a situation made possible by the existence of reliable contraception. Children are now "planned," and if the planning fails to result in pregnancy, there are various commodities available as a solution, including the virtual "purchase" of a child for adoption.

Since reproduction is neither an economic benefit nor the necessary result of satisfying sexual urges, people now want children for reasons similar to those they have for wanting to marry or form other intimate relationships. While the traditional belief that reproduction represents a form of immortality persists, childbirth and child rearing are now more often "experiences" that are sought for their own sake. The continued breakdown of other kinds of social relations means that those with children become potentially more valuable as respite from the loneliness and alienation of life in the market. If the desire to form an intimate relationship is itself rooted in the experience of childhood attachments, the desire to raise children can also be seen as a way to reproduce the experience of those bonds.

Paradoxically, however, as the exchange value of babies has climbed, the level of social investment in children continues to decline. The problem is that the love of children is not regarded as fundamentally different from the love of wine, automobiles, or any other object in which one might be emotionally invested. As social relations erode, the idea of a common responsibility for the next generation loses force. Thus, the very problems that follow from divorce—economic and emotional—are less likely to be mitigated by other institutions because of capitalism's relentless attack on all nonmarket social relations.

There is no question that divorce is difficult for children, just as it is difficult for their parents. It can have a lasting impact on all involved. Rather than asking people to stay in unhappy marriages—a strategy that, however noble, is unlikely to work—social reformers ought to be thinking about how society might make it easier for children of divorce to recover from the loss. Ideally, children should have the emotional support of other adults within their communities to help them through their loss. But given the general lack of real community, such support is no doubt often lacking. Under current social conditions, then, the public needs to pay for such support in the form of counseling and other programs. The economic consequences of divorce, now unequally borne by women, need also to be addressed. Genuine pay equity would be the best remedy, but in the meantime more stringent rules for child support are needed. For example, instead of making the amount of such support simply a matter for negotiation, laws could prescribe amounts or percentages—which might be routinely collected by payroll deduction as income taxes are.

Historian Nancy Cott concludes her book about the central role that marriage has played in American public life by observing that "it seems dubious that conventional legal marriage can recover the primacy it once had" but that state-sanctioned, monogamous marriage has not been disestablished. "If disestablishment of formal and legal Christian model monogamy were real, public authorities would grant the same kind of imprimatur to every kind of couple's marriage."[15] Marriage is still encouraged and promoted by the state. But Cott also observes that "marriage also continues to appeal subjectively, despite the alternatives visible, because of the relief it seems to offer from the ineffable coercions and insistent publicity of the postmodern world."[16] The continuing rhetoric of crisis tends to obscure the fact that marriage remains the kind of relationship the vast majority of Americans have or want. That this is true in spite of relaxed social pressure against other kinds might be taken as a reflection of the strength of marriage, at least as a desire or ideal.

The right regards this continued preference for marriage as a source of optimism and as evidence of its naturalness. Observers on the left, as duCille noted, often see it as the continuing effect of patriarchal and heterosexist ideology.[17] In my view, neither position is correct. In response to the right, one needs to note that, though marriage is no longer a requirement, it continues to be subsidized by various legal and economic benefits available only for the married. Health insurance, for example, is typically extended to spouses of employees but not to their unmarried partners. Such subtle forms of coercion are significant, and when added to the influence of the discourses I've discussed here, it is clear that the culture continues to endorse marriage strongly.

However, this picture does not tell the whole story. For one thing, it depicts discourse as existing outside the individual and imposing itself. But inner lives of individuals are developed through discourse. To a significant extent, we are what discourses like romance and intimacy have made us. We have the power to recognize and question these discourses, but we cannot escape into some purely natural realm. Moreover, as I have argued, these discourses are constructed on human capacities and drives. They channel our energies and our needs rather than manufacturing them out of whole cloth. Our desires for romance and intimacy cannot be dismissed as unreal, whatever critique we might make of these discourses. Moreover, marriage retains its allure not merely because of the promises of romance and intimacy but also because it provides much more basic benefits. For example, marriage continues to be identified with the emotional security of regular companionship. In whatever form it takes, it promises a continuing connection to another human, thus satisfying a desire that doubtless has roots in humans' fundamentally social characters but is made all the more pressing by the diminution of all other kinds of relationships. The desire for marriage is at least partly a function of its providing emotional benefits not otherwise available in contemporary America.

The continued popularity of marriage also stems from its being a reliable way to satisfy sexual desire. Marriage is "safe sex" in more than just limiting exposure to disease. In spite of popular representations of the single life, statistics show that married people typically have sex more frequently than do the unmarried. Moreover, a strong case can be made that the desire to have sex exists in psychic tension with the felt need to control that desire. Michel Foucault, in investigating the sexual practices of ancient Greece and Rome, discovered that these cultures had different sexual regulations than more recent Christian and post-Christian cultures in the West but that they did have regulations.[18] Foucault had expected to find limitless sex, something that he believed himself to have experienced in the pre-AIDS gay subculture. But he came to realize, not only that such a vision of limitlessness was an illusion but that ethical considerations could not be seen merely as an instance of repression. The monogamous relationship, whether gay or straight, is our culture's dominant form of sexual regulation. In the absence of other ethics, marriage will be seen by most as the only one available.

Despite the decline in the percentage of those who marry, a strong case could be made that the ideal of marriage remains too strong and that many people continue to marry who should not. While those whose orientation is primarily homosexual are less likely today to enter into heterosexual marriages because of social stigma (one of the chief reasons for the overall decline in marriage, but one not usually acknowledged by the crisis mongers), others who are otherwise unsuited to marriage probably still marry in large numbers. The problem is that while marriage no longer is required, alternatives to it barely exist. The major heterosexual alternatives to marriage are cohabitation and being single, and both are defined in relation to marriage. It should be obvious that to be "single" means at least "not coupled," but usually "not married." Cohabitation is most often understood as a prelude to marriage, and when it is not, it is often merely marriage without legal sanction. If we accept the idea that marriage is not the best arrangement for everyone regardless of his or her sexual orientation, then we as a society need to develop better conventions to accommodate people's differing needs. We generally accept the idea that single people are sexual, but we seem to forget that they have other needs. That someone does not want to be married does not mean that that person does not want or need emotional ties. That resources for the unmarried have declined is not, perhaps, a certainty, but there is strong evidence in studies such as Robert Putnam's *Bowling Alone* to support the contention.[19] It would seem that the "everyday social experiments" Giddens names need to be more experimental.

Nevertheless, it is clear that such experiments do routinely occur. Jane Smiley begins her essay "Why Marriage" with an account of a dinner with a new sort of extended family: "you know, me, my boyfriend, his daughter and son by his second wife, my daughters by my second husband, and my seven-year-old son by my third husband."[20] What Smiley's example shows is that divorces can create families.[21] Moreover, her example excludes the ex-mates who might also be regarded as part of the circle. Because divorce is always painful, but also because of the stigma attached to it, we still speak as if divorce inevitably means the end of a family. But often even the divorced couple continue to have emotional ties to each other and remain committed to their children—as Updike's Maples illustrate.

Divorce-extended families are fairly common. Smiley's current relationship is by comparison, an unusual experiment:

> When I began seeing my current boyfriend, he had another girlfriend, who was seeing another guy. Since the very thing that broke up my last marriage was my former husband's infidelity, it seemed to me that I was putting myself right back into danger, and so for a long time we refrained from identifying our relationship even as a "relationship." We were friends, then "all-inclusive friends." A turning point came about six months in, when the other girlfriend broke up with her other boyfriend and said to Jack, "Well, I guess it's just you and me again," and he said to her, "Well, you, me, and Jane." Within a few weeks, she had another boyfriend. Sometimes we would have dinner together, all four of us, but our dinners were, to say the least, volatile. Even so, all of the relationships, mine with him, his with her, hers with the other guy, endured, and not without pain and jealousy on the part of every single one of us. But we had a principle. We were not married, and, further, we didn't wish to take marriage as our paradigm.[22]

To recognize that marriage is a paradigm and not an inevitable, natural state is, as I have been arguing, one of the implications of the discourse of intimacy. Smiley here describes what might be another paradigm, the committed relationship not defined by fidelity. It is something other than the marriage/adultery model, since none of the relationships is illicit. Such multiply committed relationships, however, run counter to most of the intimacy literature, which continues to assume the marital dyad as its norm. The advisers assume that if it requires work to maintain intimacy in one relationship, the labor to maintain it in more than one would be at least double. But perhaps more close relations would relieve the burden that now rides on the marital one. The investment of intimacy advice literature in the one "right" person or relationship means that it cannot take seriously the possibility that human emotional needs might be better met under another paradigm.

The discourses of romance and intimacy both assume marriage as a paradigm, but they also bear paradigms for relations within and around marriage. Such paradigms are cultural constructions, but it is in the nature of culture to construct them. Recognizing their historical contingency does not mean that we can put them behind us and move on to some better construction, much less to nature itself. Discovering their internal contradictions will not inevitably lead us to a new, logically consistent way of thinking about love. But these discoveries can help us begin the work of constructing alternatives, while at the same time recognizing that our own expectations and desires are very likely to have been shaped by the discourses the culture has given us. Awareness of this shaping may not change what we expect and want, but it may make it easier to understand and to live with them. Moreover, the discourse of intimacy itself contains the possibility of overcoming its own bias toward marriage and of evolving paradigms for relationships better suited to the diversity of individual needs, including the need for social bonds. It is true that such paradigms must develop in spite of capitalism, but perhaps the relentless dissolution of all previously existing bonds will be the condition for their emergence.

In the meantime, we should recognize that it is as illegitimate to condemn marriage out of hand as it is to impose it on everyone. While it is clear that one size does not fit all when it comes to relationships, marriage does fit many. The "witness" couples in *When Harry Met Sally* reflect a reality as genuine as that of the failed relationships in Woody Allen films. That not everyone needs, wants, or can have long-lasting, happy marriages does not negate their value to those who do. There will remain many who do want such relationships but who fail to have them. Moreover, as long as intimacy remains the only alternative to the utter isolation of the market, the load it must bear will often be too much. Nevertheless, the emergence of the discourse of intimacy is an encouraging development, not only for intimate relationships, but also for gender relations and, ultimately, social relations. It shows that, despite the commodification of romance, there remain spaces where the market does not reign. What is needed now is to translate the high value that intimacy places on relatedness beyond the intimate sphere to relations in communities and society at large.

Notes

NOTES TO THE INTRODUCTION: A BRIEF HISTORY OF LOVE

1. John Gray, *Men Are from Mars, Women Are from Venus: A Practical Guide for Improving Communication and Getting What You Want in Your Relationship* (New York: HarperCollins, 1992), was *USA Today*'s number one best-seller for the years 1994–1998. "John Gray Atop Our List of 100," *USA Today*, Feb. 11, 1999, 5D.

2. See Shulamith Firestone, *The Dialectic of Sex: The Case for a Feminist Revolution* (1970; reprint, New York: Bantam, 1972); Juliet Mitchell, *Women: The Longest Revolution* (New York: Pantheon, 1984); and Ann duCille, *The Coupling Convention: Sex, Text, and Tradition in Black Women's Fiction* (New York: Oxford University Press, 1993).

3. See Jo Loudin, *The Hoax of Romance* (Englewood Cliffs, N.J.: Prentice Hall, 1981), for an example of this tendency.

4. Michel Foucault, *The Archaeology of Knowledge*, trans. A. M. Sheridan Smith (New York: Pantheon, 1972), 55.

5. Pierre Bourdieu, "Marriage Strategies as Strategies of Social Reproduction," in *Family and Society: Selections from the Annales*, ed. Robert Foster and Orest Ranum, trans. Elborg Foster and Patricia M. Ranum (Baltimore: Johns Hopkins University Press, 1976), 141.

6. Virginia Wright Wexman, *Creating the Couple: Love, Marriage, and Hollywood Performance* (Princeton, N.J.: Princeton University Press, 1993), 5.

7. Anthony Giddens, *The Transformation of Intimacy: Sexuality, Love, and Eroticism in Modern Societies* (Stanford, Calif.: Stanford University Press, 1992), 45. Giddens calls romance "the counterfactual thinking of the deprived."

8. Sharon Thompson, *Going All the Way: Teenage Girls' Tales of Sex, Romance, and Pregnancy* (New York: Hill and Wang, 1995), 26.

9. Ibid., 27.

10. Ibid., 31.

11. Ibid., 32–33.

12. Ibid., 39.

13. Giddens, *The Transformation of Intimacy*, 59.

14. Anthony Giddens and Christopher Pierson, *Conversations with Anthony Giddens: Making Sense of Modernity* (Stanford, Calif.: Stanford University Press, 1998), 145.

15. duCille, *The Coupling Convention*, 14.

16. Ibid., 143.

17. Some examples include *How Stella Got Her Groove Back* (Forest Whitaker, 1995), *The Wood* (Rick Famuyiwa, 1998), and *The Best Man* (Malcolm D. Lee, 1999).

18. The first interracial-relationship film was *Guess Who's Coming to Dinner* (Stanley Kramer, 1967). Other examples include *Mississippi Masala* (Mira Nair, 1992), *Bullworth* (Warren Beatty, 1998), and *Monster's Ball* (Marc Foster, 2001). It is worth remarking, however, that the films I call relationship stories, as well as recent novels and stories about marriage, seem to be especially monocultural, often lacking any characters of color. This surely reflects in part the reality of racial divisions, but it may also reveal generic or even artistic limitations.

19. See William Jankowiak, ed., *Romantic Passion: A Universal Experience?* (New York: Columbia University Press, 1995).

20. Helen Fisher, *Anatomy of Love: The Natural History of Monogamy, Adultery and Divorce* (New York: Norton, 1992), 19–58.

21. I follow Giddens, *The Transformation of Intimacy*, 37–38, on this point, though his choice of terms is somewhat misleading. He wants to name the universal experience "passionate love," but *passion* has a particular meaning and significance in the discourse of romance. I therefore prefer Fisher's term, *infatuation*.

22. Denis de Rougemont, *Love in the Western World*, rev. ed., trans. Montgomery Belgion (1956; reprint, Princeton, N.J.: Princeton University Press, 1983).

23. Joseph Allen Boone, *Tradition Counter-Tradition: Love and the Form of Fiction* (Chicago: University of Chicago Press, 1987) shows that the connection between romantic love and marriage is a feature specific to English and American fiction. Wexman, *Creating the Couple*, demonstrates that Hollywood films present us with a variety of conceptions of love and marriage, including not only patriarchal dynastic marriage and the more egalitarian companionate couple but also more radical alternatives, thus finding that love's various historical phases continue to live on in cinema. What *Modern Love* adds to the contributions of these studies is the treatment of romantic love as a discourse that has itself undergone historical change and the identification of intimacy as a new discourse.

24. Niklas Luhmann, *Love as Passion: The Codification of Intimacy*, trans. Jeremy Gaines and Doris L. Jones (Cambridge, Mass.: Harvard University Press, 1986), 130.

25. Paul Veyne, *A History of Private Life*, vol. 1, *From Pagan Rome to*

Byzantium, trans. Arthur Goldhammer (Cambridge, Mass.: Harvard University Press, 1987), 40.

26. See María-Rosa Menocal, *Shards of Love: Exile and the Origins of the Lyric* (Durham, N.C.: Duke University Press, 1994), 142–52, for an extended reading of *Layla and Majnun* that explores its historical influence up through Eric Clapton.

27. R. Howard Bloch, *Medieval Misogyny and the Invention of Western Romantic Love* (Chicago: University of Chicago Press, 1991), 10.

28. Georges Duby, ed., *A History of Private Life,* vol. 2, *Revelations of the Medieval World,* trans. Arthur Goldhammer (Cambridge, Mass.: Harvard University Press, 1988), 145.

29. Andreas Capellanus, *The Art of Courtly Love,* ed. John Jay Parry (New York: Columbia University Press, 1941), 100.

30. Boone, *Tradition Counter-Tradition,* 34.

31. Duby, *History of Private Life,* vol. 2, 82.

32. The long history of debate among medievalists includes, on the one hand, C. S. Lewis's *The Allegory of Love* (New York: Oxford University Press, 1938), which argues that courtly love is about adultery, and, on the other hand, E. Talbot Donaldson's "The Myth of Courtly Love," in *Speaking of Chaucer* (London: Athlone Press, 1970), and Denis de Rougemont's *Love in the Western World,* which hold that it is about unfulfilled desire. More recent studies have argued for some middle position. See Boone, *Tradition Counter-Tradition,* 34–43.

33. In the 1970s, school districts actually began to use specially produced formula romances to teach love and values in what were called "sex education" classes. Teenage girls were now being told that romance was the truth pure and simple. See Thompson, *Going All the Way,* 44. Still, it was fiction that conveyed this truth.

34. Donald Maddox, "Triadic Structure in the *Lais* of Marie de France," *Assays* 3 (1985): 22–29.

35. Rougemont, *Love in the Western World,* 15.

36. Germaine Greer, *The Female Eunuch* (New York: McGraw Hill, 1971), 204.

37. Lawrence Stone, "Passionate Attachments in the West in Historical Perspective," in *Passionate Attachments: Thinking about Love,* ed. William Gaylin and Ethel Person (New York: Free Press, 1988), 20.

38. Richard Adair, *Courtship, Illegitimacy and Marriage in Early Modern England* (Manchester, England: Manchester University Press, 1996), 134.

39. Lawrence Stone, *The Family, Sex and Marriage in England 1500–1800* (New York: Harper and Row, 1977), 99–105; David Cressy, *Birth, Marriage, and Death: Ritual, Religion, and the Life-Cycle in Tudor and Stuart England* (New York: Oxford University Press, 1997), 261.

40. Stone, *Family, Sex and Marriage,* 103.

41. Alan Macfarlane, *Marriage and Love in England: Modes of Reproduction 1300–1840* (Oxford: Blackwell, 1986), 174–89.

42. There is disagreement about the date of its emergence and the degree of novelty. Stone fixes the date at 1660, while others find companionate marriage in the late 1500s. See Adair, *Courtship, Illegitimacy and Marriage,* and Cressy, *Birth, Marriage, and Death.*

43. Stone, *Family, Sex and Marriage,* 392. This use of *companionate marriage* is confusing because it ignores the introduction of the term in the 1920s to define a new form of marriage that not only assumed romance as the basis for the choice of spouse but also reflected the breakdown of rigid gender roles.

44. Nancy Armstrong, *Desire and Domestic Fiction: A Political History of the Novel* (New York: Oxford University Press, 1987), 41.

45. Luhmann, *Love as Passion,* 63.

46. Ibid., 45, italics in original.

47. Stone, "Passionate Attachments," 18–19.

48. See Ellen K. Rothman, *Hands and Hearts: A History of Courtship in America* (New York: Basic, 1984), and Karen Lystra, *Searching the Heart: Women, Men, and Romantic Love in Nineteenth-Century America* (New York: Oxford University Press, 1989), for such evidence.

49. Luhmann, *Love as Passion,* 129, 150.

50. See Stone, *Family, Sex and Marriage;* Boone, *Tradition Counter-Tradition;* Luhmann, *Love as Passion;* and Giddens, *The Transformation of Intimacy.*

51. John R. Gillis, "From Ritual to Romance: Toward an Alternative History of Love," in *Emotion and Social Change: Toward a New Psychohistory,* ed. Carol Z. Stearns and Peter N. Stearns (New York: Holmes, 1988), 87–121.

52. Elaine Tyler May, *Great Expectations: Marriage and Divorce in Post-Victorian America* (Chicago: University of Chicago Press, 1980), 2.

53. Ibid., 167.

54. See Ernest R. Mower, *Family Disorganization: An Introduction to Sociological Analysis* (Chicago: University of Chicago Press, 1927), and Ernest W. Burgess, "The Romantic Impulse and Family Disorganization," *Survey* 57 (1926): 290–94.

55. Luhmann, *Love as Passion,* 151, 233, n.32.

56. May, *Great Expectations,* 75.

57. Ibid., 76.

58. Francesca M. Cancian, *Love in America: Gender and Self-Development* (New York: Cambridge University Press, 1987), 17.

59. Lystra, *Searching the Heart,* 205.

60. Peter N. Stearns, *American Cool: Constructing a Twentieth-Century Emotional Style* (New York: NYU Press, 1994), 52, 24–25.

61. Francine Klagsbrun, *Married People: Staying Together in the Age of Divorce* (1985; reprint, New York: Bantam, 1986), 21.

62. On the commodification of romance, see Eva Illouz, *Consuming the Romantic Utopia: Love and the Cultural Contradictions of Capitalism* (Berkeley: University of California Press, 1997).

NOTES TO CHAPTER 1:
ROMANCE IN THE ROMANCE AND THE NOVEL

1. Ian Watt, *The Rise of the Novel* (1957; reprint, London: Hogarth Press, 1987), 205.

2. See Watt, *Rise of the Novel*; Joseph Allen Boone, *Tradition Counter-Tradition: Love and Form in Fiction* (Chicago: University of Chicago Press, 1987); Nancy Armstrong, *Desire and Domestic Fiction: A Political History of the Novel* (New York: Oxford University Press, 1987); Evelyn J. Hinz, "Hierogamy versus Wedlock: Types of Marriage Plots and Their Relationship to Genres of Prose Fiction," *PMLA* 91 (1976): 900–13; and Tony Tanner, *Adultery in the Novel: Contract and Transgression* (Baltimore: Johns Hopkins University Press, 1979).

3. On the fairy-tale qualities of *Pride and Prejudice*, see Claudia L. Johnson, *Jane Austen: Women: Politics, and the Novel* (Chicago: University of Chicago Press, 1988), 73–92.

4. The historical romances discussed in this chapter are Lew Wallace, *Ben-Hur: A Tale of the Christ* (New York: Harper, 1880); Charles Major, *When Knighthood Was in Flower* (Indianapolis: Bowen-Merill, 1898); Edward Noyes Wescott, *David Harum* (New York: Appleton, 1899); Paul Leichester Ford, *Janice Meredith* (New York: Dodd, Mead, 1900); Winston Churchill, *Richard Carvel* (New York: Macmillan, 1900); and Winston Churchill, *The Crisis* (New York: Macmillan, 1901).

5. Frank Luther Mott, *Golden Multitudes: The Story of Best Sellers in the United States* (New York: Macmillan, 1947), 311–13.

6. Amy Kaplan, *The Social Construction of American Realism* (Chicago: University of Chicago Press, 1988), 17.

7. William Dean Howells, "Editor's Study," *Harper's Monthly* 74 (April 1887): 824.

8. John Tebbell, *A History of Book Publishing in the United States*, vol. 2 (New York: Bowker, 1975), 170, 171, italics in original.

9. Raymond Williams, *Marxism and Literature* (New York: Oxford University Press, 1977), 45–54; David R. Shumway, *Creating American Civilization: A Genealogy of American Literature as an Academic Discipline* (Minneapolis: University of Minnesota Press, 1994), 26–40.

10. Richard Ohmann, *Selling Culture: Magazines, Markets, and Class at the Turn of the Century* (London: Verso, 1996), 297–339, read "all of the stories in

the same volumes" of these periodicals from 1895 to 1897 and from 1902 to 1903 and found that over one hundred of the nearly two hundred stories fit the courtship formula (297).

11. Ibid., 305.

12. Northrop Frye, *Anatomy of Criticism: Four Essays* (Princeton, N.J.: Princeton University Press, 1954), 163.

13. For examples of such instruction, see J. H. Kellogg, *Plain Facts for Young and Old* (1877; reprint, New York: Arno, 1974); Sylvannus Stall, *What a Young Man Ought to Know* (Philadelphia: Vir, 1904); and Mary Wood-Allen, *What a Young Woman Ought to Know* (Philadelphia: Vir, 1905).

14. Mott, *Golden Multitudes*, 212.

15. Major, *When Knighthood Was in Flower*, 33.

16. Robert A. Lively, *Fiction Fights the Civil War: An Unfinished Chapter in the Literary History of the American People* (Chapel Hill: University of North Carolina Press, 1957), 57. These banal but affirmative descriptions disguise the racism that the rehabilitation of the South entailed. The vision of "healed wounds" and sectional "reunion" asked Northerners to embrace Southern whites as brothers and to ignore the continuing oppression of blacks.

17. Churchill, *The Crisis*, 514.

18. Ibid., 519.

19. Frye, *Anatomy of Criticism*, 33.

20. Ibid., 33–34.

21. William Dean Howells, "Editor's Study," *Harper's Monthly* 76 (December, 1887): 11–12.

22. In this regard, *The Crisis* fits perfectly Frye's definition of the genre of romance (the romance novel) in *Anatomy of Criticism*: "The romancer does not attempt to create 'real people' so much as stylized figures" (304).

23. This reading of the triangle has been given its most familiar exposition in René Girard, *Deceit, Desire and the Novel: Self and Other in Literary Structure*, trans. Yvonne Freccero (Baltimore: Johns Hopkins University Press, 1965), 1–52. In spite of the subtitle, triangular desire is treated here as a figural element of novels, rather than as proper to their narrative structure. For other readings, see Eve Kosofsky Sedgwick, *Between Men: English Literature and Male Homosocial Desire* (New York: Columbia University Press, 1985), who reads it as expressing otherwise repressed homoerotic desire, and Peter Gay, *The Tender Passion* (New York: Oxford University Press, 1986, 131–32), who sees it as a reflection of the Oedipal triangle.

24. See Donald Maddox, "Triadic Structure in the *Lais* of Marie de France," *Assays* 3 (1985): 22–29.

25. Frye, *Anatomy of Criticism*, 43–44.

26. Ibid., 163–64.

27. Anthony Giddens, *The Transformation of Intimacy: Sexuality, Love, and*

Eroticism in Modern Societies (Stanford, Calif.: Stanford University Press, 1992), 39–40.

28. Frye, *Anatomy of Criticism,* 44.

29. Karen Tracey, "'Little Counterplots' in the Old South: Narrative Subterfuge in Caroline Hentz's Domestic Fiction," *Journal of Narrative Technique* 28 (Winter 1998): 1–20.

30. Stephanie Coontz, *The Social Origins of Private Life: A History of American Families 1600–1900* (New York: Verso, 1988), 251–86.

31. Stephanie Coontz, *The Way We Never Were: American Families and the Nostalgia Trap* (New York: Basic Books, 1992), 107–8.

32. The repetition of this anachronism may also be explained by Pierre Bourdieu's point in "Marriage Strategies as Strategies of Social Reproduction," in *Family and Society: Selections from the Annales,* ed. Robert Foster and Orest Ranum, trans. Elborg Foster and Patricia M. Ranum (Baltimore: Johns Hopkins University Press, 1976), 141, that matrimonial choice can never be absolutely free since the constraints involved are too numerous and complex to be mastered by the conscious, rational mind.

33. Shulamith Firestone, *The Dialectic of Sex: The Case for a Feminist Revolution* (1970; reprint, New York: Bantam, 1972), 146.

34. See Janice Radway, *Reading the Romance* (Chapel Hill: University of North Carolina Press, 1984); and Jean Radford, ed., *The Progress of Romance: The Politics of Popular Fiction* (New York: Routledge, 1986).

35. Churchill, *The Crisis,* 167.

36. Giddens, *The Transformation of Intimacy,* 39–40.

37. Ibid., 45.

38. R. W. B. Lewis, introduction to *The House of Mirth,* by Edith Wharton (Boston: Houghton, 1963), vi.

39. This is exactly where Richard Chase comes down in *The American Novel and Its Tradition* (Baltimore: Johns Hopkins University Press, 1957), 162–67, which claims the book for the American tradition of romance while conceding that it is a novel of manners.

40. Giddens, *The Transformation of Intimacy,* 59.

41. Tanner, *Adultery in the Novel,* 12.

42. Ibid., 15.

43. Mark Twain, *The Adventures of Tom Sawyer,* in *The Works of Mark Twain,* vol. 4 (1876; reprint, Berkeley: University of California Press, 1980), 237.

44. Edith Wharton, *The Age of Innocence* (1920; reprint, New York: Macmillan, 1993), 43–44.

45. Ibid., 44.

46. Ibid., 168.

47. On identification and point of view in Hollywood cinema, see Robert

Ray's discussion of *Casablanca* in *A Certain Tendency of the Hollywood Cinema, 1930–1980* (Princeton, N.J.: Princeton University Press, 1985), 48–54.

48. Wharton, *The Age of Innocence,* 150.

49. R. W. B. Lewis, introduction to *The Age of Innocence* (New York: Macmillan, 1993), xvi.

50. Elaine Tyler May, *Great Expectations: Marriage and Divorce in Post-Victorian America* (Chicago: University of Chicago Press, 1980), 75–76.

51. F. Scott Fitzgerald, *The Great Gatsby* (New York: Scribner's, 1925), 14.

52. Ibid., 19.

53. Leslie Fiedler, *Love and Death in the American Novel,* rev. ed. (New York: Stein and Day, 1966), 316.

54. Scott Donaldson, *Fool for Love: F. Scott Fitzgerald* (New York: Congdon, 1983).

55. Fitzgerald, *The Great Gatsby,* 75.

56. Roland Barthes, *A Lover's Discourse: Fragments,* trans. Richard Howard (New York: Hill and Wang, 1978), 14.

57. Fitzgerald, *The Great Gatsby,* 73.

58. Giddens, *The Transformation of Intimacy,* 59.

59. Fitzgerald, *The Great Gatsby,* 4.

NOTES TO CHAPTER 2: ROMANCING MARRIAGE

1. Elinor Glyn, *The Philosophy of Love* (New York: Authors' Press, 1923), 197.

2. Since my primary concern is the United States, I've given the dates for publication in this country.

3. Steven Seidman, *Romantic Longings: Love in America, 1830–1980* (New York: Routledge, 1991), 65–91.

4. Ibid., 81.

5. Pamela S. Haag, "In Search of 'The Real Thing': Ideologies of Love, Modern Romance, and Women's Sexual Subjectivity in the United States, 1920–40," *Journal of the History of Sexuality* 2 (1992): 548.

6. Beth Bailey, *From Front Porch to Back Seat: Courtship in Twentieth-Century America* (Baltimore: Johns Hopkins University Press, 1988), 15.

7. Ibid., 23–24.

8. One of the most economically important of the new consumer goods, the automobile, doubtless contributed to this new freedom, but Bailey observes that dating was already on its way to becoming the norm before cars became widely available to the middle class (ibid., 19).

9. John C. Spurlock, "Problems of Modern Married Love for Middle-Class

Women," in *An Emotional History of the United States,* ed. Peter N. Stearns and Jan Lewis (New York: NYU Press, 1998), 325.

10. Ibid., 321.

11. Francesca M. Cancian, *Love in America: Gender and Self-Development* (New York: Cambridge University Press, 1987), 34, quoting Ernest Burgess.

12. Spurlock, "Problems," 320.

13. Ben B. Lindsey and Wainright Evans, *The Companionate Marriage* (1927; reprint, New York: Arno, 1972), v.

14. John D'Emilio and Estelle B. Freedman, *Intimate Matters: A History of Sexuality in America* (New York: Harper, 1988), 265–66.

15. Elaine Tyler May, *Great Expectations: Marriage and Divorce in Post-Victorian America* (Chicago: University of Chicago Press, 1980), 69, 75–76.

16. Ernest W. Burgess, "The Romantic Impulse and Family Disorganization," *Survey* 57 (1926): 290–94; and Ernest R. Mower, *Family Disorganization: An Introduction to Sociological Analysis* (Chicago: University of Chicago Press, 1927).

17. Ernest R. Groves, *The Marriage Crisis* (New York: Longmans, 1928), 46.

18. Ibid., 32, 44.

19. Ibid., 52–53.

20. See also Sylvester Graham, *A Lecture to Young Men on Chastity* (Boston: Charles Pierce, 1848), and Sylvannus Stall, *What a Young Man Ought to Know* (Philadelphia: Vir, 1904), 203, who urges that a wife be selected on the grounds of her health and abilities as a housekeeper, and counsels, "Don't fall in love."

21. Cancian, *Love in America,* 29.

22. Peter N. Stearns, *American Cool: Constructing a Twentieth-Century Emotional Style* (New York: NYU Press, 1994), 36–37, quoting Orson Fowler, *Love and Parentage* (1856).

23. Seidman, *Romantic Longings,* 47.

24. Byron Caldwell Smith, letter, 1874, quoted in ibid., 42.

25. Mary Wood-Allen, *What a Young Woman Ought to Know* (Philadelphia: Vir, 1905), 205.

26. Seidman, *Romantic Longings,* 50.

27. Glyn, *The Philosophy of Love,* 47.

28. Niklas Luhmann, *Love as Passion: The Codification of Intimacy,* trans. Jeremy Gaines and Doris L. Jones (Cambridge, Mass.: Harvard University Press, 1986), 130.

29. May, *Great Expectations,* 71. This view is often repeated in advice literature of the period. See, e.g., Laura Hutton, *The Single Woman and Her Emotional Problems* (1935; reprint, Baltimore: William Wood, 1937), 25.

30. Marie Carmichael Stopes, *Married Love: A New Contribution to the Solution of Sex Difficulties* (1918; reprint, New York: Eugenics Publishing, 1931), 116, 160.

31. Glyn, *The Philosophy of Love,* 14–15.

32. Ibid., 62.

33. Seidman, *Romantic Longings,* 84.

34. Lesley A. Hall, "Uniting Science and Sensibility: Marie Stopes and the Narratives of Marriage in the 1920s," in *Rediscovering Forgotten Radicals: British Women Writers, 1889–1939,* ed. Angela Ingram and Daphne Patai (Chapel Hill: University of North Carolina Press, 1993), 128.

35. Stopes, *Married Love,* 2.

36. Ibid., 3–8.

37. Ibid., 12.

38. Ibid., 13, italics in original.

39. Ibid., 37.

40. Ibid., 77.

41. Ibid., 158.

42. Ibid., 96.

43. Marie Carmichael Stopes, *Enduring Passion: Further New Contributions to the Solution of Sex Difficulties, Being the Continuation of* Married Love (London: Putnam, 1928), v, italics mine.

44. Ibid., 3.

45. Ibid., 9.

46. Ibid., 11, 21.

47. Ibid., 15.

48. Joan Hardwick, *Addicted to Romance: The Life and Adventures of Elinor Glyn* (London: André Deutsch, 1994), 63.

49. Elinor Glyn, *Three Weeks* (1907; reprint, New York: Macaulay, 1924), 5–6.

50. Ibid., 108–9.

51. Hardwick, *Addicted to Romance,* 117.

52. Glyn, *Romantic Adventure,* quoted in ibid.

53. Richard Ohmann, *Selling Culture: Magazines, Markets, and Class at the Turn of the Century* (London: Verso, 1996), 175–218.

54. May, *Great Expectations,* 63–67.

55. Glyn, *The Philosophy of Love,* 214.

56. Ibid., 212, italics in original.

57. Ibid., 213.

58. Peter Sloterdijk, *Critique of Cynical Reason,* trans. Michael Eldred (Minneapolis: University of Minnesota Press, 1987), 5.

59. Dix quoted in May, *Great Expectations,* 70.

60. Glyn, *The Philosophy of Love,* 62.

61. Ibid., 69.

62. Ibid., 68–69, 61, italics in original.

63. Ibid., 79.

64. Ibid., 95.

65. Ibid., 97.

66. Stopes, *Enduring Passion*, 12–13.

67. This is true of earlier advisers, such as Kellogg and Stall as well as later ones, e.g., Ernest R. Groves, *Marriage* (New York: Holt, 1933).

68. By 1933, even a social scientist like Groves (in *Marriage*) had to concede that the "romantic element" of courtship and marriage, since this "emotional attitude, now a convention in our culture, is too well established to be shaken by any sort of intellectual activity" (18).

69. Anthony Giddens, *The Transformation of Intimacy: Sexuality, Love, and Eroticism in Modern Societies* (Stanford, Calif.: Stanford University Press, 1992), 58.

70. It is worth remembering, however, as Cancian reminds us, that the actual course of most marriages during this period did not conform to the model that Glyn and Stopes proposed, and that a "family ideal" continued to be endorsed by many social scientists (*Love in America*, 35–37).

71. D'Emilio and Freedman, *Intimate Matters*, 266.

72. Groves, *The Marriage Crisis*, 194–95.

NOTES TO CHAPTER 3: MARRIAGE AS ADULTERY

1. My focus will be on the following films made between 1934 and 1949: *It Happened One Night, His Girl Friday, The Awful Truth, The Philadelphia Story, The Lady Eve,* and *Adam's Rib*. Others regarded as typical include *The Twentieth Century* (1934), *The Thin Man* (1934) and its sequels, *My Man Godfrey* (1936), *Bringing up Baby* (1939), *Ninotchka* (1939), *My Favorite Wife* (1940), *Woman of the Year* (1942), and *Unfaithfully Yours* (1948).

2. For a brief but thorough account of the conventions of screwball comedy, see Tina Olsen Lent, "Romantic Love and Friendship: The Redefinition of Gender Relations in Screwball Comedy," in *Classical Hollywood Comedy,* ed. Kristine Brunovska Karnick and Henry Jenkins (New York: Routledge, 1995), 327–28. Scholars have had a difficult time defining screwball comedy. For discussions of this difficulty, see Wes D. Gehring, *Screwball Comedy: A Genre of Madcap Romance* (New York: Greenwood, 1986), 3–12; Thomas Schatz, *Old Hollywood/New Hollywood: Ritual, Art, and Industry* (Ann Arbor: UMI, 1983), 94–97, 158–63; and Brian Henderson, "Romantic Comedy Today: Semi-Tough or Impossible?" in *Film Genre Reader,* ed. Barry Keith Grant (Austin: University of Texas Press, 1986), 311–13. James Harvey, *Romantic Comedy in Hollywood from Lubitsch to Sturges* (New York: Knopf, 1987), on the other hand, simply identifies screwball comedy as romantic comedy during Hollywood's classic period (xi–xii). For my purposes, it is important that screwball

comedy is a recognizable kind of Hollywood product distinct from other versions of romantic comedy.

3. Stanley Cavell, *Pursuits of Happiness: The Hollywood Comedy of Remarriage* (Cambridge, Mass.: Harvard University Press, 1981), 85.

4. Ibid., 48–49.

5. Stanley Cavell, "Two Cheers for Romance," in *Passionate Attachments: Thinking about Love,* ed. William Gaylin and Ethel Person (New York: Free Press, 1988), 85–100. According to Sturges's biographer, Sturges did not see *The Lady Eve* as a critique of romantic love but rather as "a paean to . . . the mysterious compulsion and mixed motives that, rather than certitude, propel romantic love." Diane Jacobs, *Christmas in July: The Life and Art of Preston Sturges* (Berkeley: University of California Press, 1992), 239.

6. See, e.g., Colin McCabe, "Theory and Film: Principles of Realism and Pleasure," *Screen* 17, no. 3 (1976): 11–29; Bill Nichols, *Ideology and the Image* (Bloomington: Indiana University Press, 1981); John Ellis, *Visible Fictions: Cinema, Television, Video* (London: Routledge and Kegan Paul, 1982).

7. On Hollywood's "invisible style," see Robert Ray, *A Certain Tendency of the Hollywood Cinema, 1930–1980* (Princeton, N.J.: Princeton University Press, 1985), 32–55.

8. David Bordwell, Janet Staiger, and Kristin Thompson, *The Classical Hollywood Cinema: Film Style and Mode of Production to 1960* (New York: Columbia University Press, 1985), 16. Their study of an "unbiased sample" of one hundred Hollywood films made between 1915 and 1960 showed eighty-five to have heterosexual romantic love as the leading line of action. Of course, some studio-era films, such as *Citizen Kane* (Orson Welles, 1939), depict romantic love critically or unromantically. Others, as Virginia Wright Wexman has shown, depict marriage in terms of social conventions that differ from those dominant in twentieth-century America. Virginia Wright Wexman, *Creating the Couple: Love, Marriage, and Hollywood Performance* (Princeton, N.J.: Princeton University Press, 1993; see esp. 39–129). D. W. Griffith's melodramas, such as *Way Down East* (1920), represent more traditionally patriarchal marriages and families than do most Hollywood films. In many Westerns, such as *Red River* (Howard Hawks, 1948) and *The Searchers* (John Ford, 1956), a focus on issues of inheritance or "blood" ties implies the residual conventions of marriage as alliance.

9. Peter Sloterdijk, *Critique of Cynical Reason,* trans. Michael Eldred (Minneapolis: University of Minnesota Press, 1987), 5; Slovoj Žižek, *The Sublime Object of Ideology* (London: Verso, 1989), 29.

10. Northrop Frye, *Anatomy of Criticism: Four Essays* (Princeton, N.J.: Princeton University Press, 1954), 163. I owe this point to James Naremore.

11. I am arguing that the conditions of production contributed to the prevalence of heterosexual love stories in Hollywood films much more than the conditions of reception. Film theorists (the seminal argument is Jean-Louis Baudry,

"The Apparatus: Metapsychological Approaches to the Impression of Reality in the Cinema," *Camera Obscura*, no. 1 [Fall 1976]: 104–28, but it is widely assumed by other theorists such as Laura Mulvey, "Visual Pleasure and Narrative Cinema," *Screen* 16, no. 3 [1975]: 6–18) have attributed extraordinary effect to what they call the "apparatus" of cinema, asserting that viewing larger-than-life images unfolding in darkened theaters is inherently dreamlike and thus readily allows the viewer's unconscious to evade its usual repression. However, Noël Carroll has demolished this theory in *Mystifying Movies: Fads and Fallacies in Contemporary Film Theory* (New York: Columbia University Press, 1988), 9–52. In light of Carroll's argument, we have no reason to think that watching a movie is inherently more erotic than reading a novel—though the theater certainly has been a convenient space for audience members to ignore the screen and engage in their own erotic activities.

12. Woody Allen, "Interview," *Rolling Stone*, no. 665 (September 16, 1993): 50.

13. See John Cawelti, *Adventure, Mystery, and Romance: Formula Stories as Art and Popular Culture* (Chicago: University of Chicago Press, 1976.

14. Wexman, *Creating the Couple*, 32.

15. I agree with Harvey, *Romantic Comedy*, 76, that the screwball comedy emerges in 1934 as an innovation in the larger genre of romantic comedy, though on somewhat different grounds. Harvey sees the chief innovation in the finding of the right tone for American audiences in which to present sophisticated comedy about the rich. I see the remarriage plot as the most significant innovation, replacing the traditional matter of comedy—getting a young man and woman together for the first time in the face of parental opposition—or of farce—the incompatibility of romance and marriage. As an example of the former, see *Fast and Loose* (1930), Preston Sturges's second screenplay, and of the latter, *Platinum Blonde* (1931), Frank Capra's first romantic comedy, in which divorce is depicted as the solution to the bad marriage that provides much of the film's laughs. However, in the "family resemblance" theory of genre I am assuming, no single feature—or even a list of features—must be present in every example. There are screwball comedies that are not comedies of remarriage.

16. Cavell, *Pursuits of Happiness*, 49, 88.

17. Frye, *Anatomy of Criticism*, 182.

18. Harvey, *Romantic Comedy*, 381.

19. "Bliss of genitality" is a paraphrase of Eric Erikson, *Childhood and Society*, 2d ed. (New York: Norton, 1963), 264. Erikson argues that genitality, as the stage of true sexual maturity, is misunderstood as a permanent state of sexual bliss. Nevertheless, Erikson seems to contribute to this vision of heterosexual paradise when he calls genitality the "utopia" of his system (92).

20. Juliet Mitchell, *Women: The Longest Revolution* (New York: Pantheon, 1984), 106.

21. In an article written after *Pursuits of Happiness*, "Two Cheers for Romance," Cavell suggests that we read these endings as the beginning of an "adventure or quest" (95). But he doesn't demonstrate how the films render the endings as beginnings or explain how they are, or why the adventure of marriage is never shown in the films. In this article, the relevance of the feminist critique of romance is acknowledged, but Cavell does not allow it to modify his own position. In fact, he describes "romantic marriage" as an "insulation from the larger world of politics" (90–91). While Cavell quite properly connects romantic marriage to the bourgeois constructions of "privacy" and the "personal," what he apparently can't see is that these constructions are precisely political.

22. Cavell, *Pursuits of Happiness*, 85.

23. Ibid., 186.

24. Ibid., 231, 232–33.

25. Ibid., 148–50.

26. Denis de Rougemont, *Love in the Western World*, rev. ed., trans. Montgomery Belgion (1956; reprint, Princeton, N.J.: Princeton University Press, 1983), 32–34.

27. Lent, "Romantic Love and Friendship," 320, 323.

28. Cavell, *Pursuits of Happiness*, 186.

29. Ibid., 154, quoting Lionel Trilling, *Beyond Culture*.

30. Thomas Schatz, *Hollywood Genres: Formulas, Filmmaking, and the Studio System* (Philadelphia: Temple University Press, 1981), 152.

31. Ibid., 159.

32. Cavell, *Pursuits of Happiness*, 90, makes much of Gable's being "parental" in *It Happened One Night* but fails to see any connection between being parental and patriarchy.

33. Ibid., 259.

34. Dana Polan, "The Felicity of Ideology: Speech Acts and the 'Happy-Ending' in American Films of the Forties," *Iris* 3 (1985): 36.

35. Cavell, *Pursuits of Happiness*, 191.

36. Diane Carson, "To Be Seen and Not Heard: *The Awful Truth*," in *Multiple Voices in Feminist Film Criticism*, ed. Diane Carson, Linda Dittmar, and Janice R. Welsch (Minneapolis: University of Minnesota Press, 1994), 216.

37. Anthony Giddens, *The Transformation of Intimacy: Sexuality, Love, and Eroticism in Modern Societies* (Stanford, Calif.: Stanford University Press, 1992), 8.

38. Shulamith Firestone, *The Dialectic of Sex: The Case for a Feminist Revolution* (1970; reprint, New York: Bantam, 1972), 146.

39. Kathleen Rowe, "Comedy, Melodrama and Gender: Theorizing the Genres of Laughter," in Karnick and Jenkins, *Classical Hollywood Comedy*, 39–59.

NOTES TO CHAPTER 4: POWER STRUGGLES

1. *Casablanca* and *Gone with the Wind* were ranked first and second respectively in the American Film Institute's list of the hundred greatest love stories. See www.afi.com/tv/passions.asp. John Housely, "A Fine Romance: Ten Best," *Premiere* 5 (Feb. 1992): 96; Leonard Maltin, "Leonard Maltin's Ten Most Romantic Movies," *Ladies Home Journal* 110 (Feb. 1993): 66.

2. It has been argued that *Gone with the Wind* is a tragedy. See Trisha Curran, "*Gone with the Wind*: An American Tragedy," *Southern Quarterly* 19, nos. 3-4 (1981): 47–57.

3. It should be understood that *man's* and *woman's* here designate gendered roles or constructs specific to a particular culture and historical moment and that they do not refer to natural conditions or essential categories.

4. The terms *outlaw hero* and *official hero* are found in Robert Ray, *A Certain Tendency of the Hollywood Cinema, 1930–1980* (Princeton, N.J.: Princeton University Press, 1985), 58–66.

5. Mary Ann Doane, *The Desire to Desire: The Woman's Film of the 1940s* (Bloomington: Indiana University Press, 1987), 96–97.

6. Niklas Luhmann, *Love as Passion: The Codification of Intimacy,* trans. Jeremy Gaines and Doris L. Jones (Cambridge, Mass.: Harvard University Press, 1986), 129, 150.

7. Denis de Rougemont, *Love in the Western World,* rev. ed., trans. Montgomery Belgion (1956; reprint, Princeton, N.J.: Princeton University Press, 1983), 15.

8. Aljean Harmetz, *Round up the Usual Suspects: The Making of Casablanca—Bogart, Bergman, and World War II* (New York: Hyperion, 1992), 172–78.

9. Ray, *A Certain Tendency,* 89–112.

10. Ibid., 60.

11. Ray's argument owes a great deal to Leslie Fiedler's in *Love and Death in the American Novel,* rev. ed. (New York: Stein and Day, 1966), though Ray does not emphasize the homoerotic as Fiedler does.

12. Roland Barthes, *A Lover's Discourse: Fragments,* trans. Richard Howard (New York: Hill and Wang, 1978), 14.

13. See Ray, *A Certain Tendency,* 48–55, for a detailed analysis of the way *Casablanca* builds identification with Rick.

14. Sigmund Freud, "The Finding of an Object," in *Three Essays on the Theory of Sexuality,* standard ed., vol. 7, ed. and trans. James Strachey (1905; reprint, London: Hogarth Press, 1953), 222–30; Sigmund Freud, *Beyond the Pleasure Principle,* trans. James Strachey (1921; reprint, New York: Norton, 1961), 10–25.

15. Werner Sollors, *Beyond Ethnicity: Consent and Decline in American Culture* (New York: Oxford University Press, 1986), 166–67.

16. Doane, *The Desire to Desire*, 109.

17. Helen Taylor, *Scarlett's Women: Gone with the Wind and Its Female Fans* (New Brunswick, N.J.: Rutgers University Press, 1989), 94–96.

18. Jan Cohn, *Romance and the Erotics of Property: Mass-Market Fiction for Women* (Durham, N.C.: Duke University Press, 1988), 148.

19. Victoria Olwell, unpublished response to an earlier version of this chapter.

20. See John C. Spurlock, "Problems of Modern Married Love for Middle-Class Women," in *An Emotional History of the United States*, ed. Peter N. Stearns and Jan Lewis (New York: NYU Press, 1998); Elaine Tyler May, *Great Expectations: Marriage and Divorce in Post-Victorian America* (Chicago: University of Chicago Press, 1980); and John D'Emilio and Estelle B. Freedman, *Intimate Matters: A History of Sexuality in America* (New York: Harper, 1988). There is a sense in which the narrative seems to want to have it both ways, however. Melanie and Ashley are cousins, and we are told that the Wilkeses always marry within the family. This smacks of arranged marriage with the best face put on it. Moreover, Rhett's marital rape of Scarlett might be seen as the return of the repressed patriarchal model of marriage, the model that would have been dominant in the time and place the film depicts.

21. Catherine Belsey, *Desire: Love Stories in Western Culture* (Oxford, England: Blackwell, 1994), 12. Lacanian theory makes the perpetual deferral of the satisfaction of desire a constant of human nature, a fact seemingly or explicitly ignored by many of the poststructuralist critics who invoke it. In one sense, of course, this theory is merely a tautology. Desire is by definition only desire so long as it remains unsatisfied. When the term is used by Lacan or by Barthes and those they have influenced, however, it becomes synonymous with love or sex or both. This identification of desire and love should be historicized as part of the discourse of romance. While Belsey takes Lacan to explain the appeal and the meaning of texts like *Gone with the Wind*, I want to suggest that both Lacan's theory and the narrative texts in their different ways embody similar cultural assumptions. Both take love to be defined by its obstacles and thus in principle to be brief and unsatisfying.

22. Cohn, *Romance*, 163, describes Rhett as the source for the "nurturing hero" of formula romances. On the women's romance formula, see also Janice Radway, *Reading the Romance* (Chapel Hill: University of North Carolina Press, 1984).

23. Belsey, *Desire*, 41.

NOTES TO CHAPTER 5: TALKING CURES

1. William H. Masters, Virginia E. Johnson, and Robert C. Kolodny, *Heterosexuality* (New York: HarperCollins, 1994), 16.

2. On the relationship between romance and consumption, see Eva Illouz, *Consuming the Romantic Utopia: Love and the Cultural Contradictions of Capitalism* (Berkeley: University of California Press, 1997).

3. Elaine Tyler May, *Homeward Bound: American Families in the Cold War Era* (New York: Basic Books, 1988), 20.

4. Ibid., 9.

5. Earl Lomon Koos, *Marriage* (New York: Holt, 1953), 244–45.

6. For other examples of textbooks, see Judson T. Landis and Mary Landis, *Building a Successful Marriage* (New York: Prentice-Hall, 1948); Howard Becker and Reuben Hill, eds., *Family, Marriage and Parenthood*, 2d ed. (Boston: D. C. Heath, 1955); and Ruth Shonle Cavan, *American Marriage: A Way of Life* (New York: Crowell, 1959). Beneath the surface of the 1950s, changes were brewing. See Beth Bailey, *From Front Porch to Back Seat: Courtship in Twentieth-Century America* (Baltimore: Johns Hopkins University Press, 1988); Susan J. Douglas, *Where the Girls Are: Growing up Female with the Mass Media* (New York: Times, 1994); and Barbara Ehrenreich, Elizabeth Hess, and Gloria Jacobs, *Re-Making Love: The Feminization of Sex* (Garden City, N.Y.: Doubleday, 1986).

7. The books discussed in this chapter were published between 1985 and 1996, and they are meant to be a rough sample of an immense genre. Not all of my examples were widely read, but those by De Angelis, Gray, Scarf, and Tannen were best-sellers.

8. Many readers may assume that self-help writing is not worth taking seriously as a cultural phenomenon, let alone as material that might have some intellectual value. I do both take the phenomenon seriously and regard much of this work as intelligent and insightful. I have tried to avoid seeming condescending or dismissive without giving up a critical stance.

9. Maggie Scarf, *Intimate Partners: Patterns in Love and Marriage* (1987; reprint, New York: Ballantine, 1988), 109. Italics in original, quoting Sigmund Freud, *New Introductory Lectures on Psycho-Analysis*.

10. Jessica Benjamin, *The Bonds of Love: Psychoanalysis, Feminism, and the Problem of Domination* (New York: Pantheon, 1988), 17.

11. Ibid., 18.

12. Ibid., 49.

13. Scarf, *Intimate Partners*, 115.

14. Francine Klagsbrun, *Married People: Staying Together in the Age of Divorce* (1985; reprint, New York: Bantam, 1986), 311.

15. Pepper Schwartz, *Peer Marriage: How Love between Equals Really Works* (New York: Free Press, 1994), 4–5.

16. Nancy Chodorow, *The Reproduction of Mothering: Psychoanalysis and the Sociology of Gender* (Berkeley: University of California Press, 1978); Dorothy Dinnerstein, *The Mermaid and the Minotaur* (New York: Harper and Row, 1976).

17. Carol Gilligan, *In a Different Voice: Psychological Theory and Women's Development* (Cambridge, Mass.: Harvard University Press, 1982).

18. Anthony Giddens, *The Transformation of Intimacy: Sexuality, Love, and Eroticism in Modern Societies* (Stanford, Calif.: Stanford University Press, 1992), 8. For another account of these changes, see Ehrenreich, Hess, and Jacobs, *Re-Making Love.*

19. Giddens, *The Transformation of Intimacy,* 58.

20. Ibid., 8.

21. Klagsbrun, *Married People,* 21.

22. Thomas Moore, *Soul Mates: Honoring the Mysteries of Love and Relationship* (New York: HarperCollins, 1994), 23.

23. Scarf, *Intimate Partners,* 141–42.

24. Klagsbrun, *Married People,* 9.

25. Aaron T. Beck, *Love Is Never Enough: How Couples Can Overcome Misunderstandings, Resolve Conflicts, and Solve Relationship Problems through Cognitive Therapy* (New York: Harper and Row, 1988), 188.

26. Deborah Tannen, *You Just Don't Understand: Women and Men in Conversation* (New York: Morrow, 1990), 98.

27. Augustus Y. Napier, *The Fragile Bond: In Search of an Equal, Intimate, and Enduring Marriage* (New York: HarperCollins, 1990), 222.

28. Beck, *Love Is Never Enough,* 188.

29. Scarf, *Intimate Partners,* 142, italics in original.

30. Klagsbrun, *Married People,* 20.

31. Scarf, *Intimate Partners,* 402.

32. Klagsbrun, *Married People,* 21, quoting Erik Erikson, *Childhood and Society.*

33. Scarf, *Intimate Partners,* 141.

34. Ibid.

35. Barbara De Angelis, *How to Make Love All the Time* (1987; reprint, New York: Dell, 1988), 234, 238–40, italics in original.

36. Scarf, *Intimate Partners,* 61–74.

37. Napier, *Fragile Bond,* 97.

38. De Angelis, *How to Make Love,* 55.

39. Ibid., 106–27.

40. Scarf, *Intimate Partners,* 207.

41. Ibid., 209.

42. Schwartz, *Peer Marriage,* 92, 15.

43. Klagsbrun, *Married People*, 10.

44. Scarf, *Intimate Partners*, 13.

45. Hayden White, *Metahistory* (Baltimore: Johns Hopkins University Press, 1976).

46. Northrop Frye, *Anatomy of Criticism: Four Essays* (Princeton, N.J.: Princeton University Press, 1954), 134.

47. Sigmund Freud, *Three Case Histories* (New York: Macmillan, 1963).

48. Cover blurbs describe Klagsbrun's *Married People* as "riveting" and Napier's *The Fragile Bond* as "compelling."

49. Moore, *Soul Mates*, 40.

50. Tannen, *You Just Don't Understand*, 49–61.

51. It is perhaps not surprising that there seem to be male and female styles in intimacy writing. Books like Beck's are typical of male style, heavy on exercises and solutions and relatively light on case-historical material. Klagsbrun and Scarf illustrate the female style, in which the relative emphases are reversed.

52. John Gray, *Mars and Venus in Love: Inspiring and Heartfelt Stories of Relationships That Work* (New York: HarperCollins, 1996).

53. Giddens, *The Transformation of Intimacy*, 184.

54. Tannen, *You Just Don't Understand*, 283.

55. Ibid., 283–87.

56. John Gray, *Men Are from Mars, Women Are from Venus: A Practical Guide for Improving Communication and Getting What You Want in Your Relationship* (New York: HarperCollins, 1992), 10.

57. Ibid., 133.

58. Giddens, *The Transformation of Intimacy*, 182.

59. Ibid., 154.

60. Ibid., 192.

61. Michel Foucault, *Discipline and Punish: The Birth of the Prison*, trans. Alan Sheridan (New York: Pantheon, 1977).

62. Michel Foucault, *The History of Sexuality*, vol. 1, *An Introduction*, trans. Robert Hurley (New York: Pantheon, 1978), 58–65.

NOTES TO CHAPTER 6: RELATIONSHIP STORIES

1. The films discussed in this chapter are *Annie Hall, Manhattan, Husbands and Wives, Blume in Love, An Unmarried Woman*, and *When Harry Met Sally*. Other films that fit the genre include Woody Allen's *Hannah and Her Sisters* (1986), *Alice* (1990), *Everyone Says I Love You* (1996), and *Deconstructing Harry* (1997); Paul Mazursky's *Tempest* (1982) and *Scenes from a Mall* (1991); Albert Brooks's *Modern Romance* (1981) and *Defending Your Life* (1991);

David Frankel's *Miami Rhapsody* (1995); and Stephen Frears's *High Fidelity* (1999).

2. The other reason is that Allen uses events, details, and situations similar to those of his own life. According to Ralph Rosenblum, Allen said of *Annie Hall*, "It was originally a picture about me." Ralph Rosenblum and Robert Karen, *When the Shooting Stops, the Cutting Begins: A Film Editor's Story* (1979; reprint, New York: Da Capo, 1986), 283. The original title was "Anhedonia," a psychoanalytic term for the inability to experience pleasure, a condition Alvy exhibits in the finished film. The focus on Annie and Alvy's relationship developed out of Allen's collaboration with co-writer Marshall Brickman and editor Ralph Rosenblum.

3. Pauline Kael, *Reeling* (Boston: Little, Brown, 1976), 408.

4. Anthony Giddens, *The Transformation of Intimacy: Sexuality, Love, and Eroticism in Modern Societies* (Stanford, Calif.: Stanford University Press, 1992), 130.

5. Adam Gopnik, "The Outsider," *New Yorker*, October 25, 1993, 92.

6. Ibid.

7. Eva Illouz, *Consuming the Romantic Utopia: Love and the Cultural Contradictions of Capitalism* (Berkeley: University of California Press, 1997), 112–52.

8. In the documentary *How Harry Met Sally . . .*, included on the DVD version of *When Harry Met Sally*, Reiner and Ephron tell us that this argument reproduces one they had had in discussing the project. In the documentary, they make the film sound like a version of *Men Are from Mars*, insisting on the absolute differences between men and women. Reiner says that he still doesn't think that a man and woman can be friends—suggesting that the screenwriter had the greater influence on the final shape of the film, the idea for which grew out of Reiner's experiences of being single after his divorce.

NOTES TO CHAPTER 7: MARRIAGE FICTION

1. The books discussed in this chapter are Alison Lurie's *Love and Friendship* (1962; reprint, New York: Avon, 1993), *The Nowhere City* (New York: Coward-McCann, 1965), and *The War between the Tates* (1974; reprint, New York:Avon, 1991); John Updike's *Couples* (1968; New York: Fawcett, 1969), *Marry Me: A Romance* (New York: Fawcett, 1976), and *Too Far to Go: The Maples Stories* (New York: Fawcett, 1979). While *Couples* was the number two best-seller of 1968, and *Marry Me* was also a best-seller, these books were not chosen for their influence or their representativeness. Rather, they constitute a major innovation in the genre of the novel, and that innovation has more than mere aesthetic significance given the historical importance of the novel in the dis-

course of romance and the development of modern marriage. It remains to be seen if this new form will be widely practiced.

2. Tony Tanner, *Adultery in the Novel: Contract and Transgression* (Baltimore: Johns Hopkins University Press, 1979), 15, italics in original.

3. Alfred Habegger, *Gender, Fantasy, and Realism in American Literature* (New York: Columbia University Press, 1982), 72.

4. Richard Hauer Costa, *Alison Lurie* (New York: Twayne, 1992), 13.

5. Tanner, *Adultery in the Novel*, 15.

6. Ibid.

7. Joseph Allen Boone, *Tradition Counter-Tradition: Love and the Form of Fiction* (Chicago: University of Chicago Press, 1987), 124. There is no actual adultery in *A Modern Instance*, but it is an issue because Bartley appears to his wife and others to have been unfaithful.

8. Allen F. Stein, *After Vows Were Spoken: Marriage in American Literary Realism* (Columbus: Ohio State University Press, 1984), 31. Stein claims that Howells, James, Wharton, Kate Chopin, and Robert Herrick produced "marriage fiction" in the late nineteenth and early twentieth centuries (3), but his argument actually supports my own, since he sees these authors as mainly treating marriage for its social significance.

9. Stephen Kern, *The Culture of Love: Victorians to Moderns* (Cambridge, Mass.: Harvard University Press, 1992), and Boone, *Tradition Counter-Tradition*.

10. Henry James, "The Art of the Novel," in *Henry James: The Future of the Novel*, ed. Leon Edel (New York: Vintage, 1956), 8.

11. Kern, *The Culture of Love*, 361.

12. Virginia Woolf, *To the Lighthouse* (1927; reprint, New York: Harcourt, 1955), 262.

13. As a result, it is now possible to advocate adultery. See Laura Kipnis, "Adultery," *Critical Inquiry* 24 (Winter 1998): 289–327, for the academic version, and Dalma Heyn, *The Erotic Silence of the American Wife* (New York: Turtle Bay, 1992), for a popular example.

14. This attitude is apparent in those who condemned First Lady Hillary Clinton for not divorcing her husband.

15. Maggie Scarf, *Intimate Matters: Patterns in Love and Marriage* (1987; reprint, New York: Ballantine, 1988), 402.

16. John Updike, "More Love in the Western World," review of *Love Declared*, by Denis de Rougemont, in *Assorted Prose* (New York: Knopf, 1965), 289.

17. Francine Klagsbrun, *Married People: Staying Together in the Age of Divorce* (1985; reprint, New York: Bantam, 1986), 79, quoting family therapist Salvador Minuchin.

18. Updike, *Couples*, 164.

19. Ibid., 480.

20. John Updike, "One Big Interview," in *Picked-Up Pieces* (New York: Knopf, 1975), 497.

21. Ibid., 504.

22. John Updike, "Howells as Anti-Novelist," in *Odd Jobs* (New York: Knopf, 1991), 189.

23. Ibid.; Updike, "One Big Interview," 518.

24. Updike, "One Big Interview," 519.

25. Updike, *Couples*, 233.

26. Ibid., 390.

27. Ibid., 35.

28. Updike, *Marry Me*, 49.

29. Ibid., 96.

30. Lurie, *War between the Tates*, 50.

31. Ibid., 279.

32. Updike, *Couples*, 113–14.

33. Ibid., 12.

34. Ibid., 292, italics in original.

35. Ibid., 147.

36. Updike, "One Big Interview," 497.

37. Alfred C. Kinsey et al., *Sexual Behavior in the Human Male* (Philadelphia: W. B. Saunders, 1948), and *Sexual Behavior in the Human Female* (Philadelphia: W. B. Saunders, 1953); Shere Hite, *The Hite Report* (New York: Macmillan, 1976), and *The Hite Report on Male Sexuality* (New York: Knopf, 1981); Robert T. Michael et al., *Sex in America: A Definitive Survey* (Boston: Little, Brown, 1994).

38. Lurie, *War between the Tates*, 11.

39. Ibid.

40. Ibid., 100.

41. Updike, *Couples*, 87.

42. Updike, *Too Far to Go*, 10, 123–143.

43. Ibid., 201, italics in original.

44. Updike, *Marry Me*, 236, italics in original.

45. Ibid., 206.

46. Lurie, *War between the Tates*, 331.

47. Ibid., 338.

48. Kern, *The Culture of Love*, 364.

49. Updike, *Couples*, 8–9.

50. Lurie, *War between the Tates*, 71.

51. Updike, *Couples*, 205.

52. Ibid., 294.

53. Ibid., 352.

54. Ibid., 281.
55. Ibid., 222.
56. Ibid., 294, italics in original.
57. Updike, "One Big Interview," 504.
58. Lurie, *Love and Friendship*, 9.
59. Lurie, *War between the Tates*, 11.
60. Ibid., 350.
61. Updike, *Too Far to Go*, 9.
62. Ibid., 37.
63. Ibid., 72.
64. Ibid., 10.
65. Ibid., 40.
66. Ibid., 59.
67. Ibid., 10.
68. Ibid.
69. Ibid., 79.
70. Ibid., 10.
71. Roger Ebert, review of *An Unmarried Woman*, in *Cinemania 97*, CD-ROM (Seattle: Microsoft, 1996).
72. Updike, *Too Far to Go*, 204.
73. Ibid., 211.
74. Ibid., 203.

NOTES TO THE CONCLUSION:
OTHER MEDIA, OTHER DISCOURSES

1. Tamar Liebes and Sonia Livingstone, "The Structure of Family and Romantic Ties in the Soap Opera: An Ethnographic Approach," *Communication Research* 21 (1994): 725.
2. Sharon Thompson, *Going All the Way: Teenage Girls' Tales of Sex, Romance, and Pregnancy* (New York: Hill and Wang, 1995), 41.
3. David Kendall, interview, in *Making and Selling Culture*, ed. Richard Ohmann et al., (Middletown, Conn.: Wesleyan University Press, 1996), 66.
4. For an example of a Christian fundamentalist use of the discourse of intimacy, see David Ferguson et al., *The Pursuit of Intimacy* (Nashville, Tenn.: Nelson, 1993). For the complex ways these discourses can mix in practice, see Judith Stacey, *Brave New Families: Stories of Domestic Upheaval in Late Twentieth Century America* (New York: Basic Books, 1991).
5. Linda Singer, *Erotic Welfare: Sexual Theory and Politics in the Age of Epidemic* (New York: Routledge, 1993), 180.

6. Ephron wrote the screenplay for *When Harry Met Sally*, another example of the "delayed fuck."

7. Judith Wallerstein, Julia Lewis, and Sandra Blakeslee, *The Unexpected Legacy of Divorce: A 25 Year Landmark Study* (New York: Hyperion, 2000).

8. Andrew J. Cherlin, quoted in Elisabeth Bumiller, "Resolute Adversary of Divorce," *New York Times*, December 16, 2000, B11.

9. Francis Fukuyama, *The End of History and the Last Man* (New York: Free Press, 1992), and *Trust: The Social Virtues and the Creation of Prosperity* (New York: Free Press, 1995).

10. National Marriage Project, "The State of Our Unions: The Social Health of Marriage in America," July 1, 1999, retrieved from http://marriage.rutgers.edu/.

11. Ibid.

12. Helen Fisher, *Anatomy of Love: The Natural History of Monogamy, Adultery and Divorce* (New York: Norton, 1992), 103, italics in original.

13. Ibid., 106.

14. National Marriage Project, "The State of Our Unions."

15. Nancy Cott, *Public Vows: A History of Marriage and the Nation* (Cambridge, Mass.: Harvard University Press, 2000), 214, 215.

16. Ibid., 225.

17. Ann duCille, *The Coupling Convention: Sex, Text, and Tradition in Black Women's Fiction* (New York: Oxford University Press, 1993), 14.

18. Michel Foucault, *The History of Sexuality*, vol. 2, *The Use of Pleasure*, trans. Robert Hurley (New York: Pantheon, 1985).

19. Robert Putnam, *Bowling Alone: The Collapse and Revival of American Community* (New York: Simon and Schuster, 2000).

20. Jane Smiley, "Why Marriage? Matrimony at the Millennium Offers Solace to Capitalism," *Harper's* 300 (June 2000): 151.

21. For an account of such "divorce-extended families," see Stacey, *Brave New Families*.

22. Smiley, "Why Marriage," 154.

Index

About the Author

David R. Shumway is Professor of English, and Literary and Cultural Studies at Carnegie Mellon University, and Director of its Center for Cultural Analysis. He is the author of *Michel Foucault* and *Creating American Civilization: A Genealogy of American Literature as an Academic Discipline*. He has also coedited a number of volumes, including *Making and Selling Culture* and *Disciplining English*. His next book from NYU Press will be *Classic Rockers*.